ACCLAIM

"Bob Reece has written a compelling story, addressing an issue familiar to physicians who care for children, but important to all of us. A baby dies, and the question of a sad, natural death weighed against a homicide and who caused the death becomes a quagmire of truth and lies inherent in the justice system assigned to determine guilt or innocence. Characters reflect personal attitudes and emotions, creating glimpses into their humanity as the baby's case winds its way through an all-too-real courtroom drama. The narrative of witnesses in the courtroom and tactics of attorneys brings the reader face-to-face with a startling reality: sometimes criminal cases are influenced by more than "the truth, the whole truth, and nothing but the truth."

– Robert W. Block, MD, FAAP, Professor Emeritus, Pediatrics, The University of Oklahoma School of Community Medicine, Child Abuse Pediatrician and Past President (2011-2012), The American Academy of Pediatrics

"Dr. Robert Reece's moving novel is fiction based upon non-fiction. We judges grapple daily with the dilemma he depicts, as do jurors. Reece's book, besides entertaining and enlightening, is a tool for all Americans. It helps all know that the world of science has finally established not only that the world is round but also that abusive head trauma in infants and children is a scientific reality-without plausible denial! Thousands of physicians agree. Perhaps a dozen criminal defense medical witnesses would disagree. The latter testify, earning $12,000 a day in court, that infant head trauma has other causes...and presumably also that the world is flat. Reece's book supports the reality of abusive head trauma. Let there finally be justice for all, including children!"

– Judge Charles D. Gill, Connecticut Superior Court

D0107268

I finished To Tell the Truth last night. I thoroughly enjoyed it, and read it in two sittings.   I recognized a lot of people I have met in the last 55 years, accurately but generously portrayed. Knowing Dr. Reece's professional focus, I was not surprised by the larger point he made about the oddities of the judicial process and the effects of the human failings it brings out. I was surprised, however, that I grew to care about the individual main characters he created, and hoped not only that the case ended with a just result, but that the scars left on the actors al were not too deep.

I wish I could say I am confident there is a solution to the larger problem. The adversary system creates adversary motivations, and trial lawyers are ordinarily the kind of people who don't like to lose. Lots of science questions get varying answers from varying experts, and the accepted answers sometimes evolve over the decades. In addition, we now live in a world in which, maybe because of the internet, everyone's opinions get an equal airing no matter how baseless they may be, and "common sense" all too often trumps expertise.

– Richard S. Cohen, retired judge of the Appellate Division, New Jersey Superior Court.

– At the time of this publication, *To Tell the Truth* has 4.9 star rating among Amazon reviewers.

TO TELL THE TRUTH

ROBERT M. REECE

Publisher's Information

EBookBakery Books

Author contact: michael@ebookbakery.com

ISBN 978-1-938517-37-2

© 2014 by Robert M. Reece

ACKNOWLEDGMENTS

I am grateful to many friends and loved ones who encouraged me to write. Particular thanks goes to David Deakin, who scrupulously read an early manuscript and made important suggestions; to Marcella Pixley, Mary Margaret White, Katrina Niez, Randall Alexander, Mary Case, Larry Ricci, Hugh Gibbons and Jim Anderst, all of whom read parts of early manuscripts; to Judge Charles Gill and Dr. Robert Block for reading and commenting; to David Kerns, for his valuable advice; to my many professional colleagues who have inspired me over the years by their admirable dedication to vulnerable children; to Michael Grossman for unfailing support and guidance in the publishing process; to Tracy Hart, a professional who not only edited my writing but taught me to be a better writer; and finally, to my patient and wise wife Betsy, who read and influenced the narrative in ways large and small.

DEDICATION

This work is dedicated to children everywhere and to those who advocate for them.

PREFACE

"When something is shouted loudly enough often enough and to enough people, with no checking of the accuracy of what's being shouted, a downright silly claim can come to sound like a long-suppressed truth."

Beckwith, S. *"Authorship is not the question."*
Philadelphia Inquirer, October 29, 2011

1

Luke had stopped crying. He had stopped moving. Luke was unconscious. With rising panic and alarm, Chrystal groped in her pocket for her cell phone. She managed to dial 911.

"Somebody help me," she screamed. "The baby's out. I don't know what to do!"

"Calm down, ma'am," the operator said. "Tell me where you are."

"Um, I can't think of the house number. Just a second," Chrystal said, and laid Luke down on the bathmat. She ran downstairs and outside to look at the number on the front of the house, then ran back to the phone. "43 Elderberry Street. Hurry up, the baby really looks bad."

"We've dispatched the Emergency Medical Team. They'll be there real soon. You know CPR?"

"Don't remember. Tell me how."

The woman quickly ran through the basics of CPR. Chrystal fumbled through it, trying not to cry.

"C'mon Luke, wake up," she pleaded. "Okay, she said the same thing they told us in CPR class. Push four times, blow into the mouth, press four times again," she mumbled. Again she tried: press 1-2-3-4, blow into his baby mouth, press 1-2-3-4. "What's wrong with you? How long do you think I can keep this up? Move. C'mon, move. MOVE!" She crouched over the baby, willing him to wake up and move his arms and legs. "Scream, go back into your tantrum. Please, please be all right."

But he wasn't. He remained unconscious even after the ambulance and the emergency medical technicians arrived. The emergency team, led by Rob Shaw, scrambled upstairs with their equipment, followed by Police Sergeant Danny Doyle. They saw Luke's naked body lying face up on the mat in the bathroom. The medical team went right to work.

"Christ, what happened?" said Doyle quickly scanning the scene. As sentimental as they come and a doting father of two boys, he felt sickened as he pulled out his camera and took pictures while the EMT's worked to revive Luke.

A ten-year veteran of the police force, Danny Doyle was known for his polite and considerate demeanor. A chunky man of medium height, his nickname of "Junior" had stuck with him long after his father had left the police force. Everyone liked Danny; he was one of those truly guileless nice guys.

"I was giving him a bath and he went—I don't know, he passed out. I can't remember."

One of the medics threaded a breathing tube into Luke's throat and squeezed the inflatable bag, sending pure oxygen into his lungs. They hustled him down the stairs and into the ambulance. Lights and sirens blaring, they sped to the local hospital. Several neighbors on Elderberry Street, hearing the commotion, came out on their porches to watch.

At Lakeville Hospital, the EMTs and ambulance stayed only long enough for the doctors to be sure he was medically stable. The town's services didn't compare with those at Children's Hospital, the premier children's facility in Kansas City.

Thirty minutes later they entered the sprawling complex of Children's Hospital.

Will Robbins, the Emergency Department pediatrician ran alongside the gurney carrying Luke into the resuscitation room. "What's the story?" he asked Shaw, the EMT leader.

"Picked him up in Brookside. Unconscious, low O2 sat, intubated him right away. Heart rate 40, but with O2 it came back pretty fast, up to 90 when we left the house. Babysitter looked like hell; worried, of course, but really out of it. Just stared at us while we worked on this little guy. No questions, said nothing. Well, don't know what else she could've done, but she was real spacey."

"Damn," said Robbins under his breath.

"A cop was there too, taking pictures, asking questions. He couldn't get much out of her. She told him nothing happened, said he just went limp. We scooped him up, took him to Lakeville; they took one look to be sure he was under control, and told us to ship him here," Shaw said.

As Robbins listened, the rest of the ED crew sprang into their routine, bringing hours of training to bear on the infant struggling to stay alive.

"See these marks on his back?" the intern asked. Robbins took a look.

"Yeah, look like bruises. Anything else?" Robbins said, in teaching mode.

"Well, when I lifted his head up off the gurney, I felt, like, some bogginess on the back of his head. I couldn't see anything though, no blood but it was spongy-feeling."

"Mention all of that in your note. Anything else?"

"That's it. I couldn't do a real thorough exam because everyone's all over him. I did feel his belly–nothing there. Normal genitalia, legs and arms looked OK."

The intern joined the rest of the team, who were busy drawing blood, starting intravenous lines, and assessing vital signs. They made sure his endotracheal tube was in the right place and open, monitored his oxygen saturation, and attached the endotracheal tube to the respirator.

A little later, once his circulation and breathing were stabilized, a head CT scan and an X-ray skeletal survey of his body were done. Dr. Michaelson, an old hand in the radiology department, pointed out the blood collection inside the skull to the Emergency Department team, along with a three-inch long skull fracture in the back of the head, and bleeding under the scalp overlying the skull fracture. He noted a spot on the right tibia that he said might be an old small healing fracture.

"The intern said there was bogginess in his scalp and that blood explains that," said Robbins. He turned to the team and said, "Get him up to the PICU. Ophtho and Neurosurg already know about him. Does McClure know he's coming?"

"Ten minutes ago. She's ready for him," said the ED nursing supervisor.

When Luke got to intensive care, a pediatric ophthalmologist, Dr. Stanley Garber, peered into his eyes with an ophthalmoscope. He took pictures of the interior of Luke's eyes, finished his exam, and turned to Dr. McClure and the residents.

"Must be 20-30 hemorrhages in each eye, in many layers of the retina," he said.

Dr. McClure called Dr. Sarah Coughlin, an expert in the diagnosis of child abuse, to see Luke. She examined him, looked at his X-rays and CT scan. "This is really suspicious for abusive head trauma," Coughlin said. "We need a case conference–like within the next hour. We need everyone from the ED and the PICU who's seen Luke."

Dr. McClure assembled critical staff from the Emergency Department, Radiology, Neurosurgery, Ophthalmology, Neurology, and the PICU, in the conference room.

When each had finished giving their assessment, all but one agreed that the most likely diagnosis was shaken impact syndrome. The one dissenter was Dr. Siler, of the Child Neurology department.

"We shouldn't rush to judgment. All these lesions could be explained by other conditions," Siler said. "There may've been an unrecognized accidental injury that caused this. I know when a baby has retinal hemorrhages most of you think it's due to shaking, but after being in this business for over thirty years, I still think increased intracranial pressure causes them. And all of the other things you see in this baby could be from a fall. I'm not ready to call this child abuse."

"We'll certainly take your opinion into account, Dr. Siler. But we have to file a child abuse report with Children's Protective Services–there's reasonable suspicion here of abuse," Dr. McClure said.

Siler wasn't used to having his opinion doubted. A tall, stately and handsome man, with a head full of pure-white wavy hair, he dressed fastidiously and charmed everyone in his well-controlled world. He was also stubborn, narcissistic and could be ruthless in dealing with anyone who crossed him.

"I disagree with your decision," he said as he left the room abruptly. McClure left with Sarah Coughlin.

"I'm not surprised at Siler," Sarah said. "He's always in denial about abusive head trauma. He has never–*never* filed a child abuse report. He just refuses to do it. He'll never, ever, go to court–for either side–in these abuse cases."

"I know," Ruth said. "But interesting that he seemed less emphatic in this case than usual. He's a great neurologist, but he doesn't understand the reporting law, and he's such a Pollyanna about children and their families. He simply can't conceive of anyone harming a kid.

"And that stuff about raised intracranial pressure…as a child neurologist he should know that raised intracranial pressure doesn't cause this kind of retinal hemorrhage. Drives the neurosurgeons nuts. But he always insists that's what causes them. The good news is that he won't write anything in the medical record. And he won't testify in court unless subpoenaed, and since he won't write a note in the chart, that's unlikely. So at least in the medical record, our medical staff will be in agreement."

At the university-sponsored seminar, Fred and Alison Talbot were deep into a discussion about curriculum design with other educators. The door to the room opened quietly and an administrative assistant came in and whispered in the ear of the chairman of the group. He quickly got up, went over to the Talbots, and asked them to follow him out of the conference room.

"Just got a message from Children's Hospital. Your baby's in serious condition. Better get over there right away."

"What? Luke? At the hospital?" Alison asked.

But there were no details. They ran to their car.

"My God, what could've happened?" Alison said.

Fred, frozen behind the wheel, didn't answer. As they drew closer to the hospital they saw ambulances backing into the emergency bays.

"Please God, let it be nothing serious," Allison prayed.

"I don't get it. He was perfectly OK when we left him this morning," Fred said.

Hurrying to the receptionist's desk, Fred blurted, "I'm Fred Talbot, Luke's father. Where is he?"

She turned to her computer and tapped a few keys.

"In the Pediatric ICU, 5th floor. Elevators are over there," she said, pointing to her right. "I'll let them know you're on your way."

In the elevator, Alison doubled over as if reliving her labor and the pain of birthing Luke. Fred gripped the railings, eyes closed, counting the moments until they reached their floor. Dr. McClure met them at the door to the PICU and guided them to Luke's crib.

"Sorry to meet like this," she said. "After you've had some time with Luke, let's sit down, and I'll fill you in as well as I can. We're still in the early stages of his care."

Neither Fred nor Alison could say anything. They only wanted to see their baby.

"Oh God, what've they done to you?" Alison cried when she saw gauze enveloping Luke's head.

Clutching the bedrails to steady himself, Fred's face went white. Just before the Talbots got to the hospital, a team of neurosurgeons had inserted a small cylindrical device called a "bolt" through Luke's skull to measure the pressure inside his head. The bulky bandage covered it. A tube coming out of his mouth was taped to his face. Intravenous lines carrying fluids and medications flowed into both arms and various monitoring devices on his chest and fingers kept track of his breathing, heart rate, and blood oxygen levels. His arms and legs were tethered to the bedrails in case he woke up and began to thrash about.

"I don't believe this," Fred said. "So many tubes. Our poor Luke. Look at him. Why has God allowed this to happen?"

He doesn't look human, thought Allison. *Where is our Luke? Oh God. Where is my plump, healthy baby? I can hardly see your sweet moon face and blue eyes.* Tears clouded her vision.

The cacophony of PICU reverberated around them. Alison felt her knees buckle, about to give way, when Dr. McClure put her hand under her elbow and guided her into a conference room. As the head of the PICU, McClure was often the unwelcome messenger of bad news, but the outlook for this baby would sadden even the most seasoned professional.

"I'll be straight with you," she said. "Luke's in critical condition. He's dealing with a number of things I'll try to explain. Please stop me if what I say is unclear or confusing. Do you have any questions before I start?"

"What could have happened?" Fred asked. "How did he get this way? When we left home this morning Luke was fine. He hasn't been sick, no fever, nothing. He couldn't have gone from fine to this," he said, glancing over at Luke, "without something terrible happening." Fred could feel his anger building.

"We don't have the full story yet. What we do know is this: Luke's had a serious injury to his brain. He's got a subdural hematoma–a fancy word meaning there's blood under the covering of the brain, and he's in a coma because of damage to his brain. He's got bleeding on the inside walls of his eyes. He's got a skull fracture at the back part of his head. The specialists who've examined Luke and looked at his medical data think the most likely diagnosis is shaken impact syndrome–a form of abusive head trauma. That seems to be the only thing this can be, although we'll be looking into all possibilities."

Several minutes passed in silence as the Talbots took in the information.

"I remember the nurses in maternity told me about shaken baby syndrome when I had Luke, gave me a pamphlet about it. But with so much other stuff they gave me and so many other things to think about, I forgot about it," Alison said. "It had nothing to do with me anyway, so I didn't pay attention to it."

"We've only been gone for a few hours. We left a healthy baby with the babysitter. If this is abuse, who did it?" Fred growled.

"I can't conceive of Chrystal doing that," said Alison.

"The investigation's just underway," Dr. McClure answered. "We haven't talked to the Children's Protective Services or the police yet. Our job in the PICU is to take care of Luke's medical problems. Law enforcement and social services will try to sort out how it happened. We'll know more in the next few hours, at least about how Luke is doing. But I have to be honest. It doesn't look good. Luke has life-threatening injuries. We'll do our best, but he's very sick."

As comprehension of this dreadful reality solidified, Alison moaned. Tears gathered in Fred's eyes. Jumping out of his seat, he drew back his fist to hit the wall then stopped, regaining control.

"How could anyone do this to a baby? Where's Chrystal? I want to hear what she's got to say," he shouted.

And then he asked the critical question that begged an answer.

"Is Luke going to die?"

Before Dr. McClure could answer, Alison said, "He's a strong, healthy baby. I know he'll be all right. We just have to pray and let the doctors do their jobs, and Luke will wake up soon and pull through. I just know that will be."

But he didn't wake up. Due to continuing swelling of his brain, Luke was taken to surgery as soon as the surgical team could be assembled.

Dr. Mayhew, the chief neurosurgeon, told a colleague as he left the operating room, "Horrendous case. When we cut into the dura, the blood inside was under such pressure it squirted two feet into the air. The brain rose up out of the incision like a loaf of rising bread. We can't make that swelling go down. I think he's a goner."

Within a short time of being brought back from the operating room, Luke was much worse. His neurological signs headed in the wrong direction.

"This is looking horrible," Dr. McClure told the residents. " I doubt his brain's working at all. We need the neurology people to determine if he's brain dead."

By the end of the next day the Neurology team had established that Luke's brain had no electrical activity. With that fact and the failing results of all other examinations, the team determined that his brain would not sustain life off the machines. Tubes and lines were removed.

The Talbots came into his cubicle to say goodbye. Alison held him for the last time.

"Goodbye, my precious treasure. I know there will be a special place for you in heaven. My sweet baby." She no longer had the strength to sob, but a lone tear streaked down her cheek.

Fred stroked Luke's bandaged head, but shed no tears. He fought for control. "Someone's going to pay for this," he said.

After the Talbots left, Luke's body was turned over to Dr. Sam Drago, the county assistant medical examiner. The time was at hand for the postmortem examination.

As Luke's little body was transported to the morgue, McClure gathered her residents for their version of a postmortem. It was a sad session meant to ease the emotional turmoil the clinical team invariably felt when a child died in the PICU.

"So, do you think that truth will emerge from the autopsy?" McClure asked the residents. They looked at one another, then Phil Gumbel, the third-year Fellow, spoke up.

"We know what they'll find at postmortem; we saw the clinical data. Speaking of the clinical findings, Michaelson called and said that what they thought could have been an old tibial fracture was just a roughening of the bone and not a fracture. The pathologists should easily nail the cause of death. Will they determine how it happened? The answer to that won't be found in the autopsy."

2

Janet Feingold walked out of Courtroom 6, lugging her files in a battered leather briefcase, a gift from her father when she graduated from Yale Law School. His law satchel for many years, it had carried files for dozens of high-profile criminal trials.

She'd prevailed in the case just finished. She'd shown how the cops screwed up during her client's arrest. Tyrone, free to walk, grinned, a trace of cunning in his eyes. She nodded as she passed the cops in the hall.

"Got another scumbag off?" sneered Buck Walker, one of the cops. "We'll just see'm back here next week. Hope he doesn't kill somebody before we haul'm in again."

Walker, a veteran cop who'd watched drug deals go down as a beat cop in the neighborhoods, was a fixture in court, testifying on arrests he and his partner made. Like a lot of old-time cops, he was cynical about life and the small-time criminals he dealt with every day. He ducked coming through most doors and his frame showed the effects of a lifetime of beer guzzling and high-fat snacks. Small wonder he hadn't gotten diabetes or a heart attack. In a year he'd retire and then maybe he'd take care of his weight, but for the moment, he wolfed down empty calories.

"If you guys did your job right, it would be a lot harder for me to get a 'not guilty,' verdict; but you guys keep helping me," Janet shot back. She brushed back the hair that continually fell across her eyes, and warming to the argument, said, "You guys know that kid is not the problem. Why don't you go after the big fish and do something real to get drugs off the street?"

"We're out there workin' on it all the time; you can bet your bippy on that," he said over his shoulder. His heavy footfall moved toward the door, handcuffs rattling against his belt.

Why do I let him tease me into this same conversation each time I see the guy? Janet thought. Her edge was always out front at court, and she didn't care that some of the cops felt disdain towards her. She was passionate about making the justice system work, and that meant working her butt off for her clients, always the poorest and often the most ignorant.

She spotted Mike, a friend and officemate from the Public Defender's Office, across the corridor.

"Hey Mike, got time for lunch?"

"Got a quick hearing in Room 4. Meet you at Hanrahan's," he said.

Hanrahan's, a local watering hole for lawyers, was reminiscent of the storied pub near the Old Bailey in London where Rumpole used to meet up and trade barbs with his brother and sister barristers. The soundproofing panels in the ceiling sagged out of their metal grids, and bygone leaks in the roof had left café-au-lait stains in careless art nouveau patterns. Sports banners adorned the walls, with the Kansas City Chiefs and the Royals most prominent. The bar itself was an ancient cherry behemoth, running the entire length of the back wall. Up front, the large plate glass windows allowed almost no light to filter through, so large chandeliers were hung to relieve the darkness.

Mike arrived and slid into the booth opposite Janet. "You're looking good," he said.

Janet's smile transformed her face from plain to radiant. When in court, facing off with prosecutors, her diminutive figure belied an intensity that made the beefiest of male prosecutors seem immediately smaller. High cheekbones under a crown of black hair framed a narrow nose. She was attractive, but not pretty by conventional standards.

"Have a good weekend?" Mike asked.

"An interesting weekend. Went on my first date in a while. Guy named Jeremy Burns. Know him? He's also JD-impaired."

"From the Rigsby office? How'd you meet him? Those private practice types seldom mix with us proletariat."

"A mutual friend introduced us. We had a good time. Just went to a club and heard some great piano jazz. I doubt we'll go out again. He mostly talked about making partner at his law firm."

"So what do you hear from Alex?" Mike said.

"We're still dear friends, but now he's living with his boyfriend; seems really happy. I miss him and our talks that went on for hours, the concerts, those weekend get-aways. Pretty good sex, too, ironically. I guess he's bisexual; he seemed to enjoy the sex as much as I did. Maybe he was faking it, like Sally in that movie, *When Harry Met Sally.* Not much I can do about it. I'm just glad we've stayed friends.

"How's Lynn now that the baby's walking?" Janet said, moving the discussion off herself.

"Great. She's going back to work next week. We got a new nanny. They're hard to find and really expensive, but it's either a nanny or daycare. Daycare costs almost as much as the nanny and the kids all end up sick – seems they're germ magnets and germ vectors. The whole thing about getting my kid taken care of makes me nervous as hell, but we both have to work," Mike said.

"I hope to have that problem someday. And kind of soon. I'm 33 and don't want to worry about birth defects or having enough energy to chase after toddlers. And with Mom and her Alzheimer's…who knows how I'll be as I get older. Then there's the little matter of finding a man, harder all the time. You know the 3-G rule about men: Gross, Gay, or Girl Friend."

Mike nodded, a little grin skirting across his face.

"But," Janet continued, "the good news is that work keeps me happy. You know how obsessed I am with defense work."

"I've never asked you this, but before you were hired, I saw your resume, and I wondered why you wanted to work in the Public Defender's Office. Low pay, sketchy clients, few victories, no respect. Not a good formula for someone with your brains and a Yale Law School degree," Mike said.

"A lot had to do with my Dad. You know…" She broke into a mock announcer's voice: "'Nathan Feingold, Defense Attorney Extraordinaire, of Feingold LLC, downtown Kansas City.' He was my idol. He wasn't usually home for supper, but he made sure he saw me at bedtime to ask, 'What was the best part of your day?'" Janet gazed at the bar, her mind traveling back in time. "When I was younger, he'd sometimes read to me. I know that sounds corny, but I cherish those memories."

"That's not corny. Everyone should have a father like that," Mike said.

"We loved to talk. When I got older, we'd discuss philosophy, religion, morality, and other light-hearted topics," Janet said with a laugh. "He encouraged me to question authority, give everyone a good argument." Janet paused, reflecting on her relationship with her father.

"Quite an accomplishment to get into Yale, and the Law Review to boot," Mike said. "I bet your father's proud of you."

"We're proud of each other. He's such a caring person, so dedicated to the law. If I can be half the lawyer and person he is, I'll be happy," she said, wiping away a forming tear. "Sorry, I get emotional when I talk about Dad."

"How's your mom doing?" Mike said.

"Well, she had to go into a nursing home. It's sad. She doesn't recognize me when I visit her, but I keep going anyway. "

"Boy, that whole business of dementia scares me. Thank God my parents haven't shown any signs of it," Mike said.

Mike saw Janet's mouth tighten and realized he may have put his foot in his own. "Uh, hasn't your father been active in the ACLU? I've seen him interviewed on television talking about it."

"Yes, and he writes a lot of Letters to The Editor about infringements on people's rights. Some actually get published."

"So you've got the DNA of a defense lawyer. Why not practice with your dad?" said Mike.

"If I'd joined him in his practice right out of law school I would've been 'Nate's daughter.' I wanted to get hands-on experience with real cases. He handles all the major cases himself, and he already has a couple of young associates. I would be so junior that I wouldn't be the lead lawyer in most cases. With the Public Defender's office, I do everything. It's sink or swim. I may join him later, after I'm more seasoned, if he continues to want me."

Mike nodded, knowing Janet had assessed this correctly.

"I also love to match wits with sanctimonious prosecutors. And then there's the fun of doing my own legal research," Janet said. "But I just plain like working as a public defender. Giving my clients the best defense I can satisfies my sappy idealism. I like advocating for the underdog, the mute ones with no money or power. They grow up in poverty, get marginal educational opportunities, and then walk streets where their lives are shaped by violence and threats. Often they stumble into bad situations and get caught doing what their friends have done all the time. What really makes me angry is that the rich and powerful always seem to get away with behavior that's much worse and more destructive–they have money and connections."

Realizing she was preaching, she said, "Sorry, guess I got on my soapbox."

Mike couldn't help but smile, knowing that Janet was an open book and completely guileless. She saw his smile, took a deep breath.

"But, honestly, I'm sometimes torn. Do you ever lose sleep when you've gotten someone off who then goes out and does something awful? Do you ever feel you're responsible for allowing him to be out there in human society?"

"Oh sure, that's all part of it. Law is not morality," Mike said. "What you've just said tells me why you work sixty hours a week and why your social life is–somewhat thin?" said Mike.

"Better thin than boring. So many guys I've gone out with are caught up with themselves or their favorite sports teams…conversations go downhill fast. And it's pretty clear their goal is to wrestle you into the sack. Are all you guys like that?"

"We're not all wrestlers, but testosterone is our driving hormone," Mike said. "Sorry, probably getting too personal. I just want to see you happy. You've got a lot to offer the right guy," Mike said.

"Thanks Mike. I know you're being sympathetic, but don't worry about me. If my prince comes along I'll know it. Right now I'm content with work."

But I sure would like my prince to come along soon. Maybe Alex will actually find someone for me. He promised he would, Janet thought as she walked out of Hanrahan's.

3

As the ambulance carrying Luke sped down the street, siren blaring and lights flashing, Detective Doyle turned to Chrystal. "Come with me. We're going down to the station. You'll have to ride in the back."

Chrystal said nothing, got into the police cruiser and stared out the window as they left 43 Elderberry. Doyle looked at his mirror and saw a small girl–17 or 18 years old–with short mousy hair, pinkish skin, and a broad nose.

In a few minutes they pulled behind the police station. Doyle jumped out and opened the rear door. "OK, get out. I'll follow you into that door over there," he said, indicating the way.

Doyle's typical fast gait slowed behind Chrystal's skin-tight jeans and a ragged jacket full of factory-made holes thought fashionable by the high school set.

Once inside, two cops Doyle had called from the cruiser led Chrystal into a small room with a worn table and two chairs.

"Want some coke or coffee?" asked Jesse Howard, the police sergeant.

"No," said Chrystal, plopping down in the plastic chair.

"How about a candy bar or cigarette?"

"No, nothing."

Howard pulled out a sheet of paper. "I'm going to read your Miranda warnings. I want you to put your initials after each advisory. Understand?" he said, handing her a pen.

Chrystal nodded.

"You have the right to remain silent.

"Anything you say or do may be used against you in a court of law.

"You have the right to consult an attorney before speaking to the police and to have an attorney present during questioning now or in the future.

"If you cannot afford an attorney, one will be appointed for you before any questioning, if you wish.

"If you decide to answer any questions now, without an attorney present, you'll still have the right to stop answering at any time until you talk to an attorney.

"Knowing and understanding your rights as I have explained them to you, are you willing to answer my questions without an attorney present?"

Chrystal was only half-listening, but answered the last question by saying "Yeah."

"Please sign this form saying you understand this," Howard said. "Do you have parents or a friend you want us to call?"

Chrystal gave them her mother's name and phone number.

"You want to call your mother or want us to do it?"

"You call her. I don't want to talk to anybody."

"So, tell me in your own words what happened when you were taking care of the baby."

"I already said everything I know," Chrystal said.

"I know you did. Just tell me again so I can write it down and you won't have to tell your story anymore," Howard said.

"I was feeding him cereal and he was throwin' it all around, got it all over himself and me. I didn't see how I could clean him up in the kitchen, so I carried him upstairs, took off his clothes, ran the water and stuck him in the tub. After I washed him, I pulled him out of the tub and he went limp, like a dishrag. That's all I know. Called 911 and they came and took him away."

Chrystal slumped in her chair and went silent.

"Can I go home now?" she asked.

"Afraid not. You're going to be our guest here a while. Did anything else happen?"

Chrystal didn't answer.

Howard would say later, "She seemed glazed and blank and didn't seem to be with it. She went into a shell."

When Howard left the room the Children's Protective Services social worker went in.

"My name is Linda Campion. I'm from the state Children's Protective Services. I need to talk with you about what happened. Can you speak with me now?"

"I told the cops everything I know. Ask them," Chrystal said.

Chrystal stared into the corner and ignored Linda. After waiting a few minutes, Linda sighed, seeing that she was going nowhere with this interview.

"She won't talk with me. I'll try again tomorrow," she said as she left. The cops shrugged and showed her out.

Jesse Howard phoned Chrystal's mother. "Is this June Watts?"

"Yes, who's this?" June said.

"We're holding your daughter Chrystal here at the police station. The baby Chrystal was looking after was rushed to the hospital. Can you come down here?"

"I...I don't understand. You're holding my daughter at the police station? Why?" June stammered.

"Well, we're questioning her about what might've happened to the baby. She was with him when he collapsed and we're trying to figure it out. Chrystal asked us to call you," Howard said.

"I'll have to ask Daryll, my husband, when we can get there. Hold on a minute," June said.

Howard heard some muffled conversation, and then June came on the phone.

"We'll be there as soon as we can close up the store. Where should we come?"

When June and Daryll Watts, Chrystal's stepfather, were allowed to see her, she turned her back on both of them and put her hands over her face and eyes.

Daryll glared at her. He had no idea what had gone on, but was immediately accusatory.

"What the hell happened over there?" he said.

Getting no response, he looked at June.

"Don't worry, Sweetie, this'll be over soon," June said to her daughter. "We'll go home and everything'll be fine. By tomorrow this'll all seem like a scary dream. When we get home, I'll make you some hot cocoa and we'll go to bed."

Howard overheard her. "Sorry, lady," he said, "she's not going anywhere. She's under arrest and staying here."

"Under arrest? She hasn't done anything! Oh, let us take her home," June pleaded. "She'll be fine with us. We'll keep our eyes on her. She's a good girl, never gives us any trouble."

"She's got an arraignment on Monday. There's legal counsel issues, bail-setting and other matters," Howard said.

"What's the charge? What are you accusing her of?" Daryll asked.

"She was the last one with Luke Talbot before the EMTs took him to Children's Hospital. Now he's in the intensive care unit with a bad head injury. The docs reported it as suspicious for abuse to Children's Protective Services. Because of that she's being held here while the investigation is under way. You're gonna need a lawyer. If you can't afford a lawyer, the court will appoint one on Monday at the arraignment."

"I sure can't afford a shyster, so they better appoint her a good lawyer. Who pays for that?" said Daryll.

"The state does. Taxpayer money, you know. You pay taxes, don't you?"

"You bet I do. Bastards take all my profit from the store. They tax me on everything. I can barely eke out a living because of the guvment. Great country we live in," Daryll said.

"Well, my salary comes out of taxes, so you want to do away with the police?" growled the police sergeant. "How about the firemen? The roads? The department of public works? The water department? Which one of those do you want to cut out?"

June nudged Daryll towards the door. She knew he was only going to make matters worse for Chrystal if he kept up his rant. He'd never learned to keep his mouth shut.

As they were leaving, Daryll called over his shoulder, "I know all about the graft and kickbacks you cops get. I wasn't born yesterday. Your pensions, health insurance, extra work details where you sit in your cruisers and eat donuts. So don't get all hifalutin on me." Daryll never failed to be inappropriate. "They better get my stepdaughter a good lawyer or they'll hear from me."

The two cops looked at him, turned away and shook their heads.

Early Monday morning, Janet Feingold shoved assorted papers and boxes aside as she entered her cubicle at the Public Defenders' office. Standing on the banks of the Missouri River, this warren of offices was in an old warehouse, rehabbed on the cheap.

It was in stark contrast to her father's office on the 30th floor of a downtown office building where Nathan Feingold's Oriental carpets and large mahogany desk made sure his workplace reflected his success. The only aspect of work environment he and his daughter shared was the view of the river.

Facing Janet was a morass of papers, her law books and a jumble of wires from her computer, printer and telephone. Her windows were so smudged they barely let in the morning sun.

She was glancing at the mist rising from the mud-colored river when her phone rang. Detective Bill Gould, one of her buddies at the police station was calling.

"Well, top o' the morning to you! I got a real nasty one for you today," he said.

"You always have real nasty ones for me, you turkey," Janet said.

"This one's more awful than most—an abused baby case, involving a young, clueless babysitter. Police say she's got nothing to say that's going to help her and she's really out of it. She was sitting this seven-month-old boy and says he just went limp during a bath. Trouble is, he has blood in his head and in his eyes. The docs at the hospital say it's most likely shaken baby syndrome. The DA is all over it, real worked up. CPS tried to talk with the girl, got nothing out of her, so the girl's sittin' in a cell here. She's a mess."

"Has the judge appointed me already?" Janet said.

"Yeah, you got the call. He wants you," Gould said.

"How old is the girl?" Janet asked.

"Eighteen, looks older," Gould said.

"When can I talk with her?" Janet asked.

"Anytime you want. Come now if you can. The sooner the better, for her sake. "

"OK, I'll get over there as soon as I get organized."

Janet had a pile of cases, mostly drug dealers, assaults, and petty larceny. She hurried out of the office and headed for the station. On the way, she pulled out her iPhone and called her father.

"Hi Dad, I'm on my way to the police station to talk to a girl who was babysitting a baby now in the hospital with a bad head injury. The cop I talked to said the hospital doctors think it's something called shaken baby syndrome. I've never done a child abuse case before. Any advice?"

"A shaken baby case? That's an interesting coincidence. I was recently at a conference by some defense attorneys about shaken baby cases. The doctors there said these cases are bogus."

"Really?" Janet said.

"Yeah, the docs said that the doctors who testify for the prosecution depend on junk science to make their case. The docs at this meeting go all over the country to testify for the defense. Let me know what you find out after talking to the girl," Nate said.

"Great, I'll pick your brain after I know more. Can we have dinner tonight?" Janet said.

"I'd love that. We could meet at Luigi's; say, around seven?"

"Perfect. I'll call you to confirm, but let's count on it," Janet said.

Janet wheeled her old Rav4 into the lot behind the police station. She went in the back entrance that was restricted to lawyers. The walls of the station were institutional green, the windows leaked, and the place smelled of body odor, cigarette smoke, and a miasma of dampness, cleaning solutions and sour mops.

She found Gould and they went to the cramped interview room. Ghostly, aging fluorescent tubes lit the room.

"Here's her file," Gould said, tossing a thin folder on the table as he left to get Chrystal.

Returning shortly with her, Gould made the introductions.

"Chrystal, this is Janet Feingold, one of the best lawyers around. You should tell her everything."

Chrystal said nothing, didn't look at Janet and waited to be told to sit down.

"Afternoon, Chrystal," Janet said and rose to shake Chrystal's hand. Chrystal sat down, ignored Janet's hand, and fixed her gaze on a stain on the table in front of her. Her brown hair was tangled and dark circles were under her puffy eyes.

"I'm from the Public Defender's office. I've been appointed as your lawyer to defend you in this case. Do you understand that?"

Chrystal barely moved.

"Do you understand I'm on your side? That I'm a lawyer who'll argue for you in court?"

Nothing.

"Do you understand you're charged with a serious crime?" Janet tried again.

A blink indicated that Chrystal had at last heard something. "Luke has died, did you know that?" Janet said.

Chrystal's eyes opened wider, the fear now all too apparent.

"So here's what's going to happen. I'll review the evidence the prosecution will use. You and I will talk about our defense strategy. Do you understand what I'm telling you?"

"I don't understand any of this. What did you say happened to Luke?" Chrystal asked.

Janet searched for a way to mitigate this terrible news to Chrystal. She decided the best approach was simply to tell Chrystal the facts.

"He had a broken skull, bleeding inside his head, and his brain swelled. He died from these things. The District Attorney will charge you as the person causing his death," Janet said. "

"But he just went limp. How can that be? I don't know anything else. I want to go home now," Chrystal said.

"You can't go home, Chrystal. Do you know that you're in jail because they believe you caused Luke's death?" Janet asked, realizing that Chrystal hadn't grasped the seriousness of the trouble she was in.

"I didn't do anything to Luke. How can they say that about me? Why are they after me? I'm so tired, I just want to go home and go to bed."

"Chrystal, I know you're tired and upset. I'll come back tomorrow and we'll talk some more. Listen to me." Janet fixed her gaze on Chrystal, to let her sense that she really did want to help her. "Do not talk to anyone about anything unless I'm with you. Understand? No one. Nobody who's in jail with you, or anyone else. Is that clear?"

Janet spoke firmly, seeing that Chrystal's mind was far away. Still no response.

"You know what a Miranda warning is? Did they give you one of those?"

"I don't know."

"A Miranda warning says you don't have to answer any questions when I'm not with you. If you do answer questions, your answers can be used against you during the trial. So don't answer any questions unless I'm here. OK?" Janet said.

Gould leaned in. "We already Mirandized her. She didn't seem to understand what it meant, but we read it, like the good cops we are. She initialed it and signed that she understood it."

"I got nothing to hide. I don't remember anything more than what I already told them," Chrystal said.

"It's not a matter of hiding anything," Janet said. "You could misunderstand a question and give an answer that would sound different in court from what you meant. So just wait until I'm around to help decide what questions you should answer."

"OK," Chrystal said.

"I'll be back tomorrow. Remember what I told you. Don't talk about the case with anyone," Janet said as she left.

"Sorry to be so repetitive, but she doesn't seem to hear or understand anything," Janet said to Gould. "You know, young people charged with big crimes are so bewildered, especially in cases like this where there's been an unexpected horrible outcome. They can't believe that they could've done such a terrible thing, and they've convinced themselves that they didn't."

"So, you don't think she's innocent?" said Gould.

"Doesn't matter what I think, you know that. What matters is what can be proven in court. My job is to defend my client, using whatever evidence I have to be sure no one is convicted without considering all the possibilities. We have to make the justice system work for everybody," she said. "OK, sermon's over."

"So, Bill, what can you tell me?" Janet asked.

"Not a whole lot. She's repeated the same story over and over. And we wanted to get you involved because I know you guys all say that we awful cops coerced a confession."

"Now when have I ever accused you of such an egregious thing?" Janet said with a smile.

"Every damned time we're in court, Ms. Defender of the Poor and Downtrodden," Bill said in the same teasing tone as Janet's.

"How about the CPS report?" Janet asked.

"Well, a CPS woman was here, but I don't have her report yet. My guess is Chrystal said about the same things to her," Bill said.

"Well, so far, it's hard to figure out what kind of defense we can build. I'll have to see what I can turn up when I get the hospital reports," Janet said as she headed for her car. "Talk to you later."

Janet called her paralegal before she left the parking lot. "On the Talbot case, get cracking on gathering all of the hospital records, the EMS run sheet, the statements of the detective who was first on the scene, the pediatricians' records from birth on, and when it's ready, the autopsy report. Also, call Dr. Baxley, the pediatric intensivist at St Louis Children's Hospital. Tell him I want to talk about a case and give him my cell number.

"I'll call Luke's parents myself in a few days to see if they'll talk to me," Janet said. "Thanks for all this."

The Talbots might refuse to talk to me for a couple of reasons. First, they don't want to give me any help in defending Chrystal. Secondly, and this is touchy, they might decline if one of them had injured Luke before Chrystal got there. If they refuse to talk, that could be construed to mean they're hiding something. And that could be useful during the trial.

anet walked into Luigi's with these thoughts swimming in her head. She spotted her father in his favorite back booth. Nate, in his late 60's, carried a few extra pounds. His hairline had retreated from the top of his head leaving tufts of gray hair on both temples. When he smiled, the lower portion of his face seemed engulfed by his mouth. Years of cigar smoking had stained his teeth, a habit he had recently thrown over. Part of his charm came from his hooded, bright blue eyes set in his round face, giving him a seductive look.

Nate had seen so much misery, corruption, dishonesty, and hypocritical righteous indignation, he was increasingly misanthropic as he aged. Despite this, he had strong convictions about providing a defense for those accused of crimes. Janet knew that he may have guessed at the guilt and culpability in some of his clients, but she admired how he always worked hard to insure the suspects were not put away without due process. His friends in the media gave him ample opportunity to vent his opinions in Op-Ed columns when serious moral or social issues arose in legal cases. He was an unreconstructed liberal. His work with the ACLU, his newspaper columns and television interviews confirmed that. He'd never lost his "Knight on a White Horse" fantasies, seeing himself as a rescuer of the falsely accused. Janet saw him that way too.

"Always know where to find you, Dad," Janet said.

"I like sitting here because it gives me a full view of the restaurant and there's no one behind me. It's an old habit I got from my Mafia clients. They invariably sat with their backs against the back walls of restaurants to avoid getting "whacked" by one of their enemies," Nate said. "Or their friends."

Nathan rose to hug his daughter. "Good to see you, my dear," he said.

"Same here, Dad. I wish we could spend more time together, but…"

"So how are things at the Public Defender's office? Still having money problems?" Nate asked, rescuing her from further explanation.

"Of course we're having money problems. The bozos at the state house take a perverse pleasure in cutting our funding while they increase the DA's pay. They must really despise the under-privileged who can't afford lawyers."

"Politicians posturing as they always do," Nate said. "Playing on the public's fear that 'those people' are killers, rapists, muggers, or drug dealers. Why should taxpayers subsidize their defense? Easy demagoguery.

"You know the cases I like most? When the prosecutors, looking to the next election, send up their heavy artillery, cross a few lines of legality and get caught. Love exposing politicians!"

"Back to the money issues. We're solvent. At least for now," Janet said.

"You could come and work in my office anytime you want. You would make five times as much money and have better working conditions."

"Persevering as always, Dad. But I wouldn't get the experience I need. After a few years, maybe."

"Just checking. One of these days maybe you'll accept my offer. I get it. Of course you're doing the right thing at this stage of your legal development." He sighed.

"You know, I often think back to when you were a little kid and came to my old, crappy office. You remember that place? Didn't look like much, but boy how we were buzzing in those days. Great cases and lots of razzle-dazzle in the courtroom. Seemed like I couldn't lose a case. Prosecutors were scared out of their wits when they found out I was going to be the defense.

"And you–you loved going into my library, poking around in the law books. Never understood why a twelve year-old kid would want to read a dusty old law book. But there you were," Nate said.

"I liked the smell of those old books. When I was in law school my happiest days were in the law library because of the same smell. It reminded me of you and your office."

"When you were in college, I wasn't convinced you should go to law school. You were smart enough, I knew that, but there are so many damned lawyers out there; I wasn't sure it was the best thing for you. But you really wanted it," Nate said.

"So, tell me about your case."

"Well, this is what I know." She filled him in on the bare bones.

"I'm intensely interested," said Nate. "There's new information about so-called shaken baby cases. Did you know that the American Academy of Pediatrics now says that this name shouldn't even be used anymore? It should be called "abusive head trauma" instead. You know why? Because no one can prove that shaking causes these injuries. I mean, Christ, how would you test the hypothesis? You can't test it on live babies!"

"These doctors at this conference were adamant that pediatricians are sending innocent people to jail. They believe it so deeply they call the child abuse pediatricians a 'cult.' This really captured me. It motivates me to fight to keep these people out of jail. It's the kind of thing that impelled me to go into defense work. "

"So, would you be interested in helping me on this case? I mean, actually being the lead counsel?" Janet said, mostly in jest. "Pro-bono, of course."

"Let me think about it. I might. I feel that strongly about this."

Janet, surprised at his response, waited for Nate to continue.

"Maybe I could get one of the lawyers from that conference to advise us on how best to defend your client. There's always perfectly good arguments why the accused didn't do the crime: someone else did it.; temporary insanity; cops didn't follow legal procedures or are lying. Prosecutors are withholding evidence. The other thing is that in medical cases, you can always find doctors who'll say anything you want. Besides, jurors aren't able to follow medical testimony. Much too much jargon, and there's so much disagreement amongst doctors about their science. Just look at how often old research is disproven by what's in today's medical journals. There's always a way to defend the accused in these cases.

"Love cross-examining doctors!" Nate continued. "They're so anxious about not being in control in the courtroom they get supercilious while testifying. Juries hate that."

Her father's increasing cynicism gnawed at Janet. She wanted to see him as pure and unsullied. Hopelessly idealistic, she still saw a justice system where a blindfolded woman held the scales of justice and courts objectively decided cases. To her, judges were expected to be men and women in black robes with an abundance of patience and Solomonic wisdom, their biases and prejudices left at the courtroom door. So she changed the subject.

"Have you seen Mom this week?"

"Yeah, she's about the same. Her mental capacity diminishes daily. She hardly recognized me yesterday. She's losing some weight and the nurses think that's due to her deepening depression. I think it's just her Alzheimer's getting worse. But what do I know?"

"How're you getting along at home with no one there?"

"Well, it's lonely, but I'm getting used to it. I'm working hard, staying late at the office, so I don't spend much time at home. "

The waitress's arrival interrupted the conversation. Janet ordered vegetable lasagna and Nathan asked for his favorite chicken broccoli pasta dish. Each ordered a glass of white wine, started off with the spinach salad, and finished off with crème brulee.

"I think we should do this at least once a week," Janet said. "I really miss seeing you."

"That's a deal. Let's make a pact and do it," said Nate. "Love you, kid."

"Love you, too, Dad."

They hugged a little longer than usual, then both headed for home.

The next morning Janet called her friend, Tom Baxley, a pediatric intensive care doctor at St. Louis Children's Hospital. Janet knew Tom from college and had kept in touch with him over the years.

"Tom, I'll get right to the point. I have this seven-month-old baby who died of what the doctors think was shaken baby syndrome." She told him the details that she knew. "Could you review the case?"

"Not a good time for me. I have a grant I'm working on, with a deadline in a couple of weeks. Also have to head up a curriculum group for the ICU, and I'm in charge of the next team of Residents," Baxley said.

"I won't need much from you until after your grant deadline, and all I really want is for you to review the records and tell me what you think. I won't call you to testify. I just need information, and a reference point to begin construction of my defense. Please."

Baxley liked Janet, always had. He was a sucker for her idealism, although he didn't understand how she could defend some of her clients. But he knew she was a good person. He thought about the grant, the curriculum, and the vacation that he'd put off for eight months. He really didn't want another thankless job. But it was Janet.

"OK, you're really good at manipulation. No wonder you're such a good defense attorney. Send the file when you pull it together. I definitely can't get to it until two to three weeks from now."

"Thanks Tom, I really appreciate it. You need X-rays? I can get a CD of those if you do. Anything else?"

"Yeah, I'll need birth records and the pediatric records from the baby's primary pediatrician. I'd like to have some family history if you can get that. Looking for some genetic or familial factors that might explain the case. Also it would be helpful to see the police and CPS interview transcripts. Although those aren't strictly medical, they may give me some insights that the medical records don't. If I think of anything else, I'll let you know."

Just as she hung up, her assistant said her father was on the other line.

"Hi Dad. What's up?"

"I've been thinking about your baby head injury case. I'd like to get involved. I mean, really involved. Like co-counsel. Would your office consider that? Would you consider that?"

"Absolutely! I'd love to work on a case with you. You're my hero, you know. Why don't we sit down and decide how to proceed?"

"Well, first, you need some defense medical experts," Nate said. "I'll pony up the costs for them. We might get the Court to pay some of that. I'll find out the names of some doctors who testify in these cases and get their resumes. Secondly, I'd like to be the one to question these expert witnesses. I'll start searching what's written in the medical books and journals. OK?"

"That's more than OK, Dad. That's wonderful. Then I'd be free to work with the defendant, do jury selection, and the rest of the witnesses?"

"Sounds like a partnership to me. I really want to get my teeth into this. By the way, I want to have the new guy in my office, David Weller, be an observer during this trial. He's fresh out of law school and needs to see how I operate. Any problems with that?" Nate said.

"No problem. He'll just be an observer, right?"

"Yeah, he won't make a peep during the trial. It will be a great experience for him," Nate said. "Listen, we ought to work the media a little bit. Starting right away, because the jury will be coming from the general public and the sooner we cast doubt on the theory of shaken baby syndrome in the press and on TV, the better chance we'll have."

"Really, the media? I've tried to stay away from them," Janet said.

"Oh yeah, the media can be a great help in shaping the opinion of the great unwashed out there, some who may end up in your jury pool. We should work the media hard. I've got contacts at the papers and the local TV channels. Never hurts to get public sympathy. You need all the sympathy you can get when it comes to dead baby cases."

"Hmm," said Janet. "New territory for me. Not sure I'm comfortable with that."

Then, after reflecting for a minute, she said, "OK, Dad; I'll pull the records together. I've already asked Tom Baxley, my friend at St. Louis Children's, to look them over. Always good to get an outside opinion."

5

The jail, an imposing Federal-style building built in the late 1800's, had been erected when structures were expected to last. This one had lasted, but now it was showing signs of erosive decrepitude.

The bricks were going to dust, and the mortar of the interstices was granulating and spilling out. The interior needed serious rehabilitation, but the county budget didn't allow it, so the sagging floors and peeling walls bore witness to its decay. Faulty ventilation allowed stagnant air to hold aromas of food, tobacco, sweat, and excrement. The oak beams supporting the ceilings were caked with years of moisture, stains, and old varnish. Prison cells, built for earlier, smaller human specimens, were cramped spaces for today's tenants, whose shoes stuck to grimy floors from years of dirty mops negligently passed over them in perfunctory acts of cleaning.

Janet went to the front desk after passing through the metal detector and an unnecessary body-pat-down.

"This is really 'security theater' when you pat down people you know," she said to the young female cop.

"You never know," she said, a little embarrassed. "Just doing my job."

When Janet came into the room, Chrystal actually made eye contact.

"How're you doing today?" Janet said.

"I hate it here. People hate me, give me a hard time, call me a baby-killer. How'd they find out why I'm in?" Chrystal whined.

"Jails are snake-pits of gossip. Rumors get started and get wilder with each telling. Stay away from other prisoners, and whatever you do, don't talk about your case with anybody. Someone may slip up close, pretend to be sympathetic and offer to be your friend, tell you that you can cry on her shoulder. If you fall for that, you can bet you'll see her in court telling the jury things you never said. So don't talk to anyone but me about anything unless I'm with you," Janet re-emphasized.

Chrystal looked down at her lap. "I'm so lonely here. I just want to get out. What about bail, so I could go home?"

"There'll be a bail hearing, but don't get your hopes up. They always set bail high in homicide."

Chrystal started to cry. Janet's impulse was to put her arm around her but she held back, not sure why. She waited until Chrystal regained control.

"Here's some things I need to talk to you about. The prosecutors may offer you something called a 'plea bargain.' This is an offer by them to charge you with a lesser crime, like manslaughter instead of murder if you'll plead 'guilty' instead of 'not guilty.' If you take a plea bargain you wouldn't have to have a trial at all. You'd be sentenced to some jail time–I don't know what the offer might be–but you'd avoid the stress of a trial and your jail term would be less than if you're convicted of murder."

Janet couldn't read the expression on Chrystal's tear-splotched face.

"You're telling me I should admit to doing something when I didn't? Just so I don't go to trial? I'm not gonna do that. I'd be stuck in jail for years! I'd be an old woman when I got out and I couldn't ever have a life! No, no way, I won't do that," Chrystal said.

"Just so you understand," Janet said, trying to strike a balance between recommending this and letting Chrystal make up her own mind, "your jail term would be a whole lot shorter with a plea bargain. I have to tell you that if we go to trial and lose you could be in jail for a lot longer."

"I'm innocent and I'm not pleading to nothing I didn't do. End of story," Chrystal said.

"OK, I hear you," Janet said. "Now, here's the other thing I want to tell you. My father's a well-known lawyer in town and wants to help. He's even willing to pay some expert doctors to help us in court. It's a wonderful offer. I'd still be your main lawyer. Is this agreeable to you?"

"You make it sound like I'm in real trouble. I thought this would all just, you know, go away. I need to talk to Mom about this. I guess I'll even have to talk to Daryll, but he'll be a prick as usual. "

Janet's third ear perked up when she heard Chrystal's remark. *I wish I knew more about Daryll,* she thought.

"Talk to them next time they come in. I'd like to be sure we're all on the same page about the plea bargain and about my dad helping. I'd be glad to talk with them too. Would you like me to speak with your mother?" Janet said.

Chrystal thought about it for a minute, then said she would talk to them and ask them to call Janet.

"Good," Janet said. "I'll be expecting their call." She smiled at Chrystal, trying to make eye contact. Then she gathered her papers, slid them into her briefcase, and got up to leave. "Anything else?" she asked.

Chrystal had disappeared into her inner world and was deaf to the question. Janet was beginning to recognize and accept these mood changes. She left quietly.

When June came to see Janet, Daryll was with her.

"Thanks for coming in," Janet said. *Maybe I'll get some insight into this strange man.* "I have some things I wanted to run by you. I've talked with Chrystal, and she wanted me to talk to you about her decisions."

June was short, overweight and frumpy, but bore some resemblance to Chrystal in her coloring. Daryll reminded Janet of pictures she'd seen of 1930's Welsh coalminers. He was a slight, wiry man, whose facial skin was a moonscape of old acne scars. He had a couple of days' growth of grayish-black beard, a shock of black disheveled hair, a downturned mouth, and a hooked, off-center nose. Dark circles dwelt under darting eyes, and one of his cheeks bore an ugly scar.

Janet explained what a plea bargain was and then told them, "Chrystal says she doesn't want a plea bargain."

June looked at Daryll. He didn't return her look, but leaned toward Janet. "Did you tell her to take the plea bargain?"

"No, my job is to tell her of the pros and cons, let her decide. She said that since she didn't do anything she's not going to say she did. I told her that if she's found guilty at trial, she'd face a much longer jail sentence than if she took a plea bargain. But she insisted she wouldn't plead to a lesser crime when she'd done nothing at all. So, bottom line, she turned it down.

"Here's the other thing. My father, Nathaniel Feingold, is an experienced criminal defense lawyer here in Kansas City. He's offered to be co-counsel with me, at no charge. He's also offered to pay for expert medical witnesses for the trial. Is that something you'd be interested in?" Janet asked.

Again, June looked at Daryll.

"Why do that for Chrystal? What's in it for him?" Daryll asked, looking as distrustful as he sounded.

"My father believes what killed Luke was not anything Chrystal did. He thinks medical people have made up this thing called shaken baby syndrome and there's no scientific basis for it. So he wants to use this case to help prove that idea."

"But why would doctors make up things like that?" June asked, bewildered by this unfathomable concept.

"Doctors make up stuff all the time, you know that," Daryll said to June. "You read about this stuff in the paper. The docs come into court and say whatever they please and the stupid juries eat it up. There ain't no justice in the courts. Between the doctors and the lawyers, they're all on the take, and they're always slamming innocent people in the can for crimes they didn't do. And cops lie through their teeth."

Janet knew there was no use arguing with a man like this, so she stayed silent. *Hard to conceive Tom Baxley, a well-trained, hard-working, straight-arrow intensivist, who had seen several cases of shaken baby syndrome, 'making this up.' On the other hand, Tom was the product of traditional medical training. If, as Nate claimed, the science was flawed, Tom might be working with the same incorrect information that mainstream medical opinion held as truth.*

"I think there's disagreement among doctors about how these injuries come about rather than someone 'making it up.' But my father has given a lot of thought to this, and he thinks many doctors are wrong about shaken baby syndrome. He may be right," said Janet.

"As a mother, I can't believe that skull fractures just happen. Babies don't just die. Something causes them to die. But I can't believe that my Chrystal hurt that baby. She's not like that. I know she's got a temper, but she's a good girl and wouldn't hurt a flea," June said, surprising both Daryll and Janet by her seemingly uncharacteristic intensity.

"If you think your father and his medical experts can get Chrystal off, then go for it," Daryll said.

"I guess it's our only hope. That and prayer," June said.

"So I'll ask my father to contact the medical experts and we'll go from there. Anything else you want to know?"

Daryll didn't hesitate for a moment.

"How much is this going to cost us?" he asked.

"I'm a public defender. Our office is supported by taxes so neither of you nor Chrystal will be charged anything. My father has offered to do his part without pay. Like I said, my Dad will foot the bill for the experts. So none of this will incur any costs for you."

"Well, I'll be damned. First time in my life that anyone–especially the guvment–did anything for me. What's the catch? What's your old man expecting to get out of this?" Daryll said again.

Janet let Daryll's negative comments and questions go without a response.

"Thanks for coming in. Here's my card. Call me if you have questions. I'll do my best to defend your daughter," Janet said, directing her comment to June and avoiding looking at Daryll.

"You mean my step-daughter. I'm not her real father. But I've had to foot the bill for all the stuff she wants and what thanks does she give me? None. Maybe this'll teach 'er a lesson about life. It'll be good for her. The school of hard knocks, I call it."

"I hope we all learn something from it, Mr. Watts," Janet replied. "Good bye."

After they had left, Janet slammed her folder onto the desk. "What a bloody jerk!"

As Daryll and June walked towards their car, June turned to Daryll. "I want to talk directly to Chrystal, alone."

He jerked his head around. This was the first time June had ever made a declarative statement to Daryll.

"You know she's a little liar, don't you? Don't believe anything she tells you. Go ahead, talk to her, but don't buy all the stuff she says. Especially about me. She hates my guts. No telling what she might say," Daryll said, his eyes shifting around.

June was probably the only living soul who thought of her husband as a nice guy. She knew that Daryll had a vulnerable side due, she thought, to his war experience. His attitude came as a shock.

"Chrystal lying? What in the world do you mean by that? I've never heard you talk about Chrystal that way. What's gotten into you?" June said, shaking her head in disbelief.

June went to see Chrystal the next day.

"Hi sweetie. I miss having you at home so much. How're you feeling?" June said from the visiting booth.

"Fine," Chrystal said as she adjusted the speakerphone on the other side of the thick plastic panel.

"Daryll and I talked with Miss Feingold yesterday. She seems real nice. I think she can get you off. And with her father helping, it shouldn't be as bad as we thought at first. Daryll thinks..."

Cutting June off in mid-sentence, Chrystal said, "I don't give a shit what Daryll thinks. He's mean and ugly and nothin' he would say means squat to me."

"Now honey, you know how he is," June said. "Since he's back from Iraq he has the PTSD. I don't know what that is exactly, but they say it's why he gets so mad sometimes. You know he wakes up at night sweating and yelling at the top of his lungs. It takes me a while to calm him down. He saw awful things over there, buddies blown up right beside him, really bummed him out. You know he saved one of his buddies, ran into that house, found his best friend wounded, his leg nearly shot off. He carried him out and got him back to the medics. He's told us that story a lot of times. Remember when he used to be worse–before he gave up drinking?"

June looked for sympathy from Chrystal but saw none.

"He's in therapy," June continued, "at the Veteran's Hospital and he's on some medicine. He tries hard. Sometimes I need to rock him to sleep. He can be very nice when he's calm."

"How's it going at the store?" Chrystal asked, changing the subject.

"Same ol', same ol'. We're scraping by," said June. "Some of your girlfriends came by the other day and were asking about you. I told them you were doing OK but hate being in jail. I told them to write you some notes. Got any yet?"

"Mom, kids my age don't write notes; they tweet or go on Facebook, and I ain't allowed any of that in here," Chrystal said. "Why is this taking so long? When this is over with I'm thinking about moving somewhere no one knows me."

"Oh, I'd miss you so if you went away," said June.

"Time's up," said the guard abruptly.

"See you. Thanks for coming in," was all Chrystal could muster as they led her away.

"Bye, sweetie. Keep your chin up. Everything's going to come up roses, you'll see. Love you," June said as she hung up the phone and blew Chrystal a kiss. It was hard to keep her own chin up as she trudged out of the jail. What would become of her daughter?

6

"Not guilty," Chrystal said in a quiet voice, standing before the judge's bench in her jumpsuit, wrists and ankles in shackles.

"I must advise you," Judge Higgins said, "of your rights, especially your constitutional right against self-incrimination." He enumerated other rights, but Chrystal wasn't listening.

"Because of the serious nature of this crime, I'm setting your bail at $50,000," he said.

Chrystal didn't blink. Later, Janet called Daryll to tell him about the bail.

"Are they fuckin' kidding?" he howled. "I don't have that kind of money. Nobody I know has that kind of money. She'll just have to tough it out in jail. At least she'll get free room and board. So how long will this take?"

Janet restrained herself from matching Daryll's vitriol in her response. *Free room and board? What kind of twisted thinking is that?*

"It could be months, depending on a lot of things. I'll be talking to the prosecutors later today. I'll let you know what comes of that."

Janet finished the call to Daryll and called her father.

"I'm putting you on speaker so David can listen in to the conversation, OK?" Nate said.

"Sure, that's fine," Janet said. "I think we're ready to lay out our defense strategy. Chrystal and her parents agreed to proceed with you as co-counsel and the arrangements for the experts. Talk about an offer they can't refuse. Is your enthusiasm still high, Dad?"

"You bet. I'll get on this right away. Send all the records to me and I'll get these medical experts on board. Have you talked to the prosecutors yet?"

"No, I'm meeting with them soon, probably tomorrow."

"Do you know who they are?" Nate asked.

"I assume the lead will be Mary Egan. She heads up the child abuse unit at the DA's office. I've met her, but don't know much about her. I hear she's smart and objective, but tough."

Nate turned to David. "I always do some digging on the opposing lawyers. I'll look into Mary Egan's old cases, what her style is in court, what her vulnerabilities are, and so on. I'll find out her law school record, what her social and religious orientations are. Whether she's rigid and brittle, or flexible. Figure out the best way to challenge her in court."

"OK, Dad, I'll get back to you after I've had my meeting with her and her co-counsel. Not sure who that will be," Janet said.

Janet's heart beat faster as she went through courthouse security and up to the prosecutor's conference room. Her palms were sweaty as she shook hands with Mary Egan.

"Morning, Janet, how're you doing?" Mary said.

She was taller than Janet and had straight, blond hair cut short around her face, which, like her body, was slender. Her slightly turned up narrow nose complemented a small mouth above a dimpled chin.

"Fine, getting colder outside. Parking's not getting any easier around the court house, is it?" Janet said, trying to appear nonchalant.

"Yeah, I come to the office by bus because of that. Oh, here's Albert now," Mary said.

"Hi. Don't think we've met before. Albert Polcari."

"Janet Feingold."

Janet noted his thick coal-black hair and dark beard shadow along his jaw. Albert's blue suit, white shirt, regimental striped tie and lace-up black wingtip shoes were standard issue from a local department store.

Albert took Janet's hand and gave it a gentle squeeze, not the hand mash Janet anticipated from a muscular, athletic guy.

"Shall we begin?" Mary asked.

"Sure. So, what are the charges?" Janet said.

"We decided second degree's most appropriate. We doubt your client woke up that morning and decided to kill Luke."

"What about manslaughter?" Janet said.

"We could reduce it to manslaughter on a plea bargain. Would your client consider that?" Mary replied.

"Not a chance. I've already talked with her and her parents about that," Janet said, feeling on firmer ground than when she came in.

"With all the evidence I've seen, it seems your client's really vulnerable. She still says she's innocent in the face of all that?" Mary said.

"Yes. She's adamant she did nothing to Luke. She's unlikely to change her mind, going by our conversations so far." After running through some procedural matters, Janet said "I guess all we need to discuss is dates. Oh, one other thing I need to tell you. My father, Nathan Feingold, will be my co-counsel, and he's lining up the medical experts we'll be using. And paying for them."

Mary's eyes narrowed when she heard this. She knew Nathan Feingold's reputation as a wily operator. This was a surprise, and not a pleasant one. But she wasn't going to let Janet know how she felt about it.

"I see. Send me the names and CV's of those experts when you engage them, OK? We'll mainly be using the doctors at Children's Hospital as our witnesses, although we may call in outside experts. We'll let you know as we get closer to trial."

A pause.

"Why's your father interested in this case?" Mary asked.

"You'd have to ask him. I'm pleased, of course, since our office can use his help. I'm not sure how the court would rule on payment for expert witnesses in a case like this. It could run into some real money."

For the first time, Polcari spoke up. "The court does have budget limitations, but my guess is that they'd allocate expert fees unless they're really outrageous. After all, it's a dead baby case and the media will be all over it. Any attempt by the court to limit expert testimony in a case like this would make for some interesting headlines."

"I'll let you know their names as soon as we get their confirmation," Janet said.

She paused, and tried not to appear abrupt when she said, "Do we have any other business?"

"Don't think so. I appreciate your coming over," Mary said. "Nice to meet you, Janet," Albert said as she was going out the door.

"Likewise," Janet said. She had long since stopped feeling awkward exchanging pleasantries with two people who were going to be fierce adversaries in short order. She knew it was best to maintain a good relationship with your opponents, adhering to her father's philosophy that you keep your friends close, but your enemies closer.

"Did you send the records over to my Dad?" Janet asked Melissa when she returned to her office.

"I had to," she said. "He called, so I sent them to him by messenger. I didn't even have time to make copies he was so much in a hurry. Honestly, he really made me nervous."

"He sure can be abrupt, but nothing personal. That's one reason he's so effective in court. He's a force of nature, very smart, very aggressive and a good debater. We used to have spirited discussions at home and he always encouraged me to butt heads with him."

Melissa was fascinated when her boss talked about personal things.

"Of course he always won the arguments. He loved to win, even with me when I just a kid. He had the ammunition—the knowledge, the techniques—but I learned a lot about how to win arguments. Underneath it all, though, he's a wonderfully generous, kind man, and a great father. As a matter of fact, excuse me, I have to call him."

"Hi Dad, I need to learn more about shaken baby syndrome. Some of the law journals suggest filing a pretrial motion to disallow introducing this controversial diagnosis into the trial."

"I guess that's a possibility, but I doubt you'd get the judge to rule in your favor on that one," Nate said, drawing on deep legal experience. "I've found out some interesting stuff about your prosecutor friends, Mary Egan and Al Polcari that I'll tell you about later."

7

"Hi Janet. Finished reviewing the Luke Talbot case. Want a written opinion or can we simply talk?" Tom Baxley said.

"Depends on your opinion," Janet said. "Tell me what you think by phone first. Anything written is discoverable by the prosecutors."

"Well, unfortunately for your client, I think this is a classic case of shaken impact syndrome. Right age group, no birth injuries, no history of car crashes, big falls or previous trauma. There was a subdural hematoma, bleeding under the scalp right over the skull fracture. A fracture on the backside of the head in a seven-month-old is hard to come by accidentally. Add in retinal hemorrhages and retinal folds–a slam-dunk for the prosecution. Plus, there's nothing to suggest any medical reasons, like family or genetic diseases, for any of this. Sorry to be the bearer of bad news, but I'm afraid your client is sunk."

"Bummer. My client already nixed a plea bargain."

"That's out of my league. Never understood plea bargains. You're either guilty or not. But then I'm a doctor, not a lawyer, thank God."

"Well, thanks anyhow. Don't put this in writing," Janet said.

"You know my father's a defense lawyer in town, right? He's helping me on this case, and he's really fired up."

"Yeah? Lucky for you. What's his interest in this case?" said Tom.

" I'm not sure why he's so gung-ho about this, but it's consistent with his personality of taking on causes where he thinks people haven't asked the right questions and have come to wrong conclusions. He thinks doctors are wrong about shaken baby syndrome and that most doctors make this diagnosis without looking at alternatives. So he's picked this windmill to joust."

Tom was quiet for a moment.

"I'm not a child abuse expert, only an intensive care pediatrician, so I asked our child abuse specialist to look at these records. She agreed this was shaken impact syndrome. She said there's a small contingent of doctors, most of whom have never taken care of a baby who's been shaken, who've been trying to turn this diagnosis into a controversy. Janet, everything I read in reliable, peer-reviewed journals supports the conclusion that injuries like Luke's are due to shaking and impact."

"OK, I hear you. I haven't gotten the Medical Examiner's autopsy report yet, but would that influence your analysis?"

"I kinda doubt it. The clinical stuff's most important. My guess is the ME's report will only confirm the clinical findings in the hospital."

"If it shows anything unexpected, can I send it over?" Janet asked.

"Sure, but don't get your hopes up."

"I won't. Thanks again, even though you haven't exactly made my day," Janet said. "I'm not giving up on the autopsy findings, though. Maybe something there will give us a new insight. Like setting the time of the injury or an unexpected disease in the baby. Maybe old injuries. I'm not ready to concede there can only be this one diagnosis."

"As I said, don't get your hopes up."

8

"Alex? Can you meet me for coffee? I need a break, and I'd like to see you anyway," Janet said.

Until a few months ago Alex and Janet had been dating steadily. She'd hoped he was "the one." He had made her laugh until tears rolled out, sympathized with her disappointments, and shared her passions for life and art and music. Well-educated and hard working, Alex was one of thousands of struggling jazz artists playing at small venues for little money. A warm, interesting guy in his mid-thirties, he had a god-like beauty–dark brown hair, cobalt–blue eyes, angular features, and a body kept in shape by daily exercise and weekend hiking trips. He and Janet made a great couple. Then one night, in a low voice, he'd said, "Not sure how to tell you this, but I guess the direct approach is best…" He paused. "I'm gay. I have to stop fooling myself, and you, and all my friends any longer."

Janet had looked at Alex in disbelief as this stunning disclosure flooded her senses. Her head felt light and spots bounced before her eyes.

"Are you kidding me?" she blurted.

"Janet, I wouldn't play that kind of game," Alex said.

"Oh my God, this is so embarrassing," Janet said. "I feel like a fool. All the good times we've had together," Janet said, her voice cracking. "I don't know what to say. This is off the charts. And frankly, it makes me very angry."

Alex reached across the table to take Janet's hand. She yanked it back, hurt and confused by this revelation.

"I'm sorry. I don't know what else to say," Alex said. "This is not easy for me either. I'm so fond of you. I don't want to hurt you any more than

I already have. So I hope after some time passes, you'll be able to forgive me."

After that night, it had taken her weeks to comprehend this bewildering reality. But as painful as it was for Janet to lose him as a potential long-term partner, best friend and lover, they had somehow found a way to remain caring friends. Now, months later, they got together frequently for coffee or a drink or lunch.

This time they met at Mocha Jim's, the local coffee bar. Both ordered a latte.

"So, have you sprung any axe murderers lately?"

"Very funny," she said in mock anger. "I don't want to talk about work. How's the music business?"

"Carnegie Hall is beckoning, but I don't think I'll accept. Too far to travel. Seriously, though, I do have a gig at Passori's, a little jazz nightspot where a lot of cool people hang out. But this barely pays the rent."

"How do you support your music habit? Artistically you seem to be a success, but financially you're a disaster."

"I hope to get famous someday so I won't have to rely on Randolph's support, but right now he's making a lot of money. When are you going to take a break from being a workaholic and meet him? You know, we're thinking about having a baby. We're trying to decide whether to adopt or go the surrogate mother route."

"Alex, that's great. I'm truly happy for you," Janet said, her mouth and throat dry. "Um, no time soon for the break, but I do want to meet him."

"What do you think? Surrogate mother or adoption?"

When Janet rebounded from this surprise, she said "Well, obviously if you want to pass on your own genetic material, surrogacy's the way to go. But there are a lot of wonderful babies out there who need homes and loving parents. My mom used to work for an international adoption agency, remember? Wish she were still active to give you some advice," Janet said. "Would you go domestic or international if you adopt?"

"Haven't gotten that far. We're still a little ambivalent about the whole thing. And gay and lesbian adoptions are still not main stream, so we'll have to work with an agency that isn't homophobic. Huge decision," he said.

Alex stopped as his eyes rested on Janet's immobile face. He saw his elation was having the opposite effect on her.

"So," Alex asked, flushing with embarrassment at his insensitivity, "do you have any significant other in your life?"

"Not yet," Janet said, recovering. "Too busy, and I'm not ready for a new relationship. I'm pretty comfortable right now with solitude. In fact, it's nice not having to worry about someone else. I love sleeping in on weekends and I'm reading voraciously; even cancelled my cable television. TV's simply a vehicle for advertising anyway. Even public television has so many ads, either for products or donations, I've had it with them too. And if the Republicans have their way, PBS won't have continuing government support, so they'll soon be gone. A shame, but that's the way it is."

Realizing the difference in their lives since their breakup, Alex said, "I'm sorry I got so enthusiastic about my news without thinking how it might sound to you. I'm usually more aware of other people's feelings."

"No reason to apologize. You deserve to be happy. I sometimes get kind of negative, but I don't feel depressed. More like disappointed with the way the world's working. I like to think I'm realistic, not pessimistic," Janet said.

"I put discouraging thoughts like that aside," Alex said. "Otherwise you can get way down. I stopped watching TV for the same reasons; it was making me crazy. I work a lot on my music, rehearsing, sometimes even composing new stuff. That keeps me centered and happy. I try to take care of myself–even went to a doctor the other day just to be sure I hadn't gotten HIV–I haven't–and to be sure my cholesterol was under control–it is–so I got no worries!"

"That's one of the reasons I like you, Alex. You're so upbeat. I'd love to find a guy like you who's drawn to girls."

"I hope you do, and soon. I'll keep my eyes peeled for a prospect. I'm good at that."

She laughed, and they finished their coffee, hugged, and said their good-byes.

9

When Janet got the Medical Examiner's autopsy report she skipped right to the summary:

CAUSE OF DEATH: BLUNT HEAD TRAUMA
MANNER OF DEATH: HOMICIDE

"Medical history was obtained from Children's Hospital records. The deceased, a seven-month-old white, male infant had been admitted unconscious to the hospital. A CT of the head on admission showed a subdural hematoma on the right side of the head and a skull fracture of the occipital bone. His clinical status deteriorated quickly and after being declared brain dead, life supports were removed, and he was pronounced dead two days after admission. The body was received by the Medical Examiner's office for autopsy.

"The autopsy was performed at the morgue on October 18th, beginning at 9:00 AM. Assistants were Joseph Grimsley, and Doris DiCarlo, Forensic Fellow. Also present were police officers Ted Bryce, Lars Holmgren, Jeff Spencer and Bernard Johnson."

Following this were rote entries about treatment alterations to the body and a general description of the autopsy. Janet read every word and then summarized the report.

Just like Tom said, a classic case of abusive head trauma with shaking and impact.

She called her dad and told him the findings.

"This is exactly like those cases the doctors talked about at that conference," Nate said. "They claim they can persuade most juries these injuries are caused by something other than abuse. Remember what Robert Frost said about juries: They're composed of men and women who hear a case argued and decide who's got the best lawyer. Makes no difference about guilt and innocence. Just about convincing one person out of the twelve on that jury that your client is not guilty."

Janet squirmed as she listened to her father.

Is Dad's only goal about winning cases? Doesn't he care about insuring that justice is done? I've always thought his modus operandi was to present the best possible defense, but strictly within ethical, moral and legal guidelines. Have I been wrong about that? Many of his Mafia clients were unsavory characters accused of heinous crimes...but I don't know anything about those cases, so who am I to judge?

"We'll wait for the reports from your medical experts," Janet said. "I've already heard from Tom Baxley and I don't think this autopsy report will alter his opinion."

"Ideally, you need a neurosurgeon, a radiologist, a pathologist, an ophthalmologist, a neuro-pathologist, and a biomechanical engineer."

Nate was listening to Kelly Callahan, a lawyer he'd met at the conference. She was describing the ideal cast of medical experts in shaken baby syndrome trials.

"You might also need an expert in clotting disorders and a metabolic expert. There may be other sub-specialists who could bolster your defense, depending on how the case develops. I'll email you a list of the top experts," Kelly said. "A lot of their professional activity involves testifying in baby head injury cases. But they aren't cheap. And these guys are busy, so you need to nail them down when you know the trial dates. Get their fee schedules so you know what to expect."

"Fine, great, this is terrific. Send them along. Appreciate your help." Nate turned to David Weller. "I can't tell you how exciting this is. This is the kind of cause I've always enjoyed."

"I can see that," David said. "Out of the hundreds of cases you've tried, what is it about these abuse cases that turns you on?"

"Well, you know...I'm getting to the end of the road. I'd love to have a swan song–end my career exposing a medical diagnosis that's sent a lot of innocent people to jail. I'd like to be remembered for revealing the truth about shaken baby syndrome, could be my epitaph," Nate said.

When the list came, the medical credentials of the doctors on the list dazzled Nate. Kelly had done a masterful job. Next to each expert's name she'd posted a succinct statement of his central message to the court, intended to cast doubt on the validity of shaken baby syndrome. His pulse quickened and his combative juices percolated as he visualized the possible courtroom theatrics.

"Janet, this is your father. I've got the list of medical experts. Before I contact them, any news?"

"Boy, you're really latched onto this case. You ready to do this?" Janet said.

"I'm committed all the way. Count on me."

"You're amazing. I have to run it by my boss to be sure he has no problems with your being involved."

"OK, get right back to me. I need to find out whether these doctors are available," Nate said.

Janet rang Jeff Larkin. "Hi, it's Janet. When can we talk about this abuse case?"

"How 'bout now? I've got a few minutes but then I have to meet with some reps at the State House about our budget."

Janet hurried down the hall to Jeff's office, knocked, and went in.

"This case is a hard sell," Janet began. "The jury's going to hear about a dead baby and they'll see a sullen teenager sitting at our defense table who won't talk to anyone, including me, about what happened to the kid."

"Yeah, I know this case is miserable. That's why I'm glad you're handling it. Your problem is that you're too good, so you get the tough ones. I'm re-assigning your other cases so you can spend all of your time on this one."

"That's why you pay me so well, right?"

"This case is of major importance to this office. It will demonstrate that the Public Defender's Office provides competent defense, even in cases where there have been accusations of an egregious crime. Even though your buddies will howl when I give them more cases, I think they'll understand when this case gets the media coverage I expect," Jeff said. "So what do you want to talk about?"

Janet outlined her conversations with her father.

"That's fantastic! What an offer! What's the problem?" said Jeff.

"No problem, I just wanted to be sure this was kosher with the guidelines we have for the Public Defender's Office."

"No reason not to accept this kind of offer. The Court will allocate some funds for experts' fees in this case, but maybe not the whole cost. Let's do it. Maybe we can even get your dad to come work here and give up his lucrative law practice!"

"Ok, I'll tell him he's hired." She rose to leave. "One thing bothers me, though. Dad's all worked up about shaken baby syndrome being 'junk science.' He's gone to conferences sponsored by defense lawyers and medical expert witnesses. They're claiming–and he's buying their line–that shaken baby syndrome is a trumped-up diagnosis."

She hesitated. "My friend Tom Baxley–he's an intensive care doc at Children's in St. Louis–thinks it's definitely shaken impact syndrome. It worries me that Dad's so passionate about this. I don't know where his zeal comes from."

And he seems willing to use tactics I think are maybe, I don't know, a little shady, to prove his point, she thought.

"It'll all come out in the wash, Janet. His passion could be a plus. Juries love emotion during tedious court proceedings. Remember, there's no one more savvy than Nate Feingold about court histrionics. "

"OK, as long as this works for you. Of course, I'm glad to have Dad's help. Right now I'm doing a crash course in pediatrics and neurology and pathology. I'm going cross-eyed looking at my computer screen trying to learn this stuff," Janet said.

She phoned Chrystal at the jail. Chrystal complained as soon as she came on the line.

"I'm so pissed. The women in this place are buggin' me, and I've really yelled at a couple of them. They're a bunch of whores, drunks, and crack heads. Horrible ugly old fat people. Most of them don't even know how to read and they sit around smoking their stupid cigarettes, spitting on the floor, cackling like crows, cursing. And they stink. The worst thing is, they have the nerve to call *me* names," Chrystal said. "I want you to stop them calling me a baby-killer." Chrystal's voice cracked, just a little.

"Chrystal," Janet said, "jail is a miserable place; it has some really awful people in it. Jails were not designed to be pleasant. I can't stop their teasing. But watch yourself. Don't let your temper get you into any more trouble. You're not going to make friends in jail, but try not to make enemies. They're testing you. If they get to you, they bear down even harder," Janet said.

Janet waited a few moments. Silence. "You remember anything more about what happened that day?"

"You too? Everybody keeps asking me that," Chrystal shouted. "Can't any of you guys get it that I already told you what I know? I'm sick and tired of being asked the same damned questions over and over again. I'm not sayin' anything I haven't already said. Now leave me alone!"

Is she acting moody like a regular teenager, or is there something that makes her act so defensive sometimes and withdrawn at others? I wonder what's shaped her coping mechanisms and, for that matter, her world-view.

Janet recalled her meeting with Daryll and June. Even at the safe distance Janet had from Daryll he had stirred up feelings of fear and anger in her. He seemed a wretched man, with no feelings for anyone, a dark Dickensian character.

Is Daryll a narcissistic borderline personality disorder? With his short fuse it seems he could explode at the smallest perceived slight. Or could he even be a paranoid schizophrenic? OK, Janet, back off, you're not a psychiatric diagnostician. But I sure would like to know: what is Chrystal's relationship with him? What's the marriage between Daryll and June like? Enough of this psychologizing. Chrystal gave me a metaphorical middle finger on the plea bargain, so I have to get ready to go to trial.

"Hi Nina, this is Janet. Is Dad there?" Nina Freeland had been Nate's secretary for 37 years. She knew his moods, his philosophy, his brilliance, and his blind spots. Nina's satisfaction in life arose from being Nate's perfect secretary–taking care of him when he wasn't home, which was most of the time.

"Yes, he's here. Just a minute."

"Hey, Janet. What's up?" Nate said.

"Dad, let's hire those experts. Sooner the better."

"Great, I'll get right on it." He hung up and turned to Nina.

"Here's a list of doctors I want to be medical experts for this trial. Get their addresses and send each of them the following letter:

```
"Dear Dr. So-and-So;

"I am co-counsel on a case of alleged abuse
involving a baby diagnosed with a head
injury due to shaking. I am skeptical about
the way doctors arrive at this diagnosis.
Your name has been recommended to me as
one who is highly qualified to testify as a
defense expert in cases like this. If you
are interested in helping me on this case,
please send your Curriculum Vitae and your
fee schedule. I will provide you the med-
ical records and any other case materials
you need. The trial date has not been set,
so times of your availability can help us
influence this.

"Thanks,
"Sincerely, etc., etc., my usual ending."
```

"Do you want these to go by regular mail or registered mail?" Nina asked. "Or perhaps if I can get their email addresses, send them by email?"

"Both registered mail and email. But right away. Today."

Nate went home to his silent house. He gazed into the maw of a nearly empty refrigerator for something, anything, to eat. Discouraged by the unappetizing selection and his exhaustion, he climbed the stairs to his bedroom. Without undressing, he laid down on the bed and fell asleep.

The next day, revived, Nate got to his office at his usual time of seven, the time of day he liked most. He searched the web for shaken baby syndrome. Up came dozens of links. One was entitled "the triad of shaken baby syndrome." It listed hundreds of articles and letters to the editor of medical journals, all attesting to the fact that this was the center of a controversy. Just then David Weller arrived.

"David, come in here. I'm finding stuff about shaken baby syndrome. Maybe you can help me with this," Nate said. "Dorland's Medical Dictionary defines syndrome as 'a set of symptoms which occur together.' But look at this. There's 22 pages of different syndromes, nearly a thousand syndromes. Christ, this is worse than studying law."

Nate went to another website.

"Shaken baby syndrome is a triad of medical symptoms consisting of subdural hematoma, retinal hemorrhage, and cerebral edema. In many cases there are no signs of external trauma to the head."

One medical text stated, "The outcome, when not fatal, is dismal in most cases with severe brain damage, learning disabilities, behavioral disorders, and other disabilities. Nearly a quarter of the victims die soon after the injury."

"These sources suggest a whole list of 'alternative' diagnoses that could explain the bad outcome. I can now see an emerging strategy for our defense argument: we get the medical experts to blame what happened to this baby on alternative medical conditions and then get at least one juror to doubt it was abuse. That's all we need, one 'not guilty,' and a conviction won't happen," he told David, who kept his eyes on the computer screen.

When Nina came in around nine, Nate asked her to call Kelly Callahan.

"I need a cram course on shaken baby syndrome," he told Kelly. "I've found some articles, but I need to focus on the core information. Where do I start?"

"Several law review articles cover most of the medical and legal issues. These will get you going. There are over a thousand published articles, but most of them are what we call 'junk science'," Kelly said.

"How do they get published if they're no good? What about peer-review? I thought that's how bad articles got rooted out."

"Read these law review articles and you'll get a sense of that. There's new science about shaken baby syndrome that questions past medical dogma. Doctors who routinely diagnose shaken baby syndrome are frothing at the mouth about the controversy we're stirring up. That's exactly what we want. The more they protest, the better press this builds for us. They're in high dudgeon and so the media sees them as irrational and less persuasive. When they get dogmatic and glib with a reporter, their credibility goes down. Our experts are masters of media management. They're calm, cool and self-confident. They charm the reporters, most of whom don't have a clue about the syndrome. But our doctors are still in the minority. Most child abuse pediatricians make this diagnosis with absolute certainty. As a result, kids are torn from their families and accused perpetrators convicted. Fewer now than 20 years ago, but still too many," Kelly said. "We're also making headway with re-opening old convictions, getting reversals in some of them."

"How do these quacks get away with it? Doesn't the medical licensure board punish docs who make the wrong diagnosis and cause people to go to jail?"

"You have to remember that medical licensure boards are populated with traditionalists who don't want to see the status-quo tampered with. Traditional medical teaching is that shaken baby syndrome does exist. Hard to reverse sixty years of teaching and habit. But we're trying to do that."

"Thanks Kelly. Send those law review articles to me as soon as you can."

When the articles came, Nate and David spent hours trying to digest the body of the articles. David distilled the main points of the article, picking the sentences that captured the central message.

"New science has challenged the old scientific dogma and has shown that the "triad" is also seen in accidental injury and medical disorders," David said.

Nate called Kelly.

"Thanks for sending me these articles. They're really an outline for the defense case, aren't they? It's on days like this I'm glad I'm a defense attorney. I do love to upset the apple cart. I am a real disturber of the peace!" Nate said.

"Glad you liked them. They've been a godsend to the defense. Mainstream physicians claim these authors relied exclusively on defense medical experts for their information and that the few child abuse experts who were asked for their opinions were either misquoted or quoted out of context. But we're delighted that these articles have been written.

"So, good luck in your trial. We'll be watching with great interest. May even use some of your arguments to advise future defense lawyers as we turn up the volume on this. And by the way, if you could give your arguments to the media along the way, that'll help. They've been key in turning the tide on this issue," Kelly said.

10

Chrystal peered through the bars in her cell, her temples pounded and her mouth felt like it was full of the dust under her cot. She walked around her cramped space, thoughts roiling in her mind.

What am I gonna do? I don't want to rot in jail the rest of my life. The cops say they got the goods on me, that I ought to fess up 'cause I'm gonna get convicted and if I fess up they'll go easier on me. But what's easier? Feinstein—or is her name Feingold?—says she's for me and I should tell her what happened so she can defend me best. She seems OK but I don't know. Last thing I remember was that brat screaming, loud enough to break my eardrums. Then he kicked me in my boobs—that hurt so bad. I was really pissed at the little brat.

I gotta get outta here. And then what? Go back where Daryll is and my stupid mother who can't see what an animal he is? But what's she gonna do? She's got no money and is dumb as a post. She doesn't know anything except to take orders from Daryll. If I get out of here, what'll I do? Don't even have a high school diploma. I'll end up like my dumb mom, hoping some mean creep'll take care of me.

And kids? Who'd want the little monsters anyway? After hearing Luke scream like that, I don't want to take care of any more kids, ever. Can't remember anything after he kicked me. All a blank. How can I tell Feingold—or is it Feinstein?—what happened when I can't even remember myself? It was like all those times when Daryll screwed me, I'd just go off and look down from the ceiling like it's someone else.

But...did I hurt Luke?

Wish that ugly fat bitch over there would stop looking at me—she hates me. My name's not "baby-killer." She's already decided I'm guilty. Maybe I am. I don't know. I must be or God wouldn't be doing this to me. Is this my punishment—for what? Maybe for smoking that joint? Taking a little meth once? Lots of kids do a lot worse. And they're not in jail with a bunch of ugly bitches who're here for god knows what. Maybe I should ask for a priest. But what for? A priest's not gonna get me out of here. No one'll make me feel better by talking. And he might make a move on me, like all men. Maybe they have a woman minister. There sure aren't any female priests. And from what I hear, priests are molesters. But I guess they like little boys more than girls. No, I don't think I'll ask for a minister or a priest.

The guard glanced through the bars.

"C'mon, time for your meal. Come out of your trance and march along!"

11

Within days, Nate got his first response, from Franklin Boyd, a neurosurgeon in Denver. It was short and to the point.

```
Dear Mr. Feingold,

I will be glad to assist you in your pursuit
of justice in this case.

I will review all the materials in the case
and render my opinion.

My fees are:$5,000.00 retainer fee. Fee
for review of materials:$1,000.00/hour. For
appearances in Court: $12,000 per day, plus
expenses.

Sincerely yours,
Franklin W. Boyd, MD FACS
```

Nate called Kelly.

"Hi Kelly, got the first response. From Dr. Franklin Boyd," he said. He read her the letter.

"Is this the typical arrangement and level of cost?"

"That's pretty standard. I told you they weren't cheap, but these guys are a seasoned group. They know one another and what'll be said in their testimony. That makes for consistent expert testimony."

"This is going to cost me more than I figured on," Nate said." I know, you warned me. But I'm still committed. This is the right thing to do. Thanks for all your help."

He rang off and stared into the dark for several minutes.

Over the next few days, responses from other experts came in, similar in content and cost. Zoltan Szabo, a biomechanical engineer from the Auto Safe Corporation in Maryland, said he'd "be delighted" to review the medical records and render an opinion. James Parten, a retired pathologist from Tacoma, Washington, wrote that he would "be glad to review all the records of the case and testify." Frans van Hooven, head of a neuro-pathology laboratory in Boston, and Ralph Constant, a retired Clinical Professor of Ophthalmology from McClain University School of Medicine in Tuscaloosa, Alabama, agreed. Neil Grasbauskas, a general pediatrician and Kevin Langone, an infectious disease specialist, also agreed to his offer.

He called Janet.

"Hi. How goes it?"

"Good. How're you?" Janet asked.

"I'm always good. Some days are better than others, but I can't complain," Nate said. "When can I talk to Chrystal? I've been in abstract mode, breaking one of my own rules – knowing my client. Let's set up a time when I can meet her. With or without you?"

Janet paused a moment to think about this.

"I think it should be with me. She's never met you and you might scare her. You're a pretty impressive character. I'll ask her tomorrow."

"Has she told you any more about what happened?" Nate asked.

"No, she's opaque about the whole thing, as though it's not her problem. She's rolled up like a little armadillo. Hard to craft a case if she stays so uncommunicative."

"She been in trouble before? Police involvement? Any misdemeanors? Traffic tickets? Fights in school, things like that? Drugs? Alcohol?" Nate said.

"We checked all that and it's all negative except she once got into a fight in gym during a volleyball game. Teammate shoved her out of the way on a ball return and she slugged her and broke a bone in her hand. Nothing came of it. Gym teacher said she's got a short fuse, especially when someone pushes her or bumps into her, but she's not a trouble-maker, doesn't get into any fights or anything like that."

"How about her family? Anything there?"

"Lives with her mother and stepfather. They run a convenience store downtown. She goes to a so-so high school. She clams up when I try to find anything out about her private or social life. If she won't talk to me I doubt you'll have any success. She's really paranoid."

"Maybe I can use my grandfatherly approach. Teenage girls like old guys."

"Hate to break it to you, Dad, but teenage girls are as uninterested in old guys as anybody can possibly be!"

"You've never seen me turn on the charm, m'dear. But if you don't think that'd work I won't try it. I'll take my cues from you."

"I think that would be best. I'll let you know when I set up the meeting."

Janet hung up and shook her head.

Hard to believe Dad can be so naïve. And his view of himself sometimes... kind of inappropriate. And I don't think anyone calls him on it. I'll have to stay sharp when he's with Chrystal.

Janet's eyes widened when she met Nate at the jail and she took in his look. Rather than his usual dark suit and tie, he wore a black turtleneck, khakis, and a gray tweed jacket with suede patches on the elbows.

"Well, you look like a rumpled college professor, not a big-time criminal defense lawyer," Janet said.

That old fox—dressed down to relate to Chrystal. We'll see how that goes down.

Janet twisted her hair around her index finger, an old anxious habit, as she and Nate waited to see Chrystal. She calmed herself, reasoning that since she'd gotten zilch from Chrystal so far, there was little to lose.

"Chrystal, this is my father, Mr. Feingold. Remember I told you about him? He wants to talk with you about what went on the day Luke was injured."

"Here we go again," Chrystal said. She turned toward the wall.

They waited. Finally Nate said, "C'mon Chrystal, we're the only people standing between you and a long, ugly prison sentence. It's time you stopped playing games, open up, and let us help you."

Janet waited to see what, if any, response would come from Chrystal.

"Why're you guys so interested in me? You don't know me. How could you care about me? No one else ever has."

"What about your parents?" Nate asked.

"Ha, that's a joke. My mother is a dumb wimp, never been no help to me. My stepfather is a nasty prick."

"Why do you say your stepfather is a prick?" Nate asked.

"Never mind why, he just is. Don't want to talk about him."

Without missing a beat, Nate said, "How does he abuse you?"

Janet nearly sunk to the floor. Her father could startle a rattlesnake.

Chrystal looked up quickly. "How'd you know that?"

"Just guessed. I've lived a long time and I've seen a lot of bad stuff. What's he done to you?" Nate said.

"Oh god, I don't want to talk about that. What's that got to do with all of this anyhow?"

"Just trying to understand where you might be coming from," said Nate.

"Well, let's get one thing straight. I don't know how Luke got hurt. That's my story today, yesterday and tomorrow. So if you're going to defend me, you got to believe what I tell you."

"We believe that's what you believe." Nate's voice was calm and firm. He paused. "But it'd be helpful if you tell us more why you think that's true. Was there something about that morning, or something about Luke that morning, that makes you believe it happened a different way than it appears?" Nate asked.

Chrystal lowered her voice. "Went to a concert the night before I sat Luke, got home really late. Daryll beat me with a belt when I got home for staying out so late. I had bruises all over my chest and he really hurt my boobs. I was real tired when I got up to go to the Talbots' house. I only got, like, two hours sleep. I don't remember the whole thing, but I was awake when Luke just went limp. I called 911, did what I had to do. Now everyone thinks I did something to him. Why're they doing this to me?"

"You were the last one to see Luke well," Nate said. "So you're the one people are blaming."

He waited.

Silence.

"Now, I want to tell you what we're doing." Nate continued. "We're rounding up a bunch of really smart doctors who'll talk about head injuries like Luke's and talk about the different ways this could've happened. I don't know what they're going to say yet, but when they send us their reports I want to go over what they say with you, to see if anything seems to fit what you remember. You were the only one there, so you know better than anyone what could've happened. These experts may come up with other explanations, like Luke had some sickness no one knew about, someone did this to him before you came and then his symptoms came on later, he fell, or something else happened. But you've got to think hard to recall anything that might've caused his injuries. A fall off the changing table, for example, or he slipped out of your hands when you pulled him out of the tub, or he hit his head on the tub. Keep thinking about this. We'll work with you to come up with the best story we can to get you out of this jail for good."

For the first time since Janet had met with Chrystal, she seemed to be engaged. It surprised her, because her father was not being particularly sympathetic but was forthright about the realities of Chrystal's situation.

Janet was impressed, pleased that she kept on learning from this guy. She came out of this meeting feeling a little better after the discouraging opinion she'd gotten from Tom Baxley. And she was shaping a more sympathetic view of Chrystal.

12

Janet entered the main reading room of the Health Sciences Library in the Medical School.

"I need assistance finding articles and books about shaken baby syndrome, otherwise known as abusive head trauma," she said to the librarian.

"Hmm. Your best bet is to use bibliographies in standard textbooks for older peer-reviewed literature. From those articles you can develop a group of key-words to look for more current articles."

After spending several hours at this task, Janet slumped in her chair, ran her fingers through her hair and massaged her scalp to relieve her developing headache. There was a mountain of information to master quickly.

At the same time at Children's Hospital, two lawyers had the attention of the hospital doctors.

"I'm Mary Egan and this is my co-counsel, Albert Polcari. Thanks for taking time from your patient care to meet with us. I know how much you like meeting with lawyers," Mary said with a smile, "but we need your medical input as we prepare for Chrystal Begley's trial. We're charging her with second-degree murder in Luke Talbot's death. I'm not sure where to begin," she said, looking around the room, "but anyone who wants to start, feel free."

"I guess I'll begin," said Ruth McClure. "When Luke first got to the PICU, he was barely holding on to life. Once Luke was here in the PICU, various consultants came, did their diagnostic testing and began necessary treatments. They'll tell you about what they did and why. Frank, you want to begin?"

Dr. Frank Mayhew, the neurosurgeon; Sarah Coughlin, the child abuse pediatrician; and the radiologist, Dr. Rodney Michaelson; explained their findings. Dr. Stanley Garber, who had examined Luke's eyes, described the extensive flames of blood in the sheets of tissue of the inner sphere of Luke's eyes. The distress of the ED and PICU nurses was evident as they told of viewing this seven-month-old baby as a rag doll in his unconscious and flaccid state.

"What's going on in there?" Dr. Stevens, one of the PICU Residents asked Bobbie, the Ward Clerk.

"The legal eagles from the DA's office are in there with everybody who took care of Luke Talbot, the baby who was shaken and slammed. He was here before you came on service. Been in there for over an hour and we need to get 'em outta there to get somethin' done around here. Like, we need orders on that new kid that just came up."

"Maybe if I poke my head in there they'll get the message," Stevens said.

He cracked the door open, slipped his head through, and looked at Dr. McClure. "Sorry to bother you, but we need to clear some orders on the new kid with the overdose."

"Be right with you. We're almost done here," McClure said.

"Well, I think we've got what we need for now. Thanks to all of you again. You've been great," Mary said as she gathered up her papers and reached for her briefcase. "Al, anything else?"

"Not now. Got a lot to digest," Al said.

Turning to the group he said, "We may get back with some of you to explain some of the medical complexities once we've reviewed our notes. Thanks a lot."

As they descended in the elevator, Al said to Mary, "Have you read the Medical Examiner's autopsy report? What's that ME's name again?"

"Drago. He's kinda weird. And there's some chatter about his work not being up to par. He's sort of on probation at the ME's office," Mary said.

"So, why do they give important cases like this to someone who's no good?" Al said.

"That office is so overworked and understaffed that they'll use anyone they can get their hands on to do autopsies. Did you hear about last week when they misplaced a body? And a couple of weeks before that there was a mix-up of eyes taken from one dead guy and mislabeled as belonging to another. They're totally screwed up over there," Mary said as they found their car in the mammoth garage at the medical center.

Back in their office, Egan and Polcari pulled their team together in the conference room. Because there were so many junior assistant DA's sitting in on this meeting who were eager to learn how this case was being prepared, Mary laid out the plans in detail.

"We just met with Luke Talbot's doctors at Children's Hospital," Mary said. "Here's how we're going to proceed. We'll meet with each doctor individually just before the trial to rehearse their testimony. We'll stress how important it'll be for them to use plain English, and to avoid speculation, academic musing and ambiguity. We'll also ask them to at least *act* humble even if that's not their natural pose in life.

"Doctors have a tendency to embellish, to show how smart they are, and go into more detail than we'll want. Juries don't follow rambling testimony, especially if it's technical. We don't want the doctors to unintentionally contradict each other. We must avoid unexpected and surprising statements on the stand. In short, we need to build a credible and understandable case for the jury. We have to pound home that Chrystal was the only possible perpetrator of Luke's injury. The jury needs to be convinced that this fatal head injury was not due to some weird disease or an accident or something that took place before the defendant came to babysit him. This may seem like an easy case if you look at the medical records and listen to the doctors from the hospital, but it could get dicey."

Mary paused to let what she had said sink in.

"Defense experts are being paid for by Nate Feingold, one of the wiliest criminal defense attorneys west of the Mississippi. He brings his years of criminal law trial experience into court and no doubt the experts he's buying have been in court countless times and will have polished testimony. The defense will use their medical experts to muddy the waters, to cast doubt. Experts like this in other child abuse trials have the reputation of being ingratiating, articulate, and credible because they're old pros in this game. Albert is finding out all he can about the experts Nate has gotten and what they've said in past trials. We'll challenge them hard and convincingly, do our best to destroy their credibility and try to expose them as venal. Portray them as whores in court who are being paid exorbitant fees to help Chrystal Begley walk."

She paused, gauging her effect on the assistant DA's.

"One other thing: in addition to the treating physicians at the hospital, I want to find an independent medical expert who's pre-eminent in the field. I want the jury to see him or her as a knowledgeable and sympathetic physician. I want this person to be our advisor as well as our renowned expert, perhaps a rebuttal witness."

One of the assistant district attorneys asked why there is disagreement amongst doctors about shaken baby syndrome.

"Simple. Because you can't shake healthy babies to see what happens. Only that would be irrefutable evidence. That research can never be done," Mary said. "That's all for now. Let's get to work."

Albert sat down at his computer and searched for the American Academy of Pediatrics Policy Statements about shaken baby syndrome. He then stumbled onto the website of the National Center on Shaken Baby Syndrome, whose mission was "to prevent shaken baby syndrome through education and research." The Center offered a list of articles about shaken baby syndrome and a DVD about the medical aspects of the syndrome. His knowledge about abused head injured babies was expanding.

While the prosecutors cranked up their efforts to build their case, Janet called the hospital to arrange times for depositions from the doctors.

"We have to clear our meetings with outside lawyers with our hospital legal department," Dr. McClure told Janet. "We'll work through Marie D'Agostino. If you call her she'll set things up."

Dr. McClure squirmed a little as she spoke with Janet. She couldn't be very objective about a lawyer who would try to prove Luke hadn't been abused and would attempt to discredit her and other doctors caring for Luke. She also felt especially bonded to Alison Talbot after sitting with her during the last moments she had with her baby.

Janet reached Ms. D'Agostino and identified herself as the defense attorney representing Chrystal Begley in the Luke Talbot murder trial.

"I'd like your permission to talk with the doctors involved in the care of Luke. Can that be arranged?"

"Yes, of course. I'll need to be at the meetings, but if you'll tell me when you're available, I'll arrange for the doctors to meet with you. We're very much aware of this case," Ms. D'Agostino said.

"I'll come at the doctors' convenience," Janet said.

"OK, give me a few days to organize this, and I'll get back to you."

When the times were set, both Janet and Nate went for the depositions. The deal was that she'd conduct the depositions.

"I promise I won't interfere with your style or get flippant with the doctors," Nate said. He complied, but did give her some whispered advice on the side as she proceeded.

"That wasn't as bad as I thought it might be," Janet said as they left. "Even though they uniformly said this was shaken impact syndrome, none was willing to say who they thought had done it, saying that was not their job. But they all said that someone had done this, and had done it during the time frame when Chrystal was with Luke."

When Janet and Nate got back to the office, they reviewed the report from the Medical Examiner. The second reading of it hardly raised their hopes.

Janet called Tom Baxley. "Hi Janet. How're things?"

"Pretty good. I'm working on this abuse case, you know the one I asked you to look at a few weeks ago?"

"Yeah, I remember, the one that I told you was pretty cut and dried?"

"The very one. Well, several things have happened. My dad, Nate, has offered to act as co-counsel, pro bono, and pay for all the expert defense witnesses. What do you think of that?"

"Great for you, but does he realize what you're up against? That case is so classic that it would take a miracle, or a really dumb jury, to get your client off."

"Gee, Tom, I knew I could count on you for some inspirational words."

"I'm sorry, but I like you too much to mislead you. That's a tough case for anyone to defend," Tom said. "Know anything about the defense experts?"

"I'm learning about them as I go over their CV's and previous testimony. Would you know their names?"

"Probably not. I don't testify in child abuse cases much."

"Can you give me the name of a good local expert who's not at Children's Hospital and not involved in the case?"

"Well, I know a child abuse pediatrician who collects articles about child abuse and he can lead you to the current journal articles on SBS, including review articles."

"OK, what's his name and where can I reach him?"

"Mike Greenbaum. He's in one of our affiliated hospitals." He gave her his number and email address.

"Mention that I recommended him when you call. Sometimes docs don't want to talk to defense attorneys, but he'll probably be willing to send you a list of pertinent articles. If there are things you don't understand—terminology or anatomy, whatever—he can help you there too. And if he won't, I can. But he's a really nice guy and knows a lot about abuse."

"Thanks, Tom. I'll let you know how I make out."

After a few tries, Janet reached Greenbaum. She told him the details of the case and asked if he would help her by providing some pertinent references.

"So, how is Tom? One of my favorite people," Greenbaum said.

"Well, he's fine, but since he doesn't consider himself an expert in shaken baby syndrome, he referred me to you. Can you give me a hand?" Janet said.

"Well, the current thinking is that these non-accidental head injury cases should be called abusive head trauma. This doesn't mean that shaking's not involved in some cases, but the term abusive head trauma is meant to include all kinds of non-accidental head injuries, not just those caused by a shaking mechanism. There's a rather large literature on the subject. I have a bibliography of over 5,000 articles. Not all of them are great, but some are good reviews to get you familiar with the basics. I'll put stars on the good review articles and the 50 or 60 that are good research. Where shall I send the list?"

"I'm shocked by the number of articles written about this," she said. "What will your charges be for this?"

"How about seven million dollars? If you can't come up with that, there'll be no charge. I have the list on my computer and it's easy to send over. I'm glad you're not asking me to review the records and testify. I hate court work. I try not to do it unless it's one of our own cases here in my hospital, and then I really have no choice," Greenbaum said.

"Thanks very much. You want my email or my physical address? And after I wade through this list, may I call you back if I have further questions?"

"Sure, no problem. Glad to help. Give me your email," he said. "I think I know the case you're defending. It's all over the news media. Difficult case. I don't envy your job."

"Thanks, that seems to be the general consensus. Not very uplifting, but we've got to give this young woman the best defense we can. So I'll soldier on."

This is getting depressing, Janet thought. *I wish I liked Chrystal more and I especially wish that she were more forthcoming. If she'd just give me something to work with, it might be easier.*

The list of articles came right away. She took heart that perhaps she could master this subject before the trial.

But one statement leapt out of the AAP Policy Statement:

"The existence of abusive head trauma in infants and young children is a settled scientific fact… from over 40 years of research. In April 2012, the prestigious and renowned government Center for Disease Control and Prevention reported that 'serious traumatic brain injury in young children is largely the result of abuse.' "

So why does my father think this is junk science? This seems pretty conclusive, when an organization like the American Academy of Pediatrics publishes a statement like this. Even if the majority opinion is that shaken baby syndrome is real, the state still has to prove that Chrystal was the perpetrator. That's where I have to focus my efforts. This'll be a challenge, but that's why I chose criminal defense law. The burden of proof is still on the state to convict her and that may not be as easy as everyone seems to think. So glad Jeff has reassigned my other cases.

13

"I hope my presence doesn't inhibit this interview," Detective Lundgren said as Mary Egan and Albert Polcari drove to the Talbot's home.

"The Talbots can't be completely excluded from involvement in Luke's death. We don't suspect either of them, but we need you with us to avoid any complications. If the Talbots say something exculpatory, we'd end up as witnesses in our own case," Albert said.

Discussing Luke's abuse and subsequent death with his grieving parents was the absolute worst part of this case. Mary and Albert couldn't assume they were blameless. But still, nothing could be more horrible for parents than losing a baby, especially this way. Talking with bereaved parents about their possible role in the demise of their child was an emotional valley neither wished to enter.

"How do you absorb this kind of horror?" Albert said. "When I think of my two kids, I can't imagine what it'd be like if I lost them in any way, but like this? I'd be so angry I'd want to kill the person who did it. Scary to feel that way, and normally, so unlike me."

"There's a difference between having homicidal thoughts and acting on them," Mary said. "A lot of parents feel furious when their toddlers pull their computers off the desk or defy them. Thank God, most parents have sufficient self-control and don't beat them. Figuring out what those internal mechanisms are has always intrigued me. What kind of wiring in the brain keeps most parents from doing awful things to their kids? Since I've never been a parent I don't understand it. Got any insights for me?"

"Well, I can't conceive of ever hurting my kids," Polcari said. "It just doesn't compute in my scheme of life. Sure, I get a flare of anger when the kids do something I don't like, even when they're crying like crazy, or oppositional or angry, but it doesn't occur to me to punish them physically. We've never spanked our kids. My mom used to say: 'Hitting kids only teaches them that it's OK to hit. It doesn't keep them from misbehaving and a lot of times it makes them more defiant.' " He paused, then went on, "I had a neighbor who'd feel so guilty after spanking her kid, she'd go out and buy her a new wardrobe. Dumb. The kids get mixed messages, so the whole thing is counter-productive."

They rounded the bend and saw the Talbot's house. So safe, so secure, so middle America. Within those walls, however, a baby was killed and a young babysitter now was languishing in jail awaiting trial.

"I'm trying to understand what drove Chrystal to do this," Albert said." You think she'll ever admit she did it–even to herself? Or come to terms with what she did? I wonder if she even cares."

"So far, the interviews with her–by CPS, the police, the social worker in the DA's office–have gotten nothing," said Mary. "No motive, no admission, no sense of her state of mind when this happened. She's stonewalled everyone."

"That in itself raises my suspicion," Albert said.

They lifted the brass pineapple doorknocker and tapped gently three times.

Soon they heard footsteps coming, then the door opened.

"Come in," Fred Talbot said.

He was reticent as he showed them into the parlor.

"This is Mary Egan and Detective Lundgren," Albert said to Fred, who nodded his acknowledgment.

The large bay window revealed the pin oaks in the yard, their leaves still clinging to their branches despite winter's presence. A formal dining room separated the kitchen from the parlor. The exterior of the house was so unassuming they were surprised to see a stairway with exquisitely carved balustrades supporting a cherry banister rising to the second floor from the front entry hall. Upstairs, out of their sight, they knew from police reports that there were three bedrooms, and two bathrooms.

They sat down on two wing chairs facing a camelback Victorian couch. On the floor was a small Tabriz rug between the couch and the chairs, and adorning the windows were chintz drapes. The Victoriana theme ran through all of the interior decorations.

"Your home is so warm and cozy," said Mary, trying to divert attention from the unpleasant conversation they were about to have. Alison walked in.

"I'm Alison Talbot," she said, holding out her hand to Al, then to Mary. Albert introduced her to Detective Lundgren.

Slender, Alison's blond hair was pulled back into a small pony-tail. Tired and pale, Alison's eyes appeared puffy, but she seemed more emotionally under control than Mary or Al had anticipated.

"What can we do for you?' Fred asked.

"First, let us tell you how sorry we are. There's nothing we can say to make this easy. Please understand that we need to talk to you so we can see that justice is done."

"There's no justice for Luke," said Fred, gripping the arms of his chair. "I'm still so angry about what that kid did to Luke, I have trouble even speaking her name. Our son, David, thinks that somehow Luke'll be coming back. I choke up every time I tell him Luke won't be coming home anymore, that he's in heaven. At the funeral David didn't understand why everyone was crying so much." Shaking his head, he said, "Thank God, David was at his grandmother's that day. You can imagine how my mother feels–that if only she'd taken both of them, Luke would be alive today. But spending one-on-one time with David has been a habit of hers.

"Death is a hard concept for a four-year-old to grasp. David has no idea that Chrystal did this. He still asks why Chrystal hasn't been over to babysit," Fred said.

Alison sat nearly catatonic in her chair. She'd said nothing as Fred spoke and gave no indication of her thoughts or feelings.

Mary waited a moment, then said, "Neither Mr. Polcari nor I can understand why these things happen. We know we can't begin to feel the depth of your grief." Waiting a few beats, she continued "We wish we didn't have to revisit that day with you. But to prosecute Chrystal properly we need to find out as much as we can. We need to tell our community this kind of crime won't go unpunished."

"How can we help you?" Fred said again, having calmed a bit. "I want Chrystal to be convicted. It would be small justice, but something."

"Describe what went on from, say, the night before, until you left the house," said Mary.

Alison spoke for the first time. "The night before, Luke had a little cold and woke up a few times, but had no fever, only a little runny nose. David had a little cold too. Kids have runny noses most of the time so we thought nothing of it. As you know, David went off to his grandmother's house the night before. Luke was a little fussy on Saturday morning, but nothing that would've told us not to go to our conference. We changed him just before Chrystal got here, fed him his bottle, and then told her to feed him some cereal. We left, thinking that we had taken care of everything to make it easy for Chrystal. She looked a little haggard and was quiet, but she's a teenager so we didn't pay attention to it. Nothing else that I can remember."

"Chrystal had taken care of your children before, right? Mary asked.

"Yes, but for a few hours in the evening. Luke would generally go to sleep shortly after we left for a movie or dinner and Chrystal would read to David until he got sleepy," Alison said.

"How did you find her in the first place?" Albert said.

"We asked some of our friends with children who sat for them and a couple of them suggested Chrystal. They all said she was fine. We had no reason to think she wasn't a nice young high school girl wanting to make a few extra dollars taking care of kids."

"You said she looked haggard and was quiet that morning. Did she act different in any other way?" Albert asked.

"Chrystal never seemed to like me much and sort of avoided contact with me," Fred said. "Sometimes when I took her home after baby-sitting she'd sit stone-silent, way over against the passenger door. Lately, Alison took her home because of this. I don't think I ever gave her any reason to dislike me, so I just assumed this is how some teenage girls act. They may be wary of men, what with all the attention given in movies and TV about men molesting babysitters."

He hesitated.

"Looking back on it, that morning she seemed more distant than usual. We were in a hurry and I didn't think twice about it. Maybe I should have and if I had, maybe Luke would be alive today."

"Oh Fred, you always take responsibility for everything," Allison said. "There was nothing that could've warned us that she'd do anything so horrible. She'd always been a good baby sitter for us."

"Except for a couple of weeks ago when we got back from the movies and found Luke asleep under the dining room table and Chrystal asleep on the couch," Fred said.

"That was just a happenstance," Alison said. Turning to Mary, she said, "Luke had crawled under the table and fell asleep there. Chrystal said she didn't want to wake him by taking him up to his crib."

"Well, that was her explanation, but I still think it was irresponsible," Fred said.

"Did you ever hear from David that Chrystal had done anything to make you worry?" Mary asked.

"No, not a word. David never said anything about her, neither good nor bad. But David is a bit introverted. He's a quiet observer of people around him."

Alison turned to Mary and Albert. "Fred wanted to find a new babysitter, so he feels he should've insisted. Maybe I should have listened to him but she never really did anything we know of that was outright wrong. Just a few things here and there that made Fred think she wasn't doing a great job. She was sort of distracted, spacey at times. He wondered whether she was on drugs. But we decided that she was just a typical teenager" – Alison's eyes were clear, speech coherent. "Too late now. You always look back and say: I should have listened to Fred." Her voice quivered as she spoke.

"That's a natural reaction," Mary said. "We've seen it before in other cases involving abuse by babysitters." She looked down at her legal pad for a moment. "We'd like to ask you a few questions about Luke before you left. Would that be OK with you?"

"Yes, of course," Allison said.

"When you gave him his bottle, was he fighting it or spitting up the formula?" Albert asked.

"No, he drank it right down. No spitting, no nothing," Alison said.

"Did you ever see any bruises on either of your children?" Mary said.

"No."

"Did Luke ever seem afraid of Chrystal?" Albert asked.

"Not that we noticed."

"Do you know anything about her parents?" Mary asked.

"Chrystal never spoke about her parents," Alison said. "I wondered about her relationships within her family. Her attitude toward Fred also made me speculate as to what her father was like. I think he's a stepfather. I don't know what happened to her real father. Her parents run a convenience store, but I don't know much else about them. Never met them," Alison said.

"You know, it's hard to find a Saturday babysitter," Alison said, a tear streaking down her cheek. "But we can't blame ourselves for what she did, can we?"

"You had no reason to think she would ever harm either of your children. My wife and I face the same dilemma – finding someone we trust to care for our kids, or we could never go anywhere, even to work," Albert said.

After a few moments, Mary cleared her throat.

"We need to ask a few more questions and we'll be done. We know this is painful for you," she said. "Had Luke ever had any health problems or hospitalizations other than routine childhood illnesses?"

"No."

"Are there any diseases that run in your family?"

"None that we know of."

"Any problems with the pregnancy and delivery, the first few weeks of life?"

"Everything was fine. A little morning sickness the first few months, but that settled down, and he was born on time, six pounds twelve ounces. Came home with me the day after delivery, so everyone must've thought he was OK to go. I breast-fed for a couple of months while I was on maternity leave. Luke never had any feeding problems. Gained weight well and was on the 75th percentile for everything. Got his shots on time, had no reactions."

"How did David get along with Luke?"

"David adored Luke. He always wanted to hold him. During the pregnancy I didn't think he would love him as much as he did."

Alison wept. "Losing Luke was so hard. We miss him so much and David does too. He's taking this badly. We have to stay strong so he doesn't imagine things." Taking a deep breath, she said "Our pediatrician told us that older siblings sometimes have fantasies about getting rid of a new baby. So if a baby dies, the older child may think his wish has been fulfilled and it's his fault. David's in therapy, seems better, but still asks lots of questions."

Albert swallowed hard as he thought about his own kids. To quell his emotions, he asked to see the bathroom where Luke had been bathed. Alison showed it to him, but he realized he'd have to rely on police photographs since there was nothing to see now. He came back downstairs and the four of them sat there in silence.

Finally, Mary spoke. "I think we're finished here. We'll leave our cards, so call if you want to add anything. Our secretaries will put calls from you directly through to us if we're in. If we're not, leave a message and we'll call you back as soon as we can. We'll leave our cell numbers also, but we have to turn them off when we're in court. Keep trying. We want to stay in close touch."

They said their goodbyes. As Mary and Albert went back to their office, a heavy sadness hung over both of them.

"I'm determined to make sure Chrystal is held accountable for this," Albert said, his face flushed in uncharacteristic anger. "We can't let Nate Feingold flummox the jury with his high-priced experts and leave the Talbots feeling abandoned by the justice system.

"This trial has made me even more aware that I have to use every instinct I have to protect my own children. But I'm also going to find a way to educate the public about abuse and its prevention. Did you know child abuse causes as many deaths as childhood cancer?" Albert said.

"Didn't know that," Mary said. "Winning this case is critical to me too. I've *never* felt so emotionally invested in a case."

14

"So here's the information about your prosecutors," Nate said to Janet when she came on the line. "Al Polcari grew up in Columbus Park–you know, "Little Italy" or the "North End." Garfield Elementary School, then to North Kansas City High School. His neighborhood was awash in crime and violence. Those who knew Albert say that even as a child he wasn't going to be absorbed into this. From a strict Catholic family, he has a strong sense of responsibility.

"Albert's father ran a small business machine repair shop, keeping his nose clean and paying his 'dues' to the local mobsters. His mother worked as a church secretary at the Sacred Heart Church close to home. They lived modestly, had many friends, and his childhood was uncluttered by any real sadness. One of his two younger brothers became a doctor and the other an elementary school teacher.

"In high school he was a varsity letterman in football and baseball, president of his senior class and on Student Council, then University undergrad in liberal arts, followed by entrance to its law school. After graduation, he went straight to the prosecutor's office because of high grades, macho good looks, and his general personality and demeanor. He was a natural for the Prosecutor's office," Nate said.

"Now, Mary Egan is one interesting woman. She also went to University, both for college and law school. She never married, is childless, and passionately dedicated to her job. She's several years older than Albert. They're good work partners, according to my sources; no ego problems or jealousy between them. Mary grew up in that large stew of new and old Irish immigrants where family meant everything and loyalty to the tribe was paramount. Her father was a steward in Local 203 of the Machinist's

Union and a ward-healer, the guy who made sure all the people in the district got what they needed. He probably taught Mary a lot about politics. He was the conduit for the locals to City Hall where one of the functionaries could make a problem go away. She got inspired in high school to be a lawyer when her father knocked on doors for the local DA's first campaign. He delivered votes from his ward in the DA's successful election.

"When she came to the DA's office, she tried minor cases of drunk drivers, petty thievery and other small-time crimes. When the DA decided he needed a special unit to handle the emerging caseload of child abuse cases, he put her in charge of this new office. She dove into this with characteristic zeal, despite knowing nothing about child abuse. Neither did anyone else in this new unit, so she organized a 'mini-course' on child abuse and had a local pediatrician who specialized in child abuse come and teach the staff about the medical aspects of abuse. Her child abuse office became a model for other DA's offices."

"How'd you find all this out?"

"Oh, I've got my ways. I have moles all over town, digging out information for me. You can't do criminal law without well-developed contacts," Nate said.

Mary and Al took a dinner break from their day's work on the Begley case. They were sharing some cold pizza when they mused about life in the fast lane of criminal prosecution.

"Ever wonder how you got into this area of law?" Al asked.

"Oh, I knew this was what I wanted to do since the first year of law school. Always had an over-developed sense of right and wrong. I get really upset and angry when people break the rules and get away with it."

"Guess that's why we work well together. We have a lot in common," said Al. "Kind of square, but it's what we are."

They turned their attention back to Luke Talbot.

"So all the docs say this case is classic," Mary said and reviewed the history of the case as she understood it. "Does that sound right to you? I miss anything?'"

"Not from a medical standpoint," Albert said. "The police and CPS reports, unfortunately, aren't helpful. Chrystal didn't answer any questions."

Mary nodded.

"You know," said Al, "I think we need a child abuse expert who's not involved in this case to help us understand what the medical findings mean. How does a kid get all these things? You remember Dr. Ellen Barker, the one who gave those lectures on child abuse to the unit? Think we can get her to give us a hand?"

"Never hurts to ask. I'll call her. I think she'd do it."

"What can you tell me about her?" Al asked. "I wasn't here when she gave those lectures."

"She's probably in her early 60's, sort of an academic type who's been doing child abuse diagnostic work for over 25 years across the river. She's published several textbooks on child abuse and numerous medical journal articles. I hear she's on the lecture circuit for all kinds of audiences–medical, legal, law enforcement, CPS. Plus she's good on the stand because she has gray hair and a maternal style," Mary said as she picked up her phone to call Dr. Barker. Surprisingly, she got her on the first try.

"Hi Mary, nice to hear from you. I bet I know why you're calling. I've read about your case in the newspapers," she said.

"Yeah, nasty case. I feel so bad for the Talbots. I'm calling to see if you could review the medical records and maybe even be an expert witness for us."

"From what I've read in the papers, the case seems pretty straightforward, but one never can tell from newspaper reports what the real story is. From a purely intellectual standpoint I'd like to review the records. Send them to me and I'll get back to you right away. I'm just back from a teaching trip and have time."

"Good. The records and X-rays are all on CD's. Is that OK?"

"Sure, CD's are fine. From what I read in the Kansas City News, the hospital stay was short so the records can't be that extensive."

"Not too much, but full of medical terms and lots of paper. Oh, and we just got the ME's report so I'll send that over too."

"I assume the ME report doesn't include the neuropath report yet. That would be record time if it did."

"Right, that's still to come. But the path reports are pretty definitive."

"Look forward to seeing them. Thanks for thinking of me."

"Thank you! You've been so helpful to our staff so many times. We appreciate it."

Mary tapped her off-switch, turned to Albert and said,

"That was easy. And a great idea. Let's call it a day."

15

Nina came into Nate's office carrying a folder full of letters.
"They're coming in all at once. Here's the first batch. Got five of them already."

"Terrific! Put them on the table and hold my calls until after lunch. I want to study these," Nate said.

The first was from Frank Boyd, the neurosurgeon from Denver. Nate scanned the letter and his eyes darted down to the conclusion:

"These injuries are explained by birth injury. A birth skull fracture and subdural hematoma at the time of birth lying dormant for months suddenly rebleeds and causes the attendant problems. Retinal hemorrhages result from increased intracranial pressure."

The next letter was from James Parten, the retired pathologist from Tacoma.

"Falls from short distances in this age group can cause subdural hematomas and skull fractures. Although there is no history recorded in the medical records, I believe a fall occurred and the fall explains the constellation of signs and symptoms."

Ralph Constant, the ophthalmologist, wrote in his conclusion: "The retinal hemorrhages resulted from increased intracranial pressure secondary to the brain swelling and subdural hematoma, caused by an accidental injury, most likely a fall."

Neil Grasbauskas, the only pediatrician in the group of experts, believed that Vitamin C deficiency led to coagulation problems, bleeding in the head and brain swelling. Vitamin D deficiency was also responsible, according to him, for low calcium levels leading to thinning of the skull bone, making it susceptible to fracture.

The infectious disease specialist, Kevin Langone, believed a clot in the large vein in the head, a sinus venous thrombosis, was responsible for Luke's demise.

Nate called Janet.

"I have five experts, each of whom gives an explanation other than shaken baby syndrome for the child's death. Any one of these is enough to produce serious doubt. The jury will have to think about all these other causes for the child's death. I'll send these over by messenger. This is the architecture of a sound defense for Chrystal. Let me know what you think after you look at these."

After Janet examined the letters she called her father.

"Well, as you say, they all say this was something other than shaken baby syndrome. Seems too simple to me. The doctors I've talked to think this is classic. How can these experts be on such a different track?" Janet said.

"As I told you, they think mainstream medicine is all wrong about this. And they're willing to testify to that. You got a problem with that?" Nate said.

"I feel a little uneasy about it. Maybe I'll feel better when I have a sense of how we'll craft the defense argument. I want to be sure we have credible experts who aren't crackpots. Do you have the CV's of these people?" Janet asked.

"Janet, these are people with respected positions. They've published papers on various subjects, including shaken baby syndrome, and they have a proven track record of being qualified as experts in courts in a number of states. So they're definitely not crackpots. They have status, they have reasoned opinions, and they can help us," Nate said.

"I just want to be careful. When the other opinions come in let's get together and lay out our strategy, OK?" Janet said.

"Good, I'll let you know when I get the rest of them. And Janet —relax. You sound uptight. Take the rest of the day off!" Nate said.

"OK, Dad. It's Friday. I'll try to chill out over the weekend," Janet said.

Janet wasn't sure what was worrying her. Maybe she needed to talk to Alex. He was always helpful when she needed a little psychological insight. She tapped his number on her cellphone.

"So Alex, how're you doing?" Janet said when he picked up.

"Great. What's up with you?"

"I need a dose of you. Got time to talk?"

"Always have time to talk with you," Alex said.

"First tell me about what you're doing. I need a break from what I'm doing," Janet said.

"My music is picking up—got a few regular gigs, and I'm writing a blurb once a week for the community newspaper on pop and folk concerts. So I'm really busy," Alex said. "What's with you? Why do you need a break?"

"I feel so conflicted about this case. It's a babysitter accused of shaking a baby to death. She's eighteen years old, won't talk to me, denies everything.

"My consultant, Tom Baxley—remember him?—says this case is classic for shaken impact syndrome. My dilemma is that Dad's helping me on this case. He's lined up a bunch of doctors who insist this is something else, that there's no such thing as shaken baby syndrome.

"I don't know. Dad's so committed to showing that doctors don't know what they're doing in these cases. I'm sort of stuck between the arguments. Part of me says this is clearly shaken baby syndrome and part of me wants to win this case and let Dad prove his theory." She sighed.

"He sees exposing this as a false diagnosis as his legacy. Dad's coming to the end of his career and I'd like to see him finish it on a winning note. But that's sort of nuts, isn't it?"

"I'm not a scientist, by any stretch, so I don't know anything about the medical parts. As far as your father's concerned, he's had a lot of victories from what you've told me. If he's wrong about this, won't it come out in court?" Alex said.

"That's another thing that's bothering me. I know that courts don't always get it right, despite the best efforts of good lawyers. I've found that juries are fickle, often illogical. They're susceptible to all kinds of influences: from the media, lawyers, experts who offer specious arguments, and from errant judges."

"What about the jury process—don't they discuss the evidence and come up with the right decision most of the time?" Alex asked.

"You want jurors who are discerning, but they can be anti-intellectual and emotional. Like any of us, they tend to put their personal experiences ahead of the facts in front of them to reach a verdict. And judges...humans too, with their quirks and prejudices that interfere with their—pardon the pun—good judgment. I used to think the law would trump all else, but I'm beginning to have my doubts. I've actually lost sleep worrying about the way the court system decides things."

"Hmm. Facts do seem less important to people than their belief systems," Alex said. "And you're right about many people being anti-intellectual. Take any issue: climate change, social services, the economy, gun control. I've heard people say that if the experts don't agree on these issues and if there's that much controversy, it's a toss-up. So they say they use 'common sense' to make a decision, which of course is usually wrong because it doesn't take into account-facts!"

"You remember the H.L. Mencken quote: 'For every problem, there's a solution that is simple, neat, and wrong?' " Janet said. "My job as a lawyer is to sell a set of factoids to twelve people, most of whom have no qualifications or capacity to decide about complex matters. I have enough trouble trying to figure out what shaken baby syndrome is, even with my access to a ton of information and expert opinion. And you know what? Common sense sometimes really is better than all the medical gobbledygook," Janet said.

"See what I mean?" Alex said. "Frustration and fatigue factors at work. Revert to common sense. Trouble is, common sense is based on what I mentioned earlier—belief systems. Philosophers have been trying to figure out reality since the beginning of our species. No wonder we have such trouble with it," Alex said. He chuckled. "My advice, gratuitous as usual, is: continue gathering information, know that truth is elusive, and see what kind of an understanding develops from listening to everyone's experts. As this trial moves along, you'll find out what you believe."

"Alex, how did you get so smart? You were never that smart when I was your girl friend," Janet said.

"Sure I was. You just never knew it. But speaking of being a girl friend, one of my musician friends–he's a teacher in real life–is a guy you might like. He's about 35, recently divorced, no kids, nice guy. He's even Jewish, if that matters to you. His ex-wife was a wombat, in my opinion, very difficult. Seems she was interested more in the money that he brought home than him, so she took up with a hedge fund guy. I'm glad, never did like her.

"His name is Jared Kornblath. Plays the clarinet and saxophone in our little group."

"When do I get to meet him?" Janet said.

"How about coming to the club where we're gigging this weekend? I'll introduce you. I've already mentioned you to him," Alex said.

"You have? Now I'm embarrassed."

A pause.

"But OK, sounds good. What time and where?" Janet said.

"Around nine. We have a break then. Passiros on 18th street," Alex said.

"Wonderful Alex. And thanks. You're the best," Janet said.

16

Passiro's was on 18th near Vine in Columbia Park where several clubs feed the passions of jazz aficionados. Old Kansas City had an illustrious history of jazz and a bloody history of gangland murders. Now, even though it was more gentrified, the neighborhood still felt shabby. Janet sat near the rear brick wall and wondered how many bodies were buried beneath her feet.

She settled back and watched as Alex's trio polished off "Don't Look At Me That Way." So that was Jared. Cute, she thought, taking in the full head of dark hair, with a few shimmery streaks of grey. His stooped shoulders were accentuated by his posture as he played the clarinet.

Stowing his clarinet on its stand, Jared headed to where Alex told him Janet would be. He spotted her through the haze of the dimly lit room.

"Hi, I'm Jared. You must be Janet," he said, struck by her diminutive figure and raven-dark hair. She was very appealing… potential?

"I am," said Janet. What intense eyes, she thought. Not usual for someone with an otherwise Semitic face to have such blue eyes, "Loved your playing. Cole Porter is one of my favorites," said Janet. "He never goes out of style. His lyrics, his intervals, his keys."

"He really had the touch," Jared said.

"Alex tells me you're a professor in real life. Where do you teach?" Janet asked.

"Assistant professor, actually, at Monroe on the north side. I teach physics and chemistry to a disinterested group of liberal arts students," he said.

"My worst subjects in school!" Janet said. "I never understood why I should learn all those formulas."

"Just like my students. But I have a couple of kids interested in studying chemistry. That's all I need–a precious few students whose lives I influence," Jared said. "So what do you do in real life?" he asked. "Wait, you're a lawyer, right?"

"I work for the Public Defender's Office," she said, without going into detail.

"Oh. So you're a defense lawyer?" he said.

"Yep. That's what I do," Janet said, knowing that some people couldn't understand how anyone can defend accused criminals.

"I've been following that awful case of a babysitter who killed that little kid. You know anything about that?" Jared said, stumbling into exactly the wrong territory for his first meeting with Janet.

"Well, actually, I'm the lead attorney for the defense of that babysitter. I guess Alex didn't tell you that," Janet said.

"Ugh. Sorry. No, Alex failed to give me that little insignificant bit of information. I'm really sorry. I just assumed the babysitter did it." The pitch of his voice went up a half octave and the pace doubled. "I do believe everyone is entitled to a defense. And despite what I said, I believe people are innocent until proven guilty," Jared said. He looked more than a little sheepish. "This isn't getting off to a good start, is it?"

"Could be better. But we could change the subject. Talk about jazz. Or the weather. Or Nietsche," Janet said.

"Like, read any good books lately? Okay, let's begin again. I'm a teacher, you're a lawyer. Let's have a drink. Glad you liked our last set. I have another set to do but maybe we could talk more after that. Or go to another pub?" Jared said.

"That sounds good. I'll wait here until you're finished playing," Janet said.

After Jared finished playing, they went to a different bar and their conversation was lively.

"You ever go to classical concerts? Janet asked.

"I'm trained as a classical musician, so, yes, from time to time I go to symphony concerts. I also love ballet," Jared said.

"Ballet is the most physically demanding performing art I know of, and beautiful," Janet said.

They discovered other common interests and after about an hour, they were laughing and feeling that this could, at the very least, lead to some good times together. Jared hopped into his car and followed Janet back to her apartment.

"Well, I'm glad that Alex introduced us," Jared said.

"Me, too," Janet agreed. Here was that ever-awkward moment of saying goodbye when you liked someone but were at the very, very beginning.

With little hesitation their arms encircled each other and their lips brushed lightly together. Their inhibitions melted away and a long, deep lingering kiss sent warm waves through both their bodies. After another embrace and kiss, they parted. Jared headed home and Janet, inside her apartment, leaned against the closed door, clutching her coat, confused by her fantasies of Alex mixed in with Jared. What did this feeling mean?

17

Monday, January 4th was set for trial. Janet tried to get Chrystal released to her parents with a GPS anklet while waiting for trial, to no avail.

"I'm doing time in jail and I haven't even had a trial," Chrystal moaned when Janet told her about the trial date. "How can they do that?"

"When you're the only suspect in a murder they can hold you until your trial ends unless you make bail. That's how the system works. My motion for reduction of bail was denied. I'm truly sorry," Janet said.

Chrystal paced around the room pulling at her hair. She impulsively jammed her fist hard into the unyielding cinder block wall, hurting her hand. "I'm so fed up with this shit!" she screamed. "You keep saying you've got these great experts and your Dad's helping you, and you're going to do this awesome job defending me, but what've you done so far? Nothing! I'm stuck here with these dirty old women and they rag on me all the time."

Janet barely breathed during this outburst, being the designated sponge for Chrystal's frustration. But reflected anger rose inside her. She struggled to resist the urge to scream back at Chrystal. One of them had to retain control.

"Let me see your hand," Janet said.

Now Chrystal let loose with a torrent of tears looking at her hand. Slowly, she moved over to Janet, extending her hand. It was swelling and her knuckles were bloody from the rough cinderblock. Janet touched it lightly and Chrystal drew back sharply.

"We have to get a doctor to look at this. You may've broken something," Janet said.

Chrystal continued crying, interspersed with deep-throated sobbing. Against her better judgment, Janet took Chrystal into her arms. After a few minutes, she calmed down. For the first time Janet was able to see Chrystal as a frightened, vulnerable child.

"I understand you feel persecuted and angry. I don't blame you. But if we're going to work together we can't have this kind of scene. The guards see it and that doesn't help your case. And I don't like seeing it either. If you want another lawyer I'll ask the judge to appoint someone else. But if you want me to stay with you, let's make a deal. No more outbursts like this one." She looked into Chrystal's eyes. "No more yelling at me that I'm not doing my job, because I'm working night and day to help you. I need your cooperation and your respect. I don't need you to like me, or my father. But I demand respect," Janet said, with a strong emphasis on the last word.

"My hand really hurts but I don't want to see a doctor 'cause they'll write that down on my record," Chrystal said. "They watch every little thing you do here and it'll be one more strike against me. Other people in here don't care about anything, but I feel everything. They laugh at me when I get pissed, but I can't help it."

"I'm not a doctor, but it looks like you've broken a bone. I have to report this so you can get it taken care of," Janet said. "When the doctor sees you, be cooperative. You're not doing yourself any favors by being difficult."

Chrystal didn't answer. She knew she had no choice, but she wasn't going to admit it.

The doctor saw her, found a broken bone in her hand, and sent her to an orthopedist at a local hospital who set the bone and put a plaster cast on her arm. Outside of the jail for the first time since her arrest, Chrystal wept, knowing her freedom was short-lived.

When she got back to the cell, the woman who had been giving her a hard time said, "So who did you punch, baby-killer? Somebody your own size this time? Huh?"

"Fuck you, I hate your fuckin' guts, you black bitch!"

"Oh, a baby killer and a racist too, eh?" she said.

"Just shut up and leave me alone," Chrystal said.

"It's a free country, honey, and there's a thing called the first amendment, ya know? I can say whatever I want, especially to a white cracker like you."

"So now who's the racist? Just fuck off," said Chrystal.

They both tired of the confrontation and turned inward with their thoughts. Her hand was beginning to throb now that the painkiller had worn off. Chrystal called the guard.

"I need some pain pills," she said.

"Not time yet. You'll have to put up with it for another hour. Not allowed to give them to you until 4 o'clock," the guard said.

"C'mon, you can give them to me now. You just like to see me suffer," Chrystal said.

The guard ignored her, turning back to her magazine, flipping the pages, irritating Chrystal even more. Recalling Janet's admonition to stay out of trouble Chrystal lay down on her bed, facing the wall. Soon she was asleep despite the pain in her hand. It had been a rotten day.

Mary Egan and Al Polcari talked to Danny Doyle, the police sergeant first on the scene at the Talbot's house. "We've read your report, but just tell us again about the scene at the house when you got there," said Mary.

Doyle reviewed police procedures followed that day.

"Basically she said she was feeding him, he got messed up with the cereal, so she gave him a bath and he went limp and passed out. She lifted him out of the tub, laid him on the floor and called 911. After she said that, she clammed up, got moody, and didn't talk any more," Danny said.

"The investigation turn up anything?" Albert asked.

"Well, she had a cellphone when we booked her, so we checked her phone records. There was one call from a girlfriend–Carol Smith–just before everything happened. We tracked her down and she told us she talked with Chrystal and heard Luke in the background, laughing and sounding normal. But she said Chrystal hung up 'cause she said the baby was flinging cereal all over the place. She said Chrystal sounded really stressed out. That's about all we could find out from her," Doyle said.

"This call is important because Carol Smith is an independent witness who helps us establish that Luke was acting normally before the bath,"

Albert said. "Other than Alison and Fred Talbot, whose observations could be characterized in court as self-serving, she's the only person who could confirm that Luke sounded like a normal infant before his sudden decline."

Albert took Carol Smith's name and number.

Later that afternoon, he was able to persuade Carol to testify even though she "didn't want to get Chrystal into any more trouble." Albert assured her that telling the truth was the most important thing she could do for Chrystal.

Also interviewed was Linda Campion, the CPS worker who tried to talk with Chrystal after her arrest. "She simply wouldn't talk with me," Linda told Albert. "I tried several times but she just shut me out. I also tried talking with her parents but her stepfather was so rude and scary that after several attempts, my supervisor told me to stop trying. Anyway, it was in police hands by then."

Albert went to Chrystal's high school to talk to her teachers. They described her as a quiet C-student, who seemed distracted much of the time.

"Once she had a fight with a fellow student in gym but otherwise she was sort of invisible, didn't interact much with anyone," one of them said.

Albert talked with a few of her fellow students but they all went into tight-lipped, adolescent mode, intimidated by this big guy, who they saw as a larger-than-life authority figure.

Mary Egan went to the convenience store to talk with Chrystal's parents. Daryll gave Mary a sour look, but led her to his small office in the rear of the store, sat down, and glared at her.

"So, fire away, missus DA," he said.

"Can you tell me anything about Chrystal to help us understand what might have happened?" she asked.

"I ain't telling you anything to 'help you understand'" he mimicked. "I know your game. You want to put Chrystal in the slammer for the rest of her life. You'll not get any help from me, or from June, for that matter."

After about five more minutes with Daryll, Mary concluded he was right about not giving her any help. She asked to speak with June alone.

Daryll didn't like it, but couldn't think how he could prevent her from talking with Chrystal's mother.

"Can you tell me anything that might help us?" Mary asked June.

"Chrystal's a good girl. I can't believe that she'd hurt a baby, like the papers are saying. I just know she's a sweet child and couldn't do that," June said.

After a few more questions, it was clear that she was getting nowhere with June either. Mary thanked them and headed back downtown.

When she walked into her office, her secretary jumped up. "There's this urgent message from the jail for you to call."

The message was about Chrystal's hand injury, how it happened, and also that Chrystal had been in a couple of fights with other prisoners.

"We decided to put her in a cell by herself," said one of the jail matrons when Mary reached her.

"Be sure to keep an eye on her," Mary said. "She could be a suicide risk. Sure don't want that to happen. Let me know if anything else comes up."

Well, now. Mary thought. *Sounds like Chrystal has a real anger management problem. She reacts to frustration by becoming physically aggressive. A fight in school, fighting a couple of jailmates, and now this. This sounds like the foundation for opening and closing arguments.*

18

The delay in the trial hung like soggy black crepe over Chrystal, but it was welcome news both to the prosecutors and to Janet and Nate. Everyone needed time to read, digest and analyze pounds of medical literature.

During the first week of December Janet went to her father's office now designated as "Command Headquarters." Nina brought them coffee, bagels, scones and croissants.

"The goal here is to separate the wheat from the chaff and distill the information to a critical mass," Nate said, stating the obvious, "then develop arguments and counter-arguments. We're not scientists, but this wait gives us time to learn a lot about medical jargon and the syndrome. I'm sure that Egan and Polcari have too. They're both smart and articulate," Nate said. He then recapped Chrystal's actions at the time of the incident.

"That's how I understand it, too," said Janet.. "What're your ideas about devising the best defense argument?"

"What we have to do is establish that there was an injury before that morning, maybe a couple of weeks earlier, or maybe even earlier than that, tie the subdural bleeding to that old injury temporally, and argue that on that day the old subdural burst or re-bled, leading to all his symptoms. I'm getting this explanation from the experts' letters. That old injury could have been one that someone else did, like the parents, or even the older brother."

"What about the skull fracture?" Janet asked.

"Could've also been an old injury," said Nate. "Here's the way I look at it: presume an old injury, two to three weeks before that fateful day, supported by the X-ray evidence of that old leg fracture. Those old injuries existed due to a fall that caused bleeding in his head. That blood clotted. He had no symptoms from it, or maybe he had some general symptoms that kids get from time to time, you know, like a little vomiting, some fussiness, out of sorts, that no one paid much attention to. Then, when Chrystal pulls him from the tub, he's having this tantrum. He's throwing his head around and this disrupts that clot, which bleeds causing everything else."

"OK, just for the sake of argument, explain how the autopsy report claims there was fresh bleeding under the scalp on the back of his head," Janet said.

"Easy," said Nate. "The Emergency Medical Tech's did CPR on the baby and that caused the swelling under the skin of the head, and maybe even the skull fracture. Those EMT's can get awful rough in their excitement to resuscitate a dying patient. And babies are little."

Janet looked non-committal.

"Another possibility," Nate continued, "is that we say there was a birth injury causing the original subdural hematoma, which then broke loose on that day. Or, how about this? Luke had a seizure and that caused the bleeding in the head. Or, as one of the experts said, he had a sinus venous thrombosis–whatever that is–that caused all of this. One expert suggested that the kid had a Vitamin C deficiency that weakened his blood vessels, making them easy to break," Nate said.

"Are any of these things supported by the medical literature?" asked Janet, head crooked at an angle that betrayed her skepticism about this line of logic.

"There are articles about all this. Don't ask me how good the literature is, but if we can sell it to the jury, what difference does it make?" said Nate. "All we have to do is convince one member of the jury that our client's not guilty and we're home free," Nate said.

Janet got that increasingly familiar queasy feeling.

Have Dad's ethics taken another nosedive? Would he do anything to get a "not guilty" verdict? Was everything fair in love, war and criminal defense?

"Then there are the biomechanics. I've got an engineer who's done experiments proving that shaking can't do any of the things seen in this kid. Added to that, this engineer thinks if a baby gets shaken really hard, he'd have neck injuries. His testimony will be hard for the jury to understand, so that'll make it easier to convince them that you need to see neck injuries to prove there's been shaking," Nate said. "I think we can persuade them with this line of thinking.

"The other important thing we've got to do is work the media. Of course, before the trial we can't say much to the media, but during the trial we should have an end-of-the-day session every day with the media. They'll eat that up. Before the trial we get some doctors who believe that shaken baby syndrome is baloney to write some op-eds and get interviewed on the tube questioning this diagnosis," said Nate.

"So, what should be the order of the witnesses?" Janet asked, trying to get back to the tactics of the case.

"I think after the prosecution presents their fact witnesses, we cross them and challenge their competence and diagnostic skills, and show they didn't look at all the possibilities. Then we lead off with our expert who will talk about re-bleeding of an old clot, followed by the one who will talk about the clot being caused by a short fall, like rolling off a changing table. Then we put on our expert who thinks there's a clotting disorder or a vitamin deficiency. We follow him with an expert who believes all of Luke's problems are due to lack of oxygen. We could add the testimony of the expert who will testify that venous thrombosis is the culprit. One of the experts thinks it's all due to one of the vaccines that kids get around this age," Nate said. "Then we bring in the biomechanical engineer's testimony that shaking can't cause any of this. I think bringing him in at the end is the right place because we want the last thought in the jury's minds, when they go in to deliberate, to be: shaking can't do this."

"I'll do the cross of the hospital doctors, Dad, if you'll do the heavy lifting with the defense experts, since you know what their testimony is going to be," Janet said.

"I've spent hours poring over reports and articles they've sent me. I'm beginning to understand a fair amount about this diagnosis. Doesn't mean I understand it all," Nate said. "But what I have to do is ask the questions and let the experts spin their tale. The prosecution will probably have a hard time with these experts since they're all highly qualified. When they begin attacking our experts, we need to be ready to object strenuously and cut them off."

"We can work on our opening statements next week. Should I do that, or do you want to?" Janet asked.

"You do the opening. As a woman, you're a more sympathetic figure and the jury will love you. I'm an old, hard-bitten defense attorney and juries don't immediately like me. They warm up once I get going, but I think you'd be better at softening them up," Nate said.

"So I'll work on the opening statement. I'd like you to look at my outline after I've had time to work on it," Janet said.

Nate's attention drifted out the window, his eyes on the river. A barge was motoring downstream, dragging tons of coal. The shoreline was dotted with frosty inlets. He was in a different place than a minute ago. Janet waited.

"Saw your mother last night. She's slipping, I think. Didn't recognize me. I was kind of down after seeing her. We had such a lovely life together. Now that's over and she's not going to get better, I know that," Nate said.

"You had one of those wonderful marriages where you grew closer over the years. I love her too, and it pains me that she doesn't recognize me. But I know that's how dementia works," Janet said. "How are you feeling otherwise?"

"Me? Well, now that you ask, I've sort of lost my appetite. Probably due to Naomi's decline. I've lost a little weight too. But I feel OK. Don't worry about me. I'm fine."

"I do worry about you. Can't help it. I love you. Wish I could make Mom better. You'll ask for help if you need it?"

"Not my style to ask for help, but, yes, I will, if the time comes when I think I need it," Nate said.

He's placating me, as he always does. But I can't do anything more than watch for changes in his affect and appearance. The psychologists say that melancholia is often masked by pride, so I'll have to be extra vigilant, Janet thought.

They walked arm-in-arm to the elevator. As soon as she got to the street, her phone rang.

"Hi, Jared here. How 'bout dinner tonight?"

"Just what I need," Janet said. "Where and when?"

"How about seven at 'A Touch of Thai' ?"

"Sounds just right. See you there."

It was tempting for Janet to unload her worries on Jared, but she knew if this relationship were to flourish she needed to keep an upbeat attitude and stick to positive subjects. Tonight Jared looked even better to her than when they first met.

"Wondering what you're doing for the holidays," he said as they finished up their basil-laden Thai main course. "I'm thinking about a long weekend someplace warm, like the Caribbean, getting away from the cold and all the holiday commercialism," he said.

"Oh, that does sound so appealing. But I have so much prep work to do before this trial, I don't see how I could take that time away," Janet said.

"Do you good to get away for three or four days. As the ads say, 'Recharge your batteries, go away, take a break.' We could get to know each other a little better," Jared said.

I've known this guy for less than two weeks and he wants to go away for a weekend in the Caribbean? Rushing it a little? Never done anything like that before..

"I would like a break," Janet heard herself say, "but I have to keep the momentum going on this case. If I interrupt it now I could lose steam. You know, like when you're in the middle of a riff, if you take a break it falls apart. I'm sorry," she sighed. "After the trial we can talk about where we're headed as an 'item.' For now, I better stick to my knitting. But I do appreciate the thought."

They left the restaurant and headed to Janet's apartment. Jared anticpated being invited in, but Janet was in the wrong place emotionally to become any more intimate than they had been. It would have to wait until the trial was over. Jared would have to understand. She hoped he would.

19

The prosecutors and defense now knew who the judge would be, decided by some byzantine process known only to the administrative judges in Superior Court in Kansas City. Neither side was pleased, since Judge Henry Carlsson was known as a maverick, one who delighted in doing the unexpected and whose rulings often were capricious. A fastidious man, colleagues considered him brilliant but terribly eccentric. He was a towering, slender figure who seemed taller than his six feet. A narcissist, he was probably thrilled to still boast a generous youthful shock of hair, though more silver than black. His face was striking, with a prominent patrician nose bestride sagging cheeks, thin lips that rarely smiled, and neck wattles that settled into a white collar where his signature bow tie rose up above his judicial robe.

"I've prayed for his retirement, but it hasn't worked," Mary said to Albert. "He's imperious on his perch, and doesn't tolerate any foolishness by the lawyers on either side. He was a criminal defense attorney before ascending to the bench and leans philosophically toward their side. He's also a good friend of Nathan Feingold. They belong to the same private club, The Hermits, for men only and housed in an ancient downtown building with creaky floors and cobwebs in the corners. I'm told the library is stacked high with musty, out-of-print, archaic books and antiquarian knick-knacks. When these guys pay their substantial initiation fees they pledge that what is said there stays there. So this adds one more obstacle to our mission."

On the day of jury selection, the lawyers filed into the courtroom, taking their places at the defense or prosecution table. The stenographer set up the machines of her trade. Silent participants in the courtroom drama, the stenographer still whispered into an antediluvian conical device that looked like a resuscitation cup, with this supplemented by a modern tape recorder. Water pitchers were provided for the jury, judge, and each of the lawyers' tables.

At length, the bailiff finally intoned the age-old call to order, "Hear ye, hear ye, the Jackson County Court is now in session. All rise."

The door to the left of the elevated presiding judge's bench opened and Judge Carlsson strode in, nodding to his clerk and the stenographers. He took some time settling in, part of his personal judicial choreography, rearranging his water pitcher, pulling his robes from under his backside and arranging his laptop to his satisfaction. The clerk called the case number and inquired about the attorneys' readiness to begin jury selection.

The jury pool was led into the chamber, then waited for the process that would either get them off the hook or onto it for what was certain to be a long trial. "Peremptory" challenges-where a lawyer doesn't like the looks of a prospective juror-and "cause" challenges-where a prospective juror is perceived as being biased or having a preconceived notion about the defendant or the issue to be decided before the court–consumed most of the day.

Fourteen jurors, evenly split as to gender, were acceptable to both sides: three African-Americans, two of whom were women; two Hispanics; and seven Caucasians. Two of the jury pool were alternates and twelve, the "real" jurors. The educational levels ranged from eighth grade to one PhD and one dentist.

At the conclusion of this process, Judge Carlsson instructed everyone to be ready for trial promptly at nine the following morning. He admonished the jurors not to watch television, listen to the radio, read newspapers, or talk to anyone about the case. Once the trial began, he would sequester the jury.

"What did you think?" Janet asked Nate as they went back to his office.

"Just another day in court," Nate said. "The jury looks OK. You never know about them, though. They're so fickle. They'll change their minds a dozen times during the trial. So you can't rely on one day's impressions. It's what happens in the end that matters."

"What about Judge Carlsson? He's an old friend of yours, isn't he?"

"Well, he's a loose cannon. I like him, think he's smart enough, but he sometimes gets a wild hair up his ass–excuse the French–and will do something completely daft. I've been astounded at some of the rulings he's made in my favor–and then some that went against my clients were equally puzzling. I'll try to read him as we go along, but with him it's like star gazing–sometimes you see the light, sometimes you don't."

"I'm ready with my opening statement. Want to read it?" Janet said.

"I'll read it, but I won't change it. It's you talking, not me. I don't want to interfere with your style. I've watched you in court. You're good," Nate said.

Janet flushed and looked down at her hands. She'd never been comfortable accepting compliments, especially from her father.

"If you have any suggestions, though, I want to hear them. You know the medical material better. My thought was to make the whole thing simple, but set doubt in motion," Janet said.

"Right, keep it simple. Remember that juries are made up of people who aren't smart enough to stay off jury duty," Nate said with a wink.

"Dad, sometimes you're so cynical. Two of our jurors are doctors. You think they're stupid? Or could it be that they actually consider it their civic duty to serve on a jury?"

"OK, OK, maybe I'm getting less tolerant of my fellow human beings. Your mother used to tell me that when she was still at home. Now that she's not around, I guess I've gotten grumpier. The world seems to be getting worse," Nate said.

"The world's not getting worse, Dad, if anything it's getting better. Remember what it was like during the Civil War, or the Second World War, during Nazi Germany. Surely you don't think we're as bad off as then," Janet said.

"You're right. I'll shut up. I get discouraged sometimes. I guess I brood too much. Maybe I ought to get a girlfriend!"

"Really?!" Janet said. She glanced over at her father and saw the familiar glint in his eyes.

I'm glad he's able to smile a little. But a girlfriend helping the old boy? I hope he wouldn't be like one of those rich, old men with a fashion model girl friend. No fool like an old, rich, fool. But he'd have more sense than that, right? I guess I'm getting jealous before he does such a thing.

The next morning at 9AM sharp, Judge Carlsson convened the court. Janet glanced around trying to get a sense of what kind of audience was sitting behind the rails. Directly behind the prosecutors' table were the Talbots, in seats that Mary had reserved for them. She spotted June–but no Daryll–in the back row. Chrystal was seated next to Janet. Janet noticed that when Chrystal located her mother in the back row their eyes locked and June smiled and nodded to her. Chrystal looked down, but then looked back again at her mother with a slight blink.

Reporters were scattered around the courtroom as were several ordinary citizens whose interest in the case was anyone's guess. Janet saw a man with gray hair, half-glasses near the end of his nose and a professorial demeanor sitting on the aisle near the door. He was carrying a folder and a book that looked vaguely familiar. She squinted to see the title and recognized it as one of the child abuse textbooks she'd consulted while preparing her case. She guessed he was a physician and wondered why he was there. She named him the "Professor" in her cast of characters. If this were a movie, Max von Sydow would be perfectly cast as the "Professor" she thought.

Judge Carlsson called on Mary Egan to give her opening statement.

She sidled around the prosecutor's table and looked at the judge. "Thank you, Your Honor."

Dressed in a gray suit, with a light blue silk blouse underneath, one-inch heels and no jewelry, Mary was the prototype of a competent female attorney. She looked over at Chrystal momentarily and then walked to the jury box, stood at the end of it. As she spoke, she looked each juror in the eye, one by one.

"Alison and Fred Talbot entrusted their precious seven-month-old baby Luke to the defendant, Chrystal Begley on Saturday October 16th. The Talbots, both reading specialists in the Kansas City School District, had to attend a national conference on improving reading skills on that day. Luke was well that morning, just as he had been ever since he was born. Alison had fed him a bottle of formula before she left and he had taken it eagerly. No spitting up, no throwing up. You'll hear from Chrystal's friend that when she talked to Chrystal on the phone around 8:30 on that morning, Luke sounded fine, was laughing and making baby noises. But within two hours after the defendant took charge of this baby, the Emergency Medical Service had rushed him to Children's Hospital. He was nearly dead.

"Something happened to Luke in the short time between the Talbots' leaving him perfectly well with the defendant and the time the Emergency Medical Team came.

"The doctors at the hospital examined and evaluated Luke's physical state, analyzed his X-rays and his laboratory tests. They ALL agreed that to have his specific symptoms, he had to have been shaken back and forth, back and forth many times, and then, to top it off, slammed against a hard surface.

"During this trial we'll show that this diagnosis was not only the most likely, but was the only one possible. The defendant has denied everything. But the medical evidence–bleeding under the covering of the brain, a fractured skull in the thickest part of the head, the swollen brain, and the bleeding in the back layers of the retina of the eyes–all scream 'inflicted trauma.' There's no history of an accident, no blows to the head, no falls out of second story windows. There's no history of any previous illnesses, not even mild illnesses. There's no history of ANY abnormalities in this innocent baby. He was perfect…until placed in the care–if you can call it that–of the defendant.

"Many of you in the jury have children. It's no easy task raising children. They can make you mad. Sometimes you wonder how you kept your temper in check. But you did. You didn't take a seven-month-old infant, grasp him under the arms, shake him over and over and then slam his head against a wall, or a floor, or a bathtub, until he goes as limp as a rag doll. But some people do lose their tempers and wreak havoc on anything near them.

"That's what Chrystal Begley did. She lost her temper badly and Luke paid for it with his life. He annoyed her, she became infuriated, and she lashed out, shook him until he was no more. And to finish the act, she slammed the baby's head onto a hard surface causing a three-inch skull fracture in the back of his head, and a big bruise and collection of blood over that fracture.

"You'll hear a lot of testimony during this trial about the complex medical issues this case raises. You'll hear medical experts for the defense arguing that these things were caused by something other than abuse. But keep your eyes on the ball, use your common sense, and ask: 'How can a baby go from being perfectly well to near death while in the care of one person, in two hours, unless that person caused that change?'

Mary paused and then said, "If you ask yourself that question, you can reach only one answer. That answer is the verdict of guilty. Guilty. Guilty."

Mary Egan stood still while these last words suffused the courtroom. The jury had been attentive. Two of the women dabbed their eyes with tissues as Mary described the shaking and slamming. One of the men looked queasy and pale as Mary walked slowly back to the table. She sat down silently with her head down.

Fred and Alison Talbot sat motionless as they absorbed Mary's words. Chrystal's eyes were glazed over as she fidgeted with her fingernails.

"Ms. Feingold, your opening statement?" Judge Carlsson said.

Janet, her heart pounding as she rose, felt weak as she answered, "Yes, Your Honor."

20

Janet looked at Chrystal, whose eyes were focused straight ahead. She walked to the middle of the jury box. "Losing your baby has to be the worst thing in the world. I mourn with Luke's mother and father. I have no way of knowing the pain they feel, but I think of their loss as I go to sleep each night. I'm sure you, the men and women of this jury, feel the same way. That's the human response. We all feel it. Their loss is devastating."

Janet paused for effect. Fred and Alison fought for control.

"Our job, here in this courtroom, is to decide, on the basis of the evidence presented, what caused Luke to succumb. You'll hear much medical testimony, detailing the terrible injuries in Luke's head, and some of that testimony will be confusing. No one on this jury is a medical doctor, yet most of what you'll be hearing will be medical information. Listen carefully to this, because your job is to decide which parts of the medical testimony are provable facts and which are medical speculation.

"Was Luke well when my client, Chrystal Begley took over his care? We've heard that he was well that morning, but was he really? We need to go back in time all the way to his birth. Did something happen to Luke's head as he was being born? I ask those women on the jury who have given birth to think back on how violent the birth of a baby can be. Could there have been a birth injury that went unrecognized only to come to light on that fateful morning? Did Luke have some genetic defect or medical condition that caused blood to collect in his brain? Had a fall onto his head days or weeks before caused a blood clot to form in his head? Did that blood clot in his head get ruptured and re-bleed during his temper tantrum when Chrystal tried to bathe him? Did he have some other disease that no one knew about that showed itself that morning? Did the shots he got at the pediatrician's office two days before cause the problem? Was it simply a lack of oxygen to the brain that caused all of this? These are all legitimate questions that need answers before we rush to the judgment that Chrystal was responsible for this horrible outcome.

"You'll hear testimony from the doctors from Children's Hospital, who are convinced that the diagnosis of shaken baby syndrome is the correct one. But you'll also hear from other medical experts that this diagnosis is being seriously questioned in the medical profession. You'll hear a bio-mechanical engineer, who has studied the biomechanics of such injuries, tell you these injuries can't happen as a result of shaking. That the doctors should've looked more carefully for other conditions that could have caused these findings. In short, these experts will contend that Chrystal didn't do anything to cause Luke's death and there are other explanations for this tragedy. Chrystal is not guilty of these charges. There is no convincing evidence that she did anything to harm Luke Talbot.

"When Chrystal saw that Luke was unconscious, she acted much older than her eighteen years when she quickly called 911 and followed the instructions given to her by the dispatcher. She tried her best to get help for Luke and to try to revive him with CPR.

"Please keep your minds and eyes and ears open and listen carefully. I know when all the testimony is heard that you'll come to the only reasonable and fair conclusion: The State has not proven its case beyond a *reasonable doubt* because the evidence does not support the charges. Chrystal is innocent of these charges. Thank you."

Janet sat down. Nate put his hand on her arm, looked into her eyes, and smiled.

Judge Carlsson surveyed the courtroom, his eyes sweeping from left to right. Carlsson enjoyed being the center of attention in cases in which the public showed a large interest. The people from print media were scribbling notes and the TV cameras were rolling. Nate had watched the jury during Janet's opening statement and had noticed that several of the jurors were writing on note pads, others were fiddling with their iPads and hand-held devices. He wondered when they would become inured to taking notes as the trial proceeded and the testimony became more complex and confusing.

"The state can present their first witness," the judge said.

Albert Polcari stood. "The state calls Police Sergeant Daniel Doyle of the Kansas City Police Department."

Daniel Doyle was only one of two witnesses known by Chrystal. She glanced quickly at him as he took the stand, wondering what he might say.

Danny Doyle looked uncomfortable in his "court clothes," an ill-fitting blue blazer, white shirt, a tie so ugly it must have been a castoff, and gray trousers. His shaved head and bull neck with rippling thick folds of skin running like a washboard across the back of his head, was sweating. He walked to the witness stand and took the oath.

"Officer Doyle, how long have you been a police officer?"

"Eight-and-a-half years," Doyle replied.

"What kind of training did you receive before you joined the police department?" Albert asked.

Danny Doyle described his education and his current assignment, then relaxed on the stand.

"Sergeant Doyle, did you arrive first at the Talbots' house on the morning of the 911 call?"

"Well, the EMS and I got there about the same time, sir."

"Will you describe what you found there?" Albert said.

"All of us went in at the same time. I saw the babysitter on her knees over the baby trying to give him CPR. The EMT's took over right away. I asked the girl what happened and she said she'd been giving the baby a bath and he 'went limp.' Didn't have much else to say," he said.

"What did Chrystal do while you looked around at the scene?" Albert said.

"She just sat on the floor and looked away, as far as I could tell," he said. "I took some pictures of the bathroom and asked her a few more questions but she didn't respond to any of them," he said.

"Did you see any signs of struggles or violence when you examined the scene and took those pictures?" Albert said.

"Nothing that I could see," Doyle said. "So when EMT's took the baby away in the ambulance, I took the babysitter into custody. I brought her to the station. They booked her, gave her the Miranda warning, she signed it, and they asked her a few more questions, but she didn't say anything more."

"Is that babysitter in the room today?" Albert asked.

"Yes."

"Would you point her out to us please?"

"Right over there," Danny said and pointed to Chrystal.

"No further questions, your Honor," Albert said.

"Ms. Feingold, your witness," Judge Carlsson said.

"Good morning, Sergeant Doyle, I'm Janet Feingold, Counsel for Chrystal Begley, the defendant," Janet began.

"Good morning, m'am," Doyle said.

"You said you didn't see any signs of a struggle or violence, is that right? Janet asked.

"Nothing that I could see," Danny said.

"Did the pictures you took add anything?" Janet said.

"No, not really."

"Thank you. That's all I have, your Honor," Janet said.

"You may step down, Officer," Judge Carlsson said.

"The state calls Rob Conklin," Albert said.

Rob Conklin pushed open the swinging gate behind the lawyers' tables and went to the stand, took the oath, sat down, adjusted the microphone, gave his name, and waited to be questioned.

"Mr. Conklin, please tell the members of the jury what your job is," Albert said.

"I'm an Emergency Medical Technician and a first responder to emergencies in Kansas City," Conklin said.

After establishing that he had been one of two Emergency Medical personnel to respond to the call from the Talbot's house, Albert asked, "Would you please describe what you found at the house?"

"The baby was laying on his back on the hall floor outside the bathroom. The babysitter was kneeling beside him. He wasn't breathing on his own. His color was pale. He looked bad," Conklin said.

"What happened then?"

"We immediately intubated him—put a breathing tube into his wind-pipe—and began bagging him-that is, pumping air into his lungs. He pinked up after we did that. His heart rate stabilized after the tube was in and he got some oxygen. He remained unconscious. Even though he didn't have any visible injuries, we immobilized him on a board anyway and wrapped him in warming blankets. We hustled him out to the ambulance and took off to the hospital," Conklin said.

"Did you talk to the babysitter?"

"No, the officer was talking to her. The most important thing for us was to get him to the hospital quickly because he looked so bad. Besides, the babysitter, she seemed pretty spacey," Conklin said.

"Objection," Janet said immediately.

"Sustained. Jury should disregard the witness' last statement," the judge said.

"No further questions," Albert said.

Janet rose. "I only have one question, Mr. Conklin. Did you see any indication of violence, either at the scene or on Luke's body, as you were working with him?"

"No."

"Thank you."

Albert approached the lectern. "The state calls Carol Smith."

Chrystal winced as she heard Carol's name.

What's she doing here? What's she gonna say? I thought she was a friend.

Carol appeared to be about the same age as Chrystal, shorter than average with a round face and a body to match. Her voice was small as she took her oath and stated her name.

After identifying her as Chrystal's acquaintance, babysitting in another home, Albert said, "Miss Smith, please tell the court about your phone conversation with Chrystal on the morning of October sixteenth."

"Well, we weren't talking, like, about anything in particular, you know, that I can remember. We were both babysitting, you know, and that's kind of, like, boring," she said.

"Before this trial began, when we spoke to you about your phone conversation with Chrystal, you mentioned hearing Luke in the background while you were talking with Chrystal. Is that correct?"

"Yeah, well, like, I heard Luke making baby noises and laughing. I said to Chrystal he seemed really happy."

"Then what happened?"

"Well, then Chrystal got sort of excited, you know, and said, like, Luke was happy but she wasn't, and he was throwing cereal all over her and himself and on the floor."

"Then what did she say?

"She said, 'Jesus! Gotta go,' and then just hung up."

"Did you talk to Chrystal later about this?" Albert said.

"No, haven't talked to her, or even seen her, since then."

"Thanks, Miss Smith. That's all the questions I have," Albert said.

"Miss Smith, when you say that Luke 'seemed really happy,' what do you mean by that?" Janet began.

"Oh, I don't know. You know, I mean, like, he was giggling and sorta whooping, like a happy little baby. I don't know," she said.

"Could those noises have been fussy noises as well?"

"Didn't sound fussy to me, but I guess they could've been," Carol said.

"Thank you, that's all I have for this witness," Janet said.

Chrystal watched Carol depart the stand.

What was that supposed to prove? Chrystal wondered.

"The state calls Dr. David Roby," Albert said.

Dressed in a blue blazer and khaki trousers, a button-down yellow shirt with a striped rep tie, a slender man in his forties moved fluidly through the gates and made his way to the witness stand. After taking the oath, he stated his name and occupation:

"David Roby, Luke's pediatrician," he said.

"Can you tell the court about Luke's medical history?" Albert said.

"Not much to tell, really. Normal at birth, got the usual treatment in the hospital including a circumcision and hepatitis shot. He left the hospital with his mother on the second day. Seen regularly in my office, got the usual immunizations up through his checkup just a few days before"–he paused–"all this happened. He was fine at the checkup, with no physical abnormalities, normally developing," he said.

"On his last visit to you, Doctor, did he have any signs of trauma on his head or body?" Albert asked.

"No. He was a perfect specimen. Beautiful, happy little guy, no signs of illness. We wouldn't have given him shots if he had anything wrong. I talked to Alison the day after he got his shots—that's my usual follow-up routine—and she said he had no reaction of any kind."

"Thank you doctor, no further questions," Albert said.

Janet considered what would be gained from questioning Dr. Roby and decided not to ask him any questions. It was obvious that the prosecution was trying to establish that Luke had been well prior to Chrystal's care.

"No questions, Your Honor," Janet said.

Judge Carlsson said to Dr. Roby, "Thank you, Doctor. You may step down."

"The state calls Dr. William Robbins."

Will Robbins was an elf-like man: short, wiry, and hyperactive. In his mid-thirties, he was a vibrant fellow, known for his engaging teaching style and brilliant diagnostic skills. His usual Emergency Department garb was a scrub suit, but today he wore khaki pants, tweed sports coat, plaid shirt and solid green tie—his "dress-up" clothes. His movements were brisk as he climbed into the witness chair. After being sworn in, Robbins described his education and training in pediatric emergency medicine at Children's Hospital in St. Louis and then told of his role in receiving Luke in the Emergency Department.

"As he was brought in I got the history from the EMS folks. They said he'd been unconscious at the house, not breathing well, low oxygen in his blood. Once they intubated him he perked up and his heart rate returned to normal. We noticed what looked like bruises on his back near the spine, up high. Little oval bruises, looked like they had been made with fingertips."

"Objection!" Janet said. "Pure speculation."

"Sustained. Jurors please disregard the last part of the doctor's response," said Judge Carlsson.

"Go on," said Albert.

"Well, we started intravenous lines, took blood samples, hooked up the monitors for breathing and heart, and then got a CT scan of his head," Robbins said.

"Why'd you get blood samples? What were you looking for?" Albert asked.

"We got a complete blood count to see if there might be signs of underlying infection, or anemia, and then we got blood coagulation studies to rule out clotting and bleeding disorders. We always get samples to see if there is an imbalance in the blood minerals, like sodium and potassium, things like that," Robbins said. "Sort of a survey for a wide range of things."

"Were these abnormal in any way?"

"The clotting studies were a little abnormal, but we often see mildly abnormal clotting studies when there's brain injury," Robbins said.

"What did the CT show?"

"There was a large subdural hematoma over the right hemisphere of the brain. This was a blood clot under the membrane covering of the brain. There were early signs of brain swelling, a skull fracture of the back of the head, and some blood under the scalp over that fracture."

"Then what happened?" Albert asked.

"We checked with Dr. McClure, the head of PICU, to see if they were ready to take Luke up there."

"What is PICU?" Albert asked.

"That's the Pediatric Intensive Care Unit. It's where we treat the patients with the most serious problems," Robbins answered.

"Thank you, no more questions," Albert said.

"Ms. Feingold?" Judge Carlsson said.

Janet paused, then got up and said, "Doctor, were there any abnormalities in the blood studies?"

"Yeah, he had what we call acidosis. We usually see that when someone has needed resuscitation. The blood count showed that he was a little anemic but he had no changes in his blood count that would suggest infection, and no other underlying diseases detectable by a blood count," Robbins said. "He also had some mild coagulation abnormalities, but, as I said before, these are explained by his having brain injury, which often causes some abnormality in the coagulation studies."

"No further questions. Thank you, Doctor," Janet said.

"Time for a break," Judge Carlsson announced. "We will recess for thirty minutes. Exactly thirty minutes."

As Janet turned to go out, she saw June scurrying out of the last row of the gallery. Daryll was not with her. "The Professor" was getting up from his seat with a notepad and his book. The Talbots both looked intently at Chrystal, then walked from their seats behind the prosecutor's table to the special room set up for them. Chrystal was slumped in her chair, eyes fixed on some distant place. Some faces in the jury were downcast, others stoic. No one was smiling.

What kind of signal could that be? Janet wondered.

21

"The State calls Dr. Ruth McClure," Albert said.

Dr. Ruth McClure walked through the swinging gate into the chamber where lawyers posture and display their plumage. She took the oath halfway to the witness box and alighted two steps to her seat. After adjusting the microphone she knit her hands together, ready for questions.

Even though court appearances are unnerving for most people, and testifying is frustrating, if not terrifying, for most doctors whose needs for control are legendary, Dr. McClure settled into her seat. She crossed her legs and looked as ready to sip some sherry as to give testimony.

"Please state your name, Doctor," Albert said. Then he asked about her education and training and how long she had been Chief of the PICU.

"For seven years. Before that, I was Associate Chief for four years in a PICU in Tulsa Oklahoma, where I trained," she said.

Dr. McClure had a serious bearing, wire-rim glasses firmly in place, black hair pulled into a bun. She had the reputation of efficiency, pragmatism, discipline, and brains, mitigated by a wry sense of humor. Nurses who worked with her in the PICU said that her mix of warmth, competence and honesty made her "my kind of doctor."

"Are you Board Certified in Pediatric Intensive Care?"

"Yes."

"Dr. McClure, is it fair to say that you oversee the care of the most seriously ill children at Children's Hospital?" Albert said.

"Yes, that's fair," she said.

"Can you give some examples of the types of cases that you treat in the PICU?"

"Well, we treat kids with serious traumatic injuries, like falls from upper story windows, automobile crashes, playground accidents. We take care of cases of accidental poisonings, burns, post-operative cases, and many other conditions requiring more than usual hospital care," she said.

"In your capacity as Chief of the PICU, do you also treat children who have been abused?"

"Yes, unfortunately, we take care of those kids since they're commonly in serious condition," she said.

"Objection!" Janet said as she rose from her chair.

Judge Carlsson raised his eyebrows. "Over-ruled. She was simply stating a fact," he said.

After this little flurry of excitement, Albert continued, "Did you have occasion to treat Luke Talbot on October sixteenth at the PICU at Children's Hospital?"

"Yes."

"Please describe Luke's problems and what you did for him."

"Luke was receiving intravenous fluids and was intubated when he arrived in the PICU. We checked his intubation for proper placement and his lines to insure they were running properly. The monitors were functioning well. His condition was listed as critical. After we established that he was stable, Dr. Stanley Garber, our pediatric ophthalmologist, did a funduscopic examination."

"Please describe for the court what that is," Albert said.

"Using an instrument called an indirect ophthalmoscope, the eye doctor looks through the pupil of the eye and inspects the retina, the back part of the eye."

"After that, what happened?"

"We did a bedside skeletal survey followed by a bone scan."

Anticipating his next question, she continued, "A skeletal survey is a series of individual X-rays of all the bones in the body—the skull, the spine, the ribs, the arms and the legs, the feet and hands—everything. To do a bone scan, we inject a radioactive material into the bloodstream and then watch on X-rays where the dye goes. This radioactive dye is drawn to areas in the bone where it is either actively growing, or where there has been injury and repair is underway. In other words, the dye goes to places where there is what we call high metabolic activity. This is how we can see new fractures that may not show up on planar X-rays."

"And did you see any fractures on these studies?" Albert asked.

"Yes. We saw the three-inch skull fracture at the back of the head," Dr. McClure said.

"Then what did you do?"

"We had the Child Abuse Pediatrician, Dr. Sarah Coughlin, see Luke and give her opinion about his injuries. Then everyone got together to fit the pieces of this puzzle together to reach consensus on the diagnosis and treatment plan," she said.

"Did you reach a consensus?" Albert asked.

"Yes we did."

"What was the team's diagnosis?"

"We agreed that Luke was most likely the victim of shaken impact syndrome. We filed the mandatory report with the Children's Protective Services and went about our jobs of taking care of him," Dr. McClure said.

"Thank you, Dr. McClure, I have no further questions for now," Albert said.

Janet approached the witness. "Good morning, Dr. McClure, I'm Janet Feingold, attorney for Chrystal Begley. I just have a couple of questions for you."

Ruth McClure nodded to her and adjusted the microphone.

"You testified that Luke was the victim of shaken impact syndrome. Doctor, were you there when this happened?"

"No, of course not," Ruth said.

"Then how can you be sure that shaking was the cause of the things you saw?" Janet asked.

"The diagnosis of this syndrome is inferred from a patient's history, signs, symptoms, and the clinical and radiographic findings."

"So is it fair to say that you cannot be one hundred percent sure that shaking is the mechanism of this injury?" Janet asked.

"No one can be a hundred percent sure of anything in life. But I'm as close to one hundred percent in this case as I can get," McClure said.

That wasn't exactly the answer I wanted, Janet thought. *I should have stopped her before she said that. I'll move on.*

"In your testimony, you didn't mention the old fracture of Luke's right tibia, the shin bone. Did you forget about that?" Janet said.

"I didn't forget. That area on the right tibia, initially thought to be an old fracture, was later deemed to be an artifact. So I didn't think it was worth mentioning," McClure said.

"When they reported that, how old did they estimate the fracture to be?" Janet said.

"Well, at the time, the radiologist thought it might be two to three weeks old. But then the radiology group decided it was not a fracture, just an aberration from the way the X-ray beam was projected," McClure said.

"How is it that they can make a big mistake like that?" Janet asked.

"In my opinion, it wasn't a mistake but simply a reinterpretation of the X-ray images. The radiologist can give you a more precise answer," McClure said.

"Is there anything else that you don't think is worth mentioning in your testimony?" Janet said, needing to find a soft spot in McClure's testimony and exploit it.

McClure's neck had an ascending red flush.

"I believe I've given the court as accurate a picture as I can of what we saw in the PICU. I have not purposely left anything out, and frankly, I resent your implication."

Judge Carlsson said, "Doctor, please answer the questions without editorial comment."

"Sorry, Your Honor," McClure said.

"Thank you, Doctor. I have no further questions for this witness," Janet said and sat down at the table, gratified that she had scored at least some points. She glanced at the jury and saw several making entries into their notebooks or iPads. She also caught a glimpse of the Talbots, sitting in their usual place behind the railing near the prosecutors' table. Both their faces were drawn, having heard the testimony detailing Luke's injuries, reliving those frightful hours as they watched their baby slide closer and closer to death. Chrystal seemed to be paying attention to the testimony, a departure from her detachment in the earlier segments of the court procedures.

"The State calls Dr. Sarah Coughlin," Albert said.

In response to Albert's questioning about her education and training, Dr. Coughlin reported three years of pediatric residency at the University of Arizona and a Fellowship in Child Abuse Pediatrics in California.

"Dr. Coughlin, please describe what you do at the hospital," Albert said.

"I'm the Medical Director of the Child Protection Team at Children's Hospital. I consult with the clinical team on cases where there are concerns about child abuse. I work like other consultants, such as a cardiologist when called for advice on cases in which questions arise about heart disease. My job is to take a history of the events leading to the patient's signs and symptoms, examine the patient, and review laboratory and X-ray findings. I talk with the child's parents or caretakers and discuss the case with a social worker from the state agency, the Children's Protective Services. We then hold a case conference with the clinical medical team and the Child Protection Team. Our team includes the social worker who gathers information to contribute to an accurate diagnosis. This process may produce suggestions for other tests and diagnostic procedures to help rule in or out other diseases," she said.

The jurors were listening intently to Dr. Coughlin, as this role in medical diagnosis was unfamiliar to most of them. Some were taking notes, but most were watching her as she spoke.

"Is this what you did when you were called to see Luke Talbot?" Albert asked.

"Yes. Dr. McClure called me to see Luke shortly after he was admitted to the PICU. I saw him after Dr. Garber had examined his eyes," she said.

"As an expert in child abuse, in light of your training and experience, did you come to any conclusion about Luke's case?" Albert said.

"Yes I did," she answered.

"And what was your conclusion?"

"All the elements of the case pointed to shaken impact syndrome," she said.

"Can you describe to the ladies and gentlemen of the jury what happens in shaken impact syndrome?" Albert said.

"Yes. The perpetrator grabs the infant either by the arms, or under the arms around the chest, and shakes the infant many times so that the head goes back and forth repeatedly," she said.

"How long does the shaking last?" Albert asked.

"It's variable. Sometimes it lasts for only a few seconds, sometimes as long as 10 to 15 seconds," she said.

"During that shaking, what happens to the brain itself?" Albert asked.

"The brain is quite soft in infants and it moves slightly within the skull. Much of that movement is within the gelatinous substance of the brain. Violent movement causes disruption of nerve cells and nerve fibers in the brain. The other thing that happens is that veins arising from the surface of the brain going across the subdural space to the dural membrane, called bridging veins, break and leak blood beneath this membrane covering the brain. This causes the subdural hematoma. Hematoma is a medical term that means a blood clot. 'Sub' means under and 'dural' refers to the membrane covering the brain.

"Inside the eyes, the same commotion causing the brain damage and subdural hematoma tears the tiny veins within the layers of the retina. These broken blood vessels leak blood.

"These bleeding points are what we call retinal hemorrhages. They're all over the retina and are seen clear out to the front of the globe, an area that is called the ora seratta. In severe cases the layers of the retina split apart and form cavities called retinoschisis. This in turn can cause folds in the retina, sort of like folds in fabric when it's bunched up. This all can be seen by looking at the retina with the ophthalmoscope such as the one Dr. Garber used," she said.

"What about the timing of these injuries? Can you give some idea about that?" Albert said.

"With the history of the baby being fine when he was turned over to the babysitter and then being seen near death just two hours later means to me that the shaking and the impact had to have happened in that interval," she said.

"Objection, Your Honor. She can't know that," Janet said.

"Over-ruled. He asked her about her opinion and she gave her opinion," Judge Carlsson said.

Janet made a note to ask her in the cross-examination how she could know that.

"Did you see the bruises on the baby's back?" Albert said.

"Yes. These were on the upper portion of the back, near the midline over the spine. There were three oval marks, about one-half inch by three-quarters of an inch on both sides of the spine," she said.

"How do you think these were produced?" Albert asked.

"Objection. Calls for speculation," Janet said.

"Sustained," the judge said.

"What about the skull fracture?" Albert asked.

"The skull fracture was three inches long, in the thickest portion of the skull, the occiput, back here," she said, indicating with her hand the back of her own head.

"How does a seven-month-old infant get such a skull fracture?" Albert asked

"This could only be the result of a major impact onto a hard surface or by a hard object striking the back of the head. Falling backward from a long distance, like from and upper story window onto a hard surface such as a sidewalk, could cause it. An automobile crash conceivably could cause this. But about the only other way to get this kind of a skull fracture would be if someone slammed the back of the baby's head onto a hard surface or a hard object striking the skull," she said.

"I have no further questions, Your Honor."

"Your witness, Ms. Feingold," Judge Carlsson said.

Janet stood up, went to the lectern,

"Dr. Coughlin, you're not a neurosurgeon, are you?" she said.

"No."

"You're not an ophthalmologist, are you?"

"No."

"You're not a radiologist, are you?"

"No."

"You're not a pathologist, are you?"

"No."

"You're not an intensive care specialist either, are you?"

"No."

"You're not an orthopedic surgeon who specializes in fractures?"

"No."

"You're this new thing called a child abuse pediatrician, right?" Janet pressed on.

"Yes."

"So your job in life is to find child abuse, right?"

"My job is to help the clinical team make the correct diagnosis," she said.

"But your job title–child abuse pediatrician–suggests what you're looking for, right?" Janet asked.

"No more than when a heart specialist is evaluating a child who has, say, a heart murmur. A heart specialist consults the clinical team to help establish whether the child does or does not have a heart condition. A cardiologist is happy when he finds that a child does *not* have a heart condition and a child abuse pediatrician is happy when she concludes that a child has *not* been abused. As I said, our job is to make sure that the diagnosis in any given child is correct," Dr. Coughlin said.

"During your testimony about shaking you said that the head goes back and forth during the shaking. How can you know that?" Janet asked.

"We have learned from videos of dummies being shaken that the heads of dummies go back and forth and that it rotates around the axis of the spine," Sarah answered. "More importantly, I think, is that people who have confessed to shaking describe the head as going back and forth."

"Is it fair to say, Dr. Coughlin, that dummies are not real children and that the arc seen in these dummies is not necessarily what might be seen in a real baby?"

"Yes, that's fair to say," Sarah said.

"Is it also fair to say, Doctor, that people who confess to shaking may want leniency in their sentences when they cooperate and tell of the shaking event?" Janet said.

"Objection!" cried Mary. "Counsel is not testifying."

"Sustained. Witness should not respond. Move on," Judge Carlsson said.

"Let's talk about the subdural hematoma. Aren't there other ways a subdural hematoma can be produced?" Janet asked.

"There are many ways for a subdural hematoma to happen. Accidental head injuries, such as those due to long falls from heights, or from automobile crashes, can cause these bleeds. Bleeding disorders can lead to subdural bleeding, as can infection. So yes, to your question, there are many ways subdurals happen," she said.

Satisfied that she made the point she wanted, Janet asked,

"Does the bleeding in the head cause a lot of pressure on the brain?"

"Bleeding from veins causes only a little pressure. Bleeding from veins is different from bleeding from an artery. An artery is under pressure from the pumping heart. Bleeding from veins is an oozing that stops from compression inside the closed box of the skull. And bleeds from veins don't commonly cause great pressure on the brain," Sarah said. "This bleeding is more a marker of injury to the head rather than the direct cause of damage to the brain. When we see a subdural hematoma we know that something significant has happened to the head," Dr. Coughlin said.

"Now, I'm going to pose a hypothetical question. If a seven-month-old infant had an old injury that left him with a subdural hematoma that no one knew about, and then he had a temper tantrum, kicking and screaming and flailing his arms and legs around, could that have disturbed the old clot, making it re-bleed, and leading to brain swelling, retinal hemorrhages and finally causing death?"

"I don't think that scenario has ever been reported in the scientific literature. Re-bleeding of an old subdural hematoma is a distinctly rare event and even if it happened, it would be a very slow seeping of blood from the clot. It's hard to conceive of this slow leakage of blood causing enough trouble to cause a baby to collapse and die," she said.

"Hard to conceive, or impossible?" Janet asked.

"Hard to conceive, as I said. Nothing is impossible," Dr. Coughlin said.

"So, in Luke's case, is it possible that he had an old clot that re-bled and lead to death?"

"There was no history of an old injury in Luke's case," Sarah said.

"But if he had had an old injury, say a birth injury, could that have been disrupted and re-bled?" Janet said.

"I've never seen that happen," Sarah said.

"Has it ever been reported in the medical literature?" Janet asked.

"I've never seen it in the pediatric literature," Sarah said.

"Have you seen these papers?" Janet said, handing Dr. Coughlin several articles.

Sarah looked at the papers; she only recognized one of them.

"All of these papers state that old subdurals can re-bleed. One is by a neurosurgeon, another by a radiologist, and the other two are by researchers who examined newborns with subdural bleeding. You're not familiar with these important papers?" Janet asked.

"Sorry, I only know about the one article. I've never seen the others," Sarah answered.

"So, you don't know about these peer-reviewed publications about re-bleeding of old subdural hematomas? Do you rely on the peer-reviewed literature to inform your practice, Doctor Coughlin?" Janet asked.

"Yes I do. The article I am familiar with says that subdurals seen in the newborn period resolve without incident." Sarah, having recovered a bit, recalled the findings of that article.

"May I take a look at those other articles?" Sarah said.

Janet handed her the articles and several minutes went by as Sarah looked at the papers.

"These two papers are from the mid-seventies and involved only adults, not children, certainly not infants," she said. "The two articles about newborn subdurals conclude they never become symptomatic."

"But isn't it true, Doctor, that until this moment you had not even seen these research papers published in reputable medical journals?" Janet said.

"Yes."

She paused, to let the jury think about this last question, which implied that Dr. Coughlin had not done due diligence in her reading of the literature.

"Now, about the skull fracture. How do you know that skull fracture was new?"

"The swelling of the scalp over the skull fracture was definitely new. And the autopsy report stated that the skull fracture was new," Sarah said.

"Do you know whether the pathologist made sections of the skull fracture to ascertain its age?" Janet said.

"I don't know. You'd have to ask the pathologist."

"I'm planning to do that. But in the meantime, can you say absolutely that the skull fracture was new?"

"From all of the findings, I believe it was new. That's all I can say," Sarah said.

"Are you aware that there are some who think–and have done research that supports what they think–that the brain damage and the subdural bleeding seen in cases like this is caused by lack of oxygen?" Janet said.

"Some of the brain damage in these cases *is* due to low oxygen, or hypoxia, but the initial cause of the brain damage is traumatic, followed later by hypoxia," Sarah said.

"There are papers that suggest that hypoxia causes the subdural bleeding. Would you like to see these papers?" Janet asked.

"I saw these papers when they came out. Most doctors who have experience with head injured children have firmly rejected that theory," Sarah said.

"But some believe it, right?" Janet said.

"I can't speak for other people. I don't accept the theory, but there may be some who do," Sarah said.

"So this whole area of shaken baby syndrome is quite controversial, wouldn't you say?" Janet said.

"There's always controversy in medicine. This field is no different from others in that respect," Sarah said.

"You said in your direct testimony that you thought the bruises on Luke's back were oval, on the upper part of his back. Could this be the result of my client's fingers while she was trying to lift Luke–who was having a tantrum–out of the bathtub?"

"I suppose so," Sarah said.

"Could it also be due to the fingers of the EMS people who were intubating Luke and administering CPR?"

"Not likely, but possible," Sarah said.

"Let's talk about the retinal hemorrhages for a moment. Are there other causes of retinal hemorrhages besides shaking?" Janet asked.

"Yes," Sarah said.

"Dr. Coughlin, can you tell me the things in pediatric medicine that can cause retinal hemorrhages?" Janet said.

"Bleeding disorders, infections, sometimes accidental head injuries, and vaginal births are some of the causes," Sarah said.

"So is it fair to say that a lot of things can cause retinal hemorrhages?" Janet said.

"Yes, but...."

"Thank you, Doctor. No further questions."

Albert rose to begin his redirect examination.

"Dr. Coughlin, Ms. Feingold made a lot of the fact that you are not an ophthalmologist, not a neurosurgeon, and so forth. You are Board Certified in Child Abuse Pediatrics, are you not?"

"Yes."

"How do you get certified in both pediatrics and child abuse pediatrics?" Albert asked.

"A pediatric residency is for three years after medical school. You have to finish three years of a pediatric residency to become eligible to sit for the Board exams in Pediatrics. You spend another three years in a Child Abuse Pediatric Fellowship in order to qualify to sit for the Board examination in that," Sarah said.

"And when you become Board Certified in Child Abuse Pediatrics, does that include training in those aspects of ophthalmology, neurology, orthopedics, radiology, and pathology that apply to child abuse cases?" Albert said.

"Yes, that's right."

"Is it fair to say that your specialty is the only medical specialty devoted exclusively to the diagnosis and treatment of child abuse cases?" Albert asked.

"Exactly. We are the only real specialists in this field," Sarah said.

"Could that skull fracture really be an old one?" Albert asked.

"Not likely," said Sarah. "A skull fracture like the one we saw in Luke would have required a serious event to produce it. It's hard to believe that no one would have known about such a serious fracture and that he would not have had dramatic, devastating symptoms."

"The defense has argued that Luke may have had an old subdural hematoma that started bleeding again during his temper tantrum. Wouldn't a subdural hematoma have produced symptoms?" Albert asked.

"Some small subdurals can be present without symptoms, that's true. But a re-bleed into an old subdural wouldn't act this way. As I said before, a re-bleed would be slow oozing, and wouldn't lead to a sudden collapse like what happened to Luke."

"Can hypoxia by itself cause what was seen in Luke?"

"The medical literature, the research in this area, doesn't support that theory," Sarah said.

"Since there are so many things that can cause retinal hemorrhages, how do you know these are the result of shaken baby syndrome?" Albert said.

"The retinal hemorrhages we see in shaken baby cases are unique. They're much different from the retinal hemorrhages we see from those other causes."

"Thanks, Doctor. No further questions."

"Ms. Feingold?" said Judge Carlsson.

"No more questions, Your Honor."

"Court is adjourned until nine tomorrow morning. Members of the jury are warned not to discuss this case with anyone outside the jury pool, not to watch television or read about this case," Judge Carlsson said, and walked to his chambers.

Janet watched Fred and Alison Talbot rise slowly from their chairs; they looked at one another wearily as they left. Chrystal looked over her shoulder to meet June's eyes and see her maternal, reassuring smile.

"Good job, counselor. Hope I can do as well. You really got smart about this syndrome, didn't you?" Nate said.

"Long way to go, Dad. Pretty good today though. We'll take it day to day. I wonder what Chrystal's thinking about as she listened to all this testimony."

"Ask her"

As Janet turned to gather up her files she noticed "The Professor" still sitting in the gallery, making entries onto his iPad. "*Who is that guy?*" Janet thought.

22

Janet lingered a few minutes to talk with Chrystal, who had hardly moved during the last hour of testimony. She had been picking at lint on her skirt, nibbling on her cuticles, and crossing and uncrossing her legs. Even though Janet was exhausted from questioning hostile witnesses, she decided to follow her father's advice and check in with Chrystal before another day in court.

"How're you doing?" Janet asked.

"Fine," Chrystal said, in her predictable dismissal of any effort to fathom her state of mind.

"Any questions or anything to tell me before we leave?" Janet said.

"What do you want me to say, anyhow? Those doctors think I killed Luke. You had them a little jumpy sometimes but they already got me hung," Chrystal said.

"No matter what happens in this trial, Chrystal, no one's hanging you."

"Sure seems like it. No one'll ever believe me after all these doctors say I did it. What's the use? Maybe I should have pled guilty. Too late now, huh?" she said.

"Are you saying you want to change your plea?" Janet said.

"No." Starting out in a whisper, her voice rose as she said, "I mean, could I have just blacked out and hurt Luke without knowing it, you know? Like spacing out? Can that happen?"

"Blacking out? You mean just doing things without knowing it?" Janet said. "Shrinks call that 'disassociating,' where you feel you're up in the corner of the room looking down on some other person doing things. Is that what you're talking about?"

"Yeah, you know, like when Daryll used to screw me, I'd put my mind somewhere else, sort of like outside of myself, and it wouldn't seem so awful? It seemed like it was happening to someone else that way?" Chrystal said.

Janet's body stiffened as she focused on Chrystal's face.

"Are you're telling me that Daryll sexually abused you? Your stepfather? Is that what you're saying?"

"He's been doin' it since I was 15. And he beats me up too," Chrystal said.

As Janet contemplated the implications of this revelation, her thoughts flashed back to her responses to Daryll during her encounters with him. She had attributed her strong visceral reactions to him as due to his generally loathsome personality, though, not this.

"So that's why you hate him so much," Janet said, and thought, *Was this what she was trying to tell Dad?*

"Could I have blacked out when I was taking care of Luke?" Chrystal asked again.

"I suppose it's possible. I don't know. I'm not a psychologist. If you'd be willing to talk to a psychologist, I can arrange that," Janet said.

Janet thought immediately of Nicole Driscoll, her psychologist friend, who could give her an opinion about this. Nicole was a forensic psychologist and did a lot of testifying, so she'd know what the courts were doing with this kind of argument.

Could this explain Chrystal's adamant denial of hurting Luke? Could she have been dissociated? Could this be a new defense strategy? Janet thought.

"Whoa, a shrink? Not for me. They're weirdos. Uh-Uh," Chrystal said.

Jesus, I keep trying to help this girl and she won't let me. I'll back off for now, talk to Nicole and see if she thinks it's worth pursuing.

Janet opened her mouth to speak, then closed it firmly, looking at Chrystal.

"OK, I'll see you in the morning, Hope you have a decent night."

"Fat chance of that," Chrystal said as she headed back to her cell with the matron.

Janet joined her father in the lobby and they both hurried out the door to the waiting press.

"What'd you think about this first day of trial?" one of the TV report-ers called out, thrusting a microphone in Janet's face.

"Went well. It's still the State's job to prove with solid evidence that my client is responsible for Luke's death. I don't think they can prove that beyond reasonable doubt," Janet said.

Nate stepped forward.

"You know, there's a lot of controversy about this thing called 'shaken baby syndrome.' Many doctors rely on the "triad"–the subdural bleeding, retinal hemorrhages, and brain injury. A growing number of doctors think it's junk science, not based on good research. That's where we're going in this trial, to expose shaken baby syndrome as a mistaken diagnosis. There're plenty of other ways the things they saw in Luke could've happened. Unless the State can present a lot better evidence than they did today, our client will walk out of this courthouse to take up her normal young life, surviving this horrendous experience. Take a close look at Chrystal and you'll see a teenager who's incapable of doing this, not only because of her small size, but because of her temperament. She's a sweet girl, never been in any trouble before. Now, all of a sudden she's sitting in jail, faced with these baseless accusations. We're going to insure that justice is done and she can resume her normal life," Nate said.

"Are you saying that shaking can't cause the injuries that killed this little baby?" another reporter called out from the rear of the pack.

"That's exactly what we're saying. You'll hear from eminent experts that shaking can't cause these findings, that there are plenty of other explana-tions for what killed this poor baby," Nate said. "Wait until you hear the testimony over the next few days and you'll see what I'm talking about."

"Can you tell us what the names of the experts are?" another reporter shouted.

"You'll learn all about them in the next few days," Nate said. "No further questions right now. We're all tuckered out, as you can imagine." Janet and Nate hurried down the courthouse steps with the reporters following them, yelling questions, but neither turned to respond. They reached the garage and soon escaped into the elevator.

"What a bunch of jackals," Janet said once they were safe in the elevator.

"Remember Janet, they can be of enormous help to us. Think of them as our friends. Put a bug in their ears and they'll print it. They're easily persuaded since they don't know squat about shaken baby syndrome. If they go to the usual sources of information on the internet they'll see the controversy's well covered there. Defense experts and the falsely accused have flooded the internet with their opinions and on the internet they have equal weight as the mainstream doctors. So put up with the press," Nate said, a bit peevishly. He looked straight ahead, tired but determined, then said, "About tomorrow. I think you'll finish with the docs from the hospital and the medical examiner by the end of the day. I've arranged to have a couple of my experts come in for the following day."

"Okay, Dad."

Janet, thinking about her conversation with Chrystal just before she left court, tapped through her iPhone contact list to find Nicole Driscoll's number and pressed it. Miraculously she was connected to Nicole after the second ring.

"I'm amazed. Janet Feingold here," she said. "I thought I'd get your answering service."

"I saw it was your number so I picked up. How goes it? I see that you're in the middle of a trial. Is that why you're calling?" Nicole said.

"Well, yes, matter of fact. When can I talk to you about something interesting my client said to me?" Janet said.

"How about now? I'm finished with everyone at the office and was going to stay here, do some paperwork and avoid the rush hour traffic," Nicole said."So what's going on?"

"Here's the deal," Janet said. She described the case from the outset, ending with Luke's death and the autopsy findings. "Chrystal, who's eighteen, just told me that her stepfather repeatedly sexually and physically abused her since she was fifteen years old. She says that during those assaults she feels like she goes 'outside of herself' as her way of coping. I've heard of dissociation and I wonder if that's what's going on. What can you tell me about that?"

"Well, it's not simple, as you can guess. There are essentially two distinct forms of dissociation: acute and chronic. Acute dissociation happens in the immediate context of a traumatic event, such as during sexual or physical abuse. Chronic dissociation is related to repeated, chronic maltreatment and adverse childhood events. This is called dissociative identity disorder (DID). Your case sounds like DID," Nicole said.

"So, could I use this in her defense? That she doesn't remember doing anything and that's the reason she denies doing it?" Janet asked.

"Well, she still did it, right? The fact that she doesn't remember doing it doesn't make her innocent of the act," Nicole said. "It may explain her claiming that she's not guilty and really believing that she didn't do it, but that's no defense in and of itself," Nicole said.

"Naturally, I don't know if she did it or not. That's what the court's job is. So, are you telling me I can't use dissociation as a defense?" Janet asked, disappointed that what seemed like a good strategy just evaporated.

"If a psychologist uses this argument, it wouldn't hold up under a good cross-examination. That doesn't mean you couldn't get a psychologist to testify for you, but I sure wouldn't want to try doing that," Nicole said.

"Nicole, you're a gem. Thanks so much for explaining this to me. You've just saved me a lot of time and probably some embarrassment. I owe you a meal. I'll call you after this bloody trial's over and we'll get together. I've got some personal news, too," Janet said.

"Oh, tell me now! I don't want to wait on good gossip until your trial's over," Nicole said.

"I've got a new guy. I think he may be a serious prince," Janet said.

"That's so great! Call me as soon as you can and we can talk it all over," Nicole said. "Bye now."

Janet went up the elevator to her dad's office where they dove into the evening's work. As they immersed themselves in the details of upcoming testimony, Janet said, "Chrystal, for some unknown reason, opened up to me today about Daryll's physical and sexual abuse of her." After telling Nate the substance of their conversation, she asked him if he thought pursuing the dissociation issue would be of any value to the defense strategy.

"I've never been enthusiastic about psychological factors in criminal cases. It's rare that such defenses yield positive results. Psychological influences on behavior are too amorphous for a courtroom setting and when you get dueling shrinks on the stand you end up with unintelligible gibberish. So I don't think we ought to waste any time on those kinds of theories," Nate said. "Besides, we've already built our case on the theory that shaken baby syndrome doesn't exist. If we were to use this dissociation theory to explain Chrystal's behavior we'd be admitting that she did it. We've come too far to change our strategy now."

23

Janet and her father worked until nearly midnight. Nate, despite advancing years, still pushed himself–and Janet–beyond a normal person's usual point of endurance. He often slept on a sofa bed in his office during a trial so as not to interrupt what he called his "circadian rhythm." He had installed a shower, toilet and closet for court clothes in his office years ago to accommodate his freakish night work vigils.

Having eaten quesadillas for dinner that night, Janet's stomach was churning the next morning. Despite that, she picked up a latte and scone at Starbuck's, a poor substitute for breakfast.

"Hear ye, hear ye, Court is now in session," the bailiff called out. Judge Carlsson ceremoniously took his bench and went through his ritual of settling in, and the jury took their assigned places.

Chrystal looked for June in her usual spot in the back row. Their eyes met, June smiled, Chrystal relaxed.

This morning, Mary noticed the Talbots' sagging countenances. They betrayed the toll on them of hearing the ugly details about Luke's horrendous injuries.

Albert Polcari looked fresh, clean-shaven, and ready for action. "The state calls Dr. Stanley Garber."

Dr. Garber emerged from the back row of seats and took his place in the witness box. Of medium height and slender of build, he had broad shoulders, a small head well-endowed with reddish-blonde hair, prominent ears, wide-set pale blue eyes, and smooth facial skin that made women envious. His voice was a distinct and pleasant baritone, his speech articulate and precise.

After being sworn in and his credentials recited, Albert asked him, "Dr. Garber, did you have occasion to examine Luke Talbot on October 16th at Children's Hospital?

"Yes."

"Please tell the court why you examined Luke," Albert said.

"I was asked to see Luke by Dr. McClure because she wanted me to examine his eyes for signs of injury in the retina. I used an indirect ophthalmoscope to examine and take pictures of his retinas."

"What were your findings?"

"Luke had retinal hemorrhages in both eyes. May I show you what this looks like by drawing on the flip chart?" he asked.

Judge Carlsson looked at Janet and said, "Any objections?"

"No, Your Honor," Janet said.

Drawing a large circle on the flip chart paper, Garber said,

"If you think of this–the globe of the eye–cut in half, this area here," indicating one side of the circle, "represents the front of the eye where the pupil is, called the ora serrata, and this area," pointing to the other end of the circle, "represents what is called the posterior pole, set deep in the eye socket near where the optic nerve leaves the eye globe to go to the brain. There were twenty-five to thirty hemorrhages in several layers of the retina in both eyes. They were present all the way from the posterior pole of the retina-here-the deepest part of the globe of the eye-to the ora serrata-here-the area at the front of the globe, just inside the iris. I took pictures of these hemorrhages. These pictures also showed retinal folds and what we call retinoschisis," Dr. Garber said.

The court stenographer interrupted here asking for spelling of retinoschisis and ora serrata, and some jurors jotted down the spelling as he gave it.

"If the court pleases, may we project these pictures so that Dr. Garber can explain them?" Albert asked Judge Carlsson.

"Objection, your Honor. Prejudicial," Janet called out.

After considering the basis for the objections, Carlsson said,

"Overruled. This is evidence that should be viewed. I don't consider pictures of the interior of the eyes to be prejudicial," he said.

Garber's pictures of the retinas showed brilliant red smudges covering most of both the retinas, clearly indicating the extent and numbers of these bleeding points. He pointed to several of them and in the role of teacher described what the findings indicated: blood had leaked out of the small vessels between the layers of the retina.

"What is the significance of these findings, Doctor?"

"These hemorrhages are quite numerous and they involve several layers of the retina. These ridges here," he pointed with a laser pointer, "are retinal folds. These findings all result from the shearing forces on the retina during the application of acceleration-deceleration force. These are characteristic retinal findings," Dr. Garber said.

"Do you have an opinion as to what caused Luke's retinal hemorrhages?" Albert asked.

"Yes I do."

"What is your opinion?"

"These eye findings make me ninety-nine percent sure that Luke was shaken. In his case, he was also impacted," Dr. Garber responded.

After Albert indicated he had no further questions, Janet began her cross-examination.

"Dr. Garber, would you agree that many things can cause retinal hemorrhages?" Janet said.

"Yes," he said, and before Janet stopped him, he said "but not all retinal hemorrhages are the same."

"Please just answer the question I asked you, Doctor," Janet said.

"Are you aware of the articles where crushing head injury due to a fallen television onto a child's head have resulted in this kind of retinal hemorrhages and retinal folds?" Janet asked.

"Yes, I've read those articles," he said.

"So they do happen in cases other than shaken babies, right?" Janet said.

"The number of reported cases like that is so small that we refer to these as 'outliers,' meaning they are very far from what is ordinarily seen in clinical practice. More importantly, in these articles there are clear histories of television sets falling on the children's heads. There is nothing like that in Luke's case," he said.

"Could these retinal hemorrhages be caused by the high pressure that was described within the skull?" Janet asked.

"That high pressure within the skull causes retinal hemorrhages is an old theory. Practically every week we see children with serious head injuries from other causes–falls from great heights, motor vehicle crashes, for example–who have raised pressure inside the head, measured by sensing instruments placed through the skull, but these patients don't have retinal hemorrhages. So if they were really due to high intracranial pressure alone we would see it in those cases where there is increased pressure. The fact is, we see retinal hemorrhages like these in a tiny minority of those cases. So that theory of increased intracranial pressure causing retinal hemorrhages has been discarded. It's simply not borne out by the evidence in real cases," he said.

Janet could hear her old professor saying, "one of the cardinal principles of witness examination is never ask a question to which you don't know the answer." She had gambled that Dr. Garber would waffle on this answer, but he didn't. So she decided to cut her losses here.

"Thank you doctor, no further questions."

"Any further questions from the State?" Judge Carlsson said.

"Yes, Your Honor. Dr. Garber, you began to say more when defense counsel told you to answer only the question she had asked. Would you like to say more about retinal hemorrhages caused by other conditions?" Albert said.

"Yes, thank you. There are many kinds of retinal hemorrhages. Some are little specks, like the ones we see in nearly half of all newborns delivered vaginally. Those go away by themselves and aren't a problem. Sometimes we see older patients with just a few of these scattered tiny hemorrhages. They also don't cause any trouble. Some retinal hemorrhages are obviously associated with other diseases, such as infections, say, or abnormal blood clotting. But in those cases we know exactly why they're there," he said.

"Sometimes we see retinal hemorrhages, like the ones we saw in Luke, in patients who have been in serious automobile crashes, where the victim's head has been subjected to sudden acceleration-deceleration forces, like whiplash. But in those cases we also have detailed histories from the first responders at the scene who pull the victims from the wrecked vehicles.

But in Luke's case, since there was no such history and no other medical conditions, there can only be one cause. That's shaking, because that involves acceleration-deceleration forces, or, in other words, back and forth motion of the head."

Janet looked at her father, who shook his head slightly, indicating that there was no point in objecting to this statement. He told her later that the experts he had talked to would have countervailing arguments and that no more attention should be called to Garber's testimony to avoid cementing in the juror's minds the idea that shaking was the only way this could happen.

"Thank you, Doctor," Albert said.

"The State calls Dr. Frank Mayhew."

An imposing figure rose from the rear of the courtroom and strode toward the witness box. He barely fit into the chair. Mayhew, familiar to many in Kansas City, was respected and admired for his skill with some of the most demanding neurosurgical cases in the region. The head of the hospital's Trauma Team, he had operated on Luke. Trained at Johns Hopkins Hospital, he had come directly to Kansas City to become Chair of the Department of Neurosurgery at the hospital and medical school.

At Albert's request, Dr. Mayhew recited his impressive credentials and established that he had personally operated on Luke.

"Can you describe your findings at surgery, Doctor? Albert said.

"When we exposed the dura mater under the skull, it was bulging due to the pressure under it. When we cut through the dura, blood and straw-colored fluid spewed out nearly two feet into the air. As we extended the incision, the brain rose up out of the incision like a loaf of rising bread. It was under extraordinary pressure and I thought at the time that this child's survival was doubtful. We left a section of bone out to keep the pressure from doing any more damage and closed the incision because there was nothing else we could do to help him. We sent Luke to the recovery room. We instituted the usual therapy to try to retard further brain swelling," Dr. Mayhew said.

The Talbots swayed in their seats. Alison rested her head on Fred's shoulder, their hands squeezed together as they visualized these hideous images of their baby.

"Do you have an opinion as to what caused this brain injury?" Albert asked.

"Yes."

"What is that opinion?"

"The constellation of signs, symptoms, and the clinical, radiographic and operative findings all say to me that this is a classic case of shaken impact syndrome," he said.

"No further questions, Your Honor," Albert said as he sat down.

Janet rose.

"Dr. Mayhew, you mentioned 'straw-colored fluid' in addition to blood coming out of the operative site. What does that represent?"

"That is serum, a part of the blood products that were in the head," he said.

"When bleeding first occurs, it is pretty uniform in color, it looks like blood, doesn't it?" Janet asked.

"Yes."

"If blood separates into serum and cells, then it's not uniform in color. Isn't it true that means that it is not fresh bleeding?" Janet said.

"Yes, that's generally true," Mayhew said.

"Would it be fair to say then, that the blood and straw-colored fluid that came out of Luke's head was not actually fresh blood, but blood that had been in there for a longer period of time than just a few hours? Time enough to separate into cells and serum?" Janet asked.

"The separation of the serum from the cells in this case could have been due to the extreme pressure in his head," Mayhew responded. "It's called a 'hyperacute' blood collection."

"So you cannot say with surety that these blood products were new?" Janet asked.

"I cannot say with scientific accuracy that the pressure caused the separation, but that's what I think happened," Mayhew answered.

"So, just so the members of the jury understand what you just said, is it that you don't know for sure that the blood in Luke's head was fresh blood?" Janet said.

"Objection. Asked and answered," Albert said.

"Sustained. Move on, Counselor," Judge Carlsson said.

"No more questions," Janet said. She hoped the point was made and the jurors understood it. Some of them were writing in their notebooks.

"The State calls Dr. Rodney Michaelson," Albert said.

Tall, slender, with a full gray-flecked beard and nearly all–white hair arranged over his ears and meeting his collar, Michaelson could have passed for a rabbi. Because of a chronic back problem he had asked to stand during his testimony. His voice was deep and resonant and, as he spoke, he swayed slightly. He could have been cast as Moses reading from the tablets just down from Mt. Sinai. All eyes were on his commanding presence.

"Dr. Michaelson, you read the X-rays of Luke Talbot at the time of his hospitalization, is that correct?" Albert began.

"Yes."

"Please describe what you found," Albert said.

"The computerized axial tomography of the head, the CT scan, showed a subdural hematoma over a large area of the right cerebral hemisphere, massive brain swelling, a three-inch occipital linear skull fracture with an overlying hematoma under the scalp."

His recitation sounded like he was dictating an X-ray report.

"Do you have an opinion as to how these injuries occurred?" Albert asked.

"Yes."

"What is that opinion?"

"These injuries were almost certainly caused by someone shaking and then impacting the baby's head against a hard surface," he said.

"No further questions, Your Honor," Albert said. "Your witness, Ms. Feingold."

"Dr. Michaelson, can you determine the age of the skull fracture?" Janet began.

"Skull fractures are difficult to age because there is no callus formation as there is in long bone fractures. Callus is the laying down of healing tissue followed by deposition of calcium within that healing. So I cannot be certain as to the age of this fracture on the basis of the X-rays. But the overlying scalp hematoma was fresh suggesting that those two injuries occurred at the same time."

"Thank you, Doctor," Janet said.

"Now, one thing you didn't mention was the tibial fracture. Why didn't you mention that?" Janet asked.

"We thought there might have been a tibial fracture on the skeletal survey but on further review we determined that it was an artifact," he said.

"But at first you thought it could be a fracture. What changed your mind about it?" Janet asked.

"We magnified the radiograph, looked at it with a high intensity lamp, and then we could tell it was not a fracture," he said.

"Well, it was by looking that you suspected it was a fracture originally. I will ask you once more, what changed your mind about it?" Janet said.

"As we magnified the area, it became clear that this was only a roughening of the bone and not a fracture," he said.

"I still don't see what the evidence is for changing your mind, Doctor," Janet said.

"That's the best explanation I can give you for that finding," he said.

"Isn't it true that your interpretation changed, not the actual lesion on the bone?"

"Objection, Your Honor. This has been asked and answered. Defense is badgering the witness," Albert said.

"Sustained. Move on," Judge Carlsson said.

"No further questions, Your Honor," Janet said.

Judge Carlsson noted that some of the jurors were fidgeting and whispering to one another. He looked at the clock. Time for a lunch recess.

24

"State calls Dr. Samuel Drago," Albert said.

A soft, doughy figure shuffled to the stand and lifted himself into the witness box. He had pale, papery skin, dark bags under his gray eyes, a bald shining pate, and an air of ennui. His black ill-fitting suit completed the stereotype of the rumpled medical examiner. Quincy he was not.

"Please state your name and spell it for the stenographer please," Albert said.

"Samuel L. Drago, D-R-A-G-O."

"Where do you work?"

"At the Medical Examiner's Office on 24th Street in Kansas City, Missouri," he mumbled.

The stenographer asked Dr. Drago to speak more loudly. He spoke in such low tones that his words were occasionally inaudible.

Albert shortened the usual litany of qualifications, then asked, "Did you perform the postmortem examination on the body of Luke Talbot on October 18th?"

"I did."

"What were the relevant findings?"

Drago commenced with a sing-song version of the process of doing an autopsy, beginning with the inevitable "After making a Y-shaped incision…" and it was here that Albert interrupted him.

"I'm asking you for the relevant findings, Doctor."

"Oh. OK." He read from his autopsy report: "The body is that of a seven-month-old well-developed, well-nourished infant male weighing seventeen pounds, twenty-six inches long, with a head circumference of eighteen inches. These are average measurements for an infant of this age."

Mary glanced over her shoulder to see how the Talbots were taking this impersonal recitation about their beloved Luke. Alison's eyes were wet and Fred's jaw was tight. The vicissitudes of the trial proceedings were making them obligatory stoics.

Drago droned on through the bulk of the report, essentially confirming the descriptions by the clinical doctors.

"What were the findings in the head?" Albert asked.

"They were the same things the doctors at Children's Hospital found. A right subdural hematoma and traumatic and hypoxic injuries in the brain tissue," Drago said.

"Can you tell us what you found in the eyes?"

"In the eyes? Oh, sure." He flipped a couple of sheets over and read, again in his grating monotone, more confirmation of the clinical findings.

"Is there anything else you want to add?" Albert asked.

"Think that's it," he said.

"Ms. Feingold, your witness," the judge said, arousing from his torpor caused by Dr. Drago's boring voice.

"Dr. Drago, with regards to the skull fracture. Did you do a microscopic examination of the edges of the fracture to determine whether it was a new fracture or an old one?"

"No, ma'am, I didn't."

"Why not?"

"It looked like a fresh fracture and I didn't think I needed to do that," he said.

"Could you go back and do that now?" Janet asked.

He averted his eyes and didn't answer for a moment.

"Don't think I saved that piece of bone, m'am. I vaguely recall tossing it into the bucket. I didn't save the actual specimen."

Alison grabbed Fred's hand as they both listened.

"Didn't you think it might be important to establish whether this was a new or old fracture?" Janet asked, hands outstretched, palms upward.

"I thought it was a fresh fracture so I didn't think it necessary to save the tissue. Happens all the time," Drago said. "You have to understand that when you do an autopsy, especially when there's already been a piece of the skull removed at surgery, that to get a swollen brain out of the skull you have to saw a lot of the skull away to get hold of the soggy brain, and you just toss that part of the skull into the waste bucket."

At this, even the Talbots' stoicism broke down. Alison sobbed and Fred groaned audibly.

There was a gasp from a couple of the jurors as this strange man described the performance of an autopsy with an almost ghoulish disregard for how lay people's sensitivities might be jarred by his words. Mary Egan turned to give comfort to the Talbots, but they were already on their way out of the courtroom.

Janet flushed red. *How could this guy be so bloody incompetent?*

"So essentially, you're asking the court to take your word for the fact that this was a fresh fracture?" Janet said.

"Yes."

"But you really don't know for sure that it was a fresh fracture, right?" Janet pressed.

"I'm pretty sure it was a fresh fracture. That's all I can say about it," Drago said.

Janet considered how she could further undermine the credibility of Dr. Sam Drago, but she decided he had already given her the ammunition to make the jury skeptical about the age of the skull fracture.

"No more questions for this witness, Your Honor," she said.

Albert considered trying to rescue Dr. Drago, but decided against it. He was clearly unsalvageable. If the jury saw any more of him, it could only harm their case further.

"No further questions, Your Honor," Albert said.

Dr. Drago stepped down from the stand and hurried out the door.

Judge Carlsson turned to Janet and Nate. "Are you ready to present your defense experts?"

"We expected to begin tomorrow, Your Honor. They're not in town yet."

"Alright, that's understandable considering what's gone on here today.

"Ladies and gentlemen of the jury, you're excused. We'll reconvene tomorrow morning at nine," Judge Carlsson said. He slammed down his gavel with more force than was his custom. His exasperation was matched by that of the lawyers as they left the courtroom.

Janet saw "The Professor" leaving. *Boy, would I like to know who that man is and what he is doing here.*

Janet and her father went to the hall. Since the trial was gaining widespread attention, a swarm of reporters from national wire services were there. They were shouting all at once, with the critical question being, "If that skull fracture is old, does that mean someone else did this to Luke?"

"We believe in our client's innocence. We have said from the beginning that we don't think she did this. If there were previous injuries to this baby, then obviously we have to consider that someone else must have been involved," Janet said.

"Who do you suspect?"

"That's not our job. Our job is to defend our client."

"Could one or both of the parents be the perpetrator?" one reporter called out.

"We're not going to speculate on that at this time," Nate said.

"However, we heard that Luke's four-year old brother was very undisciplined. You all know about sibling rivalry and what could happen in that situation."

Janet looked sharply at her father. That was really a cheap shot at a little kid. Where did he hear that anyway? Did he just make that up? Did he have no boundaries around his need to prove this syndrome didn't exist?

"So you suspect the little brother?" said one wag.

"I didn't say that, I only said there's a possibility, that's all," Nate said.

He had noticed Janet's reaction to his inappropriate statement.

"Do you think the ME's office screwed up?" the guy from one of the tabloid newspapers said.

"I don't think name-calling helps anything," Janet said. "But preservation of relevant evidence by the ME's office should be paramount, especially in homicide cases. The ME's office failed to do that here. It could affect the outcome of this trial. That's all I'll say about that."

Recognizing that more gold would be mined from Nate's statements than from Janet's, one of the national reporters asked, "Mr. Feingold, what did you think of the Children's Hospital doctors' testimony about shaken baby syndrome?"

"These doctors are parroting what has been the standard theory over the last fifty years. They have no proof that the triad of Luke's injuries were caused by shaking. Over the next few days some eminent medical experts will dispute everything the hospital doctors said and show that their testimony is bunk. So stay tuned folks, and you'll learn a lot in the next few days. That's all we have to say now. Thanks for your attention," Nate said, in his most mellifluous voice.

Janet and Nate headed to Nate's office to strategize about tomorrow's performance. It would be Nate's turn to show the jurors what he wanted them to see: that shaken baby syndrome was not a real medical entity.

25

The morning newspaper, in the Metro section, carried the story:

NOTED CRIMINAL DEFENSE LAWYERS: NO SUCH THING AS SHAKEN BABY SYNDROME

Childrens' Hospital doctors reviewed the medical information about Luke Talbot's injuries; they were certain the injuries were the result of shaken baby syndrome.

That's what they have said in court over the past two days. But the father-daughter team of Janet and Nathan Feingold isn't buying it. They don't believe there is a scintilla of evidence to support the theory known as shaken baby syndrome. Moreover, they maintain their client is innocent of the murder of Luke Talbot, the seven-month-old infant brought to Children's Hospital with a serious head injury on October sixteenth, who subsequently expired.

Janet Feingold grilled the hospital doctors today in court, but saved her most withering attacks for Dr. Sam Drago, the medical examiner who performed Luke Talbot's postmortem examination. Drago couldn't say whether Luke's skull fracture was new or old. More

importantly, he'd discarded the skull frag-
ments. Even Judge Carlsson was clearly impa-
tient with the pathologist's testimony.

The article went on to discuss the testimony heard so far and described Chrystal Begley as "seemingly uninterested in the proceedings" and the jury as "engaged and interested in the testimony."

That evening, a national television network had a panel of "experts" on both sides of the shaken baby syndrome argument heatedly debating the issue. Nate got his wish to use the media in his campaign to argue that the syndrome was a hoax.

His experts arrived in town; he and Janet spoke with them in their hotel rooms. At the end of the evening when they had finished rehearsing their testimonies, he was "fly'n high."

26

"You can't go to that damned trial again today," Daryll said to June. "I need you at the store. If you disobey me, I'll teach you a lesson. They'll get along without you at the Courthouse. You got nothing to add."

"I'm going, and you can't stop me. It's my flesh and blood on trial for murder, and it's my duty as her mother to go to her trial," June shouted.

Daryll moved toward her with his fists clenched, his face red and fire in his eyes. June had already called a taxi and it was honking outside their house.

"You're getting away with this today with that cab out there, but never again," Daryll screamed.

She scurried out to the cab, leaving Daryll seething with anger and frustration.

Snow fell as Janet and Nate entered the Courthouse. The media had multiplied several-fold. Television trucks and cables clogged the streets. Reporters and technicians milled about outside and inside the courthouse. Janet cast her eyes around the courtroom and noticed June skulking into the back row of the gallery, again without Daryll. She saw the ever-present "Professor" in his usual seat. She caught a glimpse of Chrystal looking at June and June smiling back.

Court resumed when Judge Carlsson turned to the defense table and instructed Nate to call his first defense witness.

He stood and said in stentorian tones, "Dr. Frank Boyd."

Heads turned and dozens of eyes fixed on a small, gaunt but sprightly mid-sixties man as he hurried to the witness box. He took the oath quickly, sat down, and adjusted the microphone. What little hair he had was swept straight back, giving his whole head and face a squirrel-like visage. His quick, jerky movements also suggested a bushy-tailed creature. His voice was a high-pitched, dry monotone.

Nate went through his qualifications with dispatch knowing that juries are not captivated by recitations of expertise. Nevertheless, Nate wanted to insure that the jury—and the media—understood that Dr. Boyd had admirable credentials.

"You are a Clinical Professor of Neurosurgery at the Citadel University in Denver, and in that capacity you see patients, do surgery and teach residents in neurosurgery, is that correct?" Nate said.

"Just so," Boyd said.

"How long have you been Board Certified in Neurosurgery?"

"For twenty-eight years," he answered.

"In your clinical practice, what kinds of patients do you regularly see?" Nate asked.

"I see adults and children with neurosurgical problems of all kinds. I operate on the heads and spinal cords of those who require surgery," he said. "My other duties include seeing patients in my private office. Part of my responsibility, I think, is to offer my expert neurosurgical testimony in cases like this. I do that in numerous states; I have also testified in Canada, the United Kingdom, Sweden and the Netherlands," he said.

Nate asked him about his hospital privileges, all current; his Board Certification in Neurosurgery; and where he was licensed to practice. Then he got into the relevant issues of Luke Talbot's case.

"Please tell the court about the materials that you reviewed in preparation for your testimony here today," Nate said.

Boyd recited a list of medical records, police reports, and children's protective services reports that he had analyzed.

"Did you reach any conclusions about the reasons Luke fell sick and later died?"

"Yes, I did," he said.

"And will you please tell the court what your conclusions are?"

"I think that Luke had a fall two to three weeks before this hospitalization causing the skull fracture and the subdural hematoma. Then, when he had that violent temper tantrum during his bath, he disrupted that clot in his head. It bled, causing the brain damage and ultimately causing his demise. His retinal hemorrhages were the direct result of the high pressure in his head from significant bleeding from the old subdural hematoma. The bruises on his upper back were undoubtedly due to resuscitation efforts when the EMT's were working on him," Boyd said.

"Now, the doctors from Children's Hospital said this was shaken baby or shaken impact syndrome. You seem to disagree with those assessments," Nate said. "Why is that?"

"Shaking couldn't have caused such extensive damage, even with impact, as they claim. There weren't any neck injuries at the postmortem examination. If there had been severe shaking you'd have to see spinal cord injury, neck fractures and bleeding into the neck muscles. There was none of that, either clinically or at autopsy."

"Do you think there is such a thing as shaken baby syndrome?" Nate asked.

"I think some people may shake their babies, and I think that's a bad idea, but I don't think the injuries seen in Luke's case were caused by shaking. May I explain to the court about the structures we're talking about and how these things happen?" Boyd said.

Judge Carlsson looked to the prosecution table and said, "Any objections to having Dr. Boyd discuss his theories about this condition?"

"No objection, Your Honor," Mary Egan said. She had reviewed Boyd's testimony from past trials. She knew almost to the letter what he'd say since he said the same things in every case.

Boyd began to lecture as though he were in a Grand Rounds at a hospital. He went into exquisite detail about the anatomy of the head. He described the structure of the brain, its gyri and sulci, and various areas named after many dead pathologists, neurologists and neuro-anatomists. As he became more and more pedantic, the jurors put down their pens and iPads. He seemed unaware of how few of the mere humans in court were able to understand, or were even interested, in what he was saying. As he plunged forward, he resembled an absent-minded professor or mad scientist. Even Nate and Janet wondered where he was going. Nate was unsure how to bring his testimony back to relevance.

Finally Nate said, "Dr. Boyd, we appreciate your enlightening us about the anatomy of the brain and spinal cord. Now that we understand better about the head and the brain, can you show us how this relates to Luke's case?"

"Sure," Boyd said, unaware that he had strayed from the point.

"Luke's old subdural resumed bleeding again and that led to a catastrophic outcome. At least three other things may have been in play: one, he might have had a birth injury that caused him to have a chronic subdural hematoma; two, he might have had an infection in the cerebrospinal fluid that aggravated the chronic subdural hematoma; and three, lack of oxygen to the brain could have done it. Sometimes those things are missed by the doctors," he said.

"Can you clarify something for me?" Nate said. "Do you think Luke had a pre-existing chronic subdural hematoma from birth, or from a fall two to three weeks prior to his presentation at the hospital?"

"It could be from either of those, but I think it's more likely that he fell since he had the skull fracture. But he could have had both. Take your pick," he said with an ingratiating smile directed towards the jury. "The whole point is, he had something other than shaking to account for his condition."

"Thank you, Dr. Boyd. No more questions for now," Nate said.

"Your witness, Ms. Egan," Judge Carlsson said.

"Dr. Boyd, you said that as a Board-Certified neurosurgeon you are also a pediatric neurosurgeon, is that right?"

"Pediatric neurosurgery is included in the Boards for Neurosurgery; yes, that's correct," he said.

"Isn't it true that pediatric neurosurgeons have a separate Board Certification from the Board of Adult Neurosurgery?"

"Pediatric neurosurgeons created their own Board certification," Boyd said. "There's a group of neurosurgeons who have anointed themselves as pediatric neurosurgical subspecialists, but they're not recognized by the real Board of Neurosurgery," he said.

"So are they quacks?" Mary said.

"Well, that's what some people think," he said.

"Is that what you think?" Mary pressed further.

"Maybe not quacks, but no more qualified to do neurosurgery on children than I am," he said.

"In your private practice of neurosurgery, what percentage of your patients are children, say, under one year of age, over the past ten years?" Mary asked.

"Well, I don't keep track of that sort of thing," he said.

"You must have some idea. Ten percent, twenty percent?"

"Under one year of age? Over the past ten years? Are you kidding? Who knows?" he said.

"Well, surely you must have a rough idea. It's *your* practice. Maybe give the court some idea of the actual number of infants you have seen. Ten, or twenty infants?" Mary said.

"Oh, at least that many over the past ten years. Yeah, probably twenty, that would be a couple a year," he said.

"And of those, how many were cases of abusive head injury?" Mary asked.

"I don't remember, but some," he said.

"But even with that small a number of patients you've seen, you still consider yourself an expert in abusive head trauma in infants?" Mary asked.

"Yes, of course I do. I'm a neurosurgeon, and this is one area of my expertise," he said.

"I see," said Mary. "Have you published research on this subject?"

"Yes, I have," he said.

"Will you please name the studies and the journals where they have been published?" Mary said.

"Sure. I published a Letter to the Editor in the journal *Neurosurgical Digest* in 1972. And I published my article on shaken baby syndrome in the journal *'Neuropathological Questions'* in 1998," he said.

"Do you think a letter to the editor is a research publication?" Mary asked.

"Published in a peer-reviewed journal, yes. It's often cited in court," he said.

"Was that second publication considered an "evidence-based" paper?" Mary asked.

"Yep."

"Isn't it true, Dr. Boyd, that publication was essentially a review article and an opinion article that evoked a strong negative response from several child abuse pediatricians who thought it was disingenuous and not arising from a good analysis of the literature?" Mary asked.

"Sure, but that's the nature of scientific discourse. My views may be controversial but that doesn't mean they're wrong. Only controversial. Besides, child abuse pediatricians are not neurosurgeons. They don't know what neurosurgeons know," he said.

Janet glanced at her father who was gazing straight ahead, always analyzing, always computing, looking for that chink in the armor where he could thrust a spear of argument to secure a point.

"Dr. Boyd, over the last ten years, how many times have you testified in court about abusive head trauma?" Mary asked.

"Oh, over the last ten years, maybe one hundred fifty times," he said without blinking.

"And in those hundred fifty times in court, how often have you testified for the defense?"

"Almost all of them. I'm seldom asked to testify for the prosecution," he said.

"And what do you charge for your testimony?" Mary asked.

"I don't charge for my testimony. I charge for my time and my expertise. My charges include a five thousand dollar retainer fee, one thousand dollars per hour to review records and develop a report, and twelve thousand dollars per day in court, plus expenses," he said.

Mary paused, to let those numbers sink into the jurors' minds. It would be an odd collection of jurors if even one of them were able to earn that much money in their jobs. Janet squirmed in her chair as the revelation about his usurious fees came out. Mary then moved from behind the lectern and stood closer to the jury box.

"You testified that one of your theories about Luke's condition was that he had fallen two to three weeks prior to his hospitalization and that fall caused his subdural hematoma and his skull fracture. Then that clot re-bled and caused all of his difficulties. Is your theory supported by *anything* in the medical literature?" Mary asked.

"Oh yes. In Japan, an eminent researcher showed that re-bleeding occurs and it can lead to all of these findings. Also, a neuropathologist reported that re-bleeding within an old subdural can lead to all of these things," he said. "One researcher who studied subdurals in newborns found that nearly half of all vaginal deliveries had subdural hematomas. Others found similar things in their studies."

"Isn't it true that in the first article you mentioned, the authors reported the re-bleeding occurred only in adults?" Mary said.

"No, there were kids in his studies too."

"I have those papers here. Would you point out to me where he discusses any children in the papers?"

Boyd studied the articles for a few minutes. "I can't find the exact place where he discusses the ages of the patients, but I remember seeing that when I looked at them before," he said.

"We can give you as much time as you need to identify that piece of information. Would you like to take a break so you can look more closely at the papers?" Mary asked.

"No, that won't be necessary Counselor. I don't want to impose on the jury in that way," he said.

"Well then, are you conceding that there were no children or infants in that paper?"

"It doesn't matter. The principal remains the same. Re-bleeding can occur in an old subdural hematoma," he said.

"Turning to the other papers you cited, isn't it true that they all concluded that the subdurals they were describing in newborns disappeared by one month of age and produced no symptoms or problems in these babies?" Mary asked.

"That doesn't mean that in some cases the subdurals couldn't have persisted and bled later. That's the nature of scientific research, you see, that even though some studies show one thing, other studies can show something else, and some things don't even get studied," he said.

Mary stood there, momentarily stupefied by Boyd's illogical responses to her questions, but then decided to go on to another subject.

"What, in your opinion, caused the retinal hemorrhages?" Mary asked.

"The increased intracranial pressure from the re-bleeding,"

he said.

The stock answer, Janet thought.

"Dr. Boyd, in some of your past testimony in other cases, you have said that you don't believe that shaking can cause subdural hematomas, is that correct?"

"That's right, I don't. And the reason is simple. It has been shown in studies that shaking can't generate enough force to cause bleeding in the central nervous system."

"And what studies are you relying on to make that statement?" Mary asked.

"A study published a few years ago and two studies in the early 2000's. They came to the same conclusion that shaking cannot generate enough force to cause subdural bleeding," he said. "And the other thing is that even if you could generate that enormous force, there would be neck injuries, and in none of the cases of alleged shaken baby syndrome are there any neck injuries."

"Isn't it true, though, that the authors didn't say that it couldn't happen, only that they were unable to demonstrate it in their studies?" Mary asked.

"Oh no, they have stuck to their assertions that shaking doesn't cause this," he said.

Mary walked back to her desk and picked up a couple of articles.

She walked back and showed them to Boyd.

"Do you recognize these papers?" she asked.

"Yeah, those are the papers we've been talking about," he said.

"Can you show me where they say unequivocally–as you are saying–that subdurals cannot be caused by shaking?" Mary asked.

Boyd flipped through the papers. Everyone waited. After about ten minutes, he said, "I can't find the exact quote."

"Moving on to the last study you cited, are you aware that the math in that paper has been successfully challenged by another group of bio-mechanical engineers, saying that a great big math error was made in the calculations?" Mary asked.

"I'm not a mathematician, so I can't answer that," he said.

"But wouldn't you agree that the research that you've cited does not do what you say it does, that is, it does not prove that shaking cannot cause subdural hematomas?" Mary said.

"I stick by my opinion. My twenty-eight years of operating on children's central nervous systems has convinced me that shaking does not cause these things," he said with finality.

Janet looked at her father to see if he was going to do redirect, but he wasn't stirring.

Is it because he knows Boyd is fatally wounded? Or does he think it's better to keep moving and hope the jurors will forget his testimony? That the next few witnesses will be better? I'll find out later, but I'm not happy with what I've heard from the eminent neurosurgeon, Dr. Franklin Boyd, Janet thought.

When court adjourned, Nate and Janet rose, spoke not a word but swept into the maelstrom of activity in the hall. Reporters gathered around, eager to hear their take on the testimony.

"A really good day in court," Nate said. "I think the jury heard a lot of things that had to make them wonder whether there's a thing called shaken baby syndrome."

Janet tried not to look surprised by her father's calling black white.

"Mr. Feingold, your expert witness was unconvincing to me and my guess is that the jurors also found him that way. How can you say that your expert persuaded the jury that shaken baby syndrome doesn't exist?" one of the TV talking heads said.

"You must not have heard the same testimony I did. I thought Dr. Boyd was very illuminating about this bogus thing called shaken baby syndrome," Nate said, using repetition, as in advertising, to secure his point.

"And wait until tomorrow when you hear some of our other experts. Then we can talk," and with that he pushed through the crowd and Janet followed in his wake, avoiding eye contact with any of the reporters.

In the car, Janet said, "You don't really believe what you just told the press, do you?"

"Doesn't matter whether I believe it or not, it's what they put out there in the form of news. I was watching the jury. A couple of them were looking quite protective towards Boyd as Egan was tearing him apart. Sometimes, my dear, discrediting a witness like she did can backfire. What appears to be a bad performance by an embattled witness may provoke sympathy in some jurors. Remember, we only need one to believe. The prosecution needs a unanimous vote to convict. I'm not worried," Nate said. "I really need to eat something, though. I feel a little hypoglycemic."

27

Max Schmidt, a provocative contrarian anchor for Channel 1, made the Luke Talbot case his lead story on the six o'clock news.

"Today in the Kansas City Courthouse, a drama is evolving, pitting the two sides in a controversial medical diagnosis against each other. 'Mainstream Medicine' versus 'The Dogma Challengers,' the 'Iconoclasts.' The Children's Hospital doctors, the police, the Children's Protective Services and the Prosecutors all say seven-month-old baby Luke Talbott died from "shaken impact syndrome." The defense claims he died from other causes.

"The father-daughter defense team of Janet and Nathan Feingold brought an eminent neurosurgeon from Denver who argued persuasively that Luke Talbot had fallen several weeks before and that his symptoms arose from that old injury. There was the inevitable strong challenge by the prosecution to his testimony, but make no mistake, his testimony raised doubts about whether the eighteen-year-old babysitter was responsible for Luke's injuries and his subsequent death. Tomorrow the defense will offer other expert witnesses to argue that Chrystal Begley did

not commit this crime and should be found not
guilty. Stay tuned for this dramatic story.
We'll bring it to you each night on the Six
O'clock News.

"Now, listen to this money-saving offer for
long-term care insurance from the offices of
Delaney and Stewart."

Nate turned to Janet as they were driving to the courthouse the next
morning. "What did I tell you? The news media are your friends. Especially Max Schmidt."

"He was a lot more impressed with Dr. Boyd than I was. Shows how
perceptions can vary. I thought Boyd was full of it, very illogical and to
top it off, supercilious. A stereotypical surgeon who thinks he rules the
world," Janet said. "And you're going to write a big fat check for that
performance?" she said, uncharacteristically scolding. "I sure hope the
rest of those experts are better than he was."

"Whoa, you're beginning to sound like a prosecutor," Nate said. "I
agree he was a little over the top but he wasn't that bad, and some of the
jurors may have believed what he was saying. The guy we have today is
Dr. Parten, who testifies about falls causing these head injuries. He will
strengthen the case that Luke fell and that it all stems from that. He's done
more research than Boyd and has a track record of pleasing juries. I think
you'll see what I mean when you hear him," Nate said.

Janet's feeling of dysphoria arose from her irritation—and even anger—
toward her father, with his talk of fooling the jury and his practice of
using the media.

*He must know that media accounts of this trial can't affect this seques-
tered jury. His dance with the media must have more to do with his need to
undermine the acceptance of shaken baby syndrome by the "great unwashed,"
possible future jurors. I know a lot of people are sympathetic to anyone accused
of crimes because of well-publicized reversals of convictions. Some people
harbor a deep-seated distrust of institutions—government, courts, bureaucrats,
police—anyone who is perceived as impeding their "rights."*

What am I supposed to do? I have to give Chrystal the most persuasive defense I can, but there's a delicate line between that and deceit. I'm glad Dad is doing the examinations of the experts. I'm not sure I could tolerate them, Janet thought.

The matrons brought Chrystal into the courtroom, and she sat next to Janet at the defense table.

"How was your night?" Janet said.

"Fine," Chrystal replied.

"Any questions for me?" Janet asked.

"How long do you think this thing is going to go on?" Chrystal said.

"Hard to say for sure, but a few more days," Janet said.

"I hate this whole thing. It's like watching a stupid television show. Except the actors are better looking on television," she said.

"Try to look interested and upbeat," Janet said, feeling disconsolate herself.

"Easy for you to say. You don't have to live in jail. I'm not interested in what these people say and I'm not upbeat. I'm pissed and I'm gonna stay pissed. Nothing you say will make things any better," Chrystal said as she looked at the back row for June.

"All rise, the court is in session."

The Judge strode in, took his place, and asked Nate to begin.

"The Defense calls Dr. James Parten."

Parten was a robust man in a tan suit. He wore a starched white shirt with a non-descript tie, and brown hiking boots. He had a shining bald-head and his green eyes were deep–set in his broad, reddish face. Under his eyes were generous folds of flesh and his nose suggested a fondness for drink.

After he answered questions about his credentials, including Board Certification in pathology, a modest list of publications and honorary society memberships, Nate asked, "Dr. Parten, what were your duties as a pathologist for Pathology Services Ltd?"

"I was in charge of running the testing labs, of analyzing biopsy specimens taken by doctors in operating rooms or clinics of our clients, and serving as a consultant to clinicians in the network served by Pathology Services. I am considered the doctors' doctor," he answered.

"And is it also true that you are a forensic pathologist?" Nate asked.
"Yes."

"What exactly is a forensic pathologist?" Nate said.

"Forensic pathologists try to figure out the true cause of various kinds of injuries and deaths. You usually see forensic pathologists involved in unexplained death investigations, poisonings, murders, that sort of thing. You know, like Quincy, CSI. We're really the medical detectives who seek out the scientific causes of things," he said.

"Do you take extra training to become a forensic pathologist?" Nate asked.

"Oh, yes indeed. Four years of pathology training plus one year of forensic pathology training. It's highly regulated," he said.

"Is it because you are a forensic pathologist that you often testify in court?" Nate said.

"That's right. We're regularly called as expert witnesses in cases where there are forensic–that is legal–implications," he said.

Nate paused a moment, then asked Dr. Parten to describe the medical materials about Luke Talbot that he had reviewed. Parten iterated all of the hospital records and the autopsy documents that he had analyzed.

"Let's go over the autopsy report on Luke first," said Nate. "I am going to give you the report so you can refer to it as you testify."

"Thank you," he said.

"The report talks about the hemorrhage under the scalp in the back of the head overlying a skull fracture. How does that happen?" Nate asked.

"Both of those things are due to trauma," Parten replied.

"Can you tell from the findings how old those traumatic events might have been?"

"No way to tell with certainty. If the pathologist had taken a section of the skull fracture and examined it microscopically, we could tell from the cellular elements as to whether it was healing or not and could assign a time to it," Parten said.

"Could the blood under the scalp also be old blood?" Nate asked.

"Maybe a couple or three weeks old, but that's hard to say. If I'd been the examining pathologist I'd be in a better position to know that. Don't understand how he could've overlooked the importance of dating the blood. That's one of the things that forensic pathologists try to teach medical examiners," he said.

"What else was shown by the autopsy?" Nate asked.

"Well, there was brain edema – swelling–and a right subdural hematoma, blood under the dura. The brain swelling during life causes raised pressure within the skull. There were also retinal hemorrhages."

"Were there any findings in the neck?" Nate said.

"Nothing of consequence," Parten said.

"What do you make of the skin bruises along the spine?" Nate said.

"Could have been due to resuscitation efforts or other kinds of handling of the baby in the hospital," Parten said.

"Dr. Parten, do you have an opinion as to how these injuries occurred?" Nate said.

"Yes, I do," he said.

"And what is that opinion?"

"I think Luke fell backwards, perhaps out of his high chair, or off a changing table, striking his head and sustaining a skull fracture two to three weeks prior to the day he was brought to the hospital. This same fall caused the subdural hematoma and it lay dormant during this lucid interval. That clot was then disturbed during his temper tantrum. It started bleeding again and this led to pressure on the brain due to what is called a 'mass effect' in the head. This causes hypoxia-decreased oxygen to the brain–and this adds to the heightened pressure within the head. That pressure prevents the blood return from the eyes, building up the pressure in the retinal vessels. They finally burst from that back pressure. That's why we see retinal hemorrhages."

"You mentioned a term "lucid interval." Nate said. "Can you explain that?"

"Sure. A lucid interval is that period of time after a head injury when the patient seems to be perfectly fine for a time before the injury catches up with them. When it does catch up with them, they deteriorate and die. It's what we call "walk and talk and die.""

"So you don't subscribe to the theory that Luke was shaken and then his head struck a hard object?" Nate asked.

"No. First of all, shaking can't cause these injuries because it's been proven biomechanically that shaking can't do these things. It would take much more force than a human being can generate to cause these injuries. Besides, there were no injuries to Luke's neck, and if a baby were shaken there would have to be injuries to the neck," Parten said.

A broken record, playing the same set of notes over and over, with no variation. These guys have their stories down pat, Janet thought.

"Do you believe that a short fall–say three to four feet–could have caused the skull fracture, the subdural hematoma, and the brain swelling that caused Luke to die?" Nate said.

"Yes I do. Exactly so," Parten said.

"No further questions, Your Honor," Nate said as he sat down.

"Your witness, Miss Egan," Judge Carlsson said.

Dr. Parten rearranged himself in the witness box as Mary Egan brought her yellow legal pad to the lectern, set it down quietly, and paused for a moment.

"Dr. Parten, you described your duties in the pathology services company earlier. Do you remember that?"

"Yes, ma'am."

"As a pathologist for a private pathology service, do you perform autopsies?"

"Not in my current job, but in the past, yes. When deaths occur in our network hospitals, the autopsies are usually done by the medical examiner," he said.

"Well, in the past five years, how many autopsies have you personally done?" Mary asked.

"In the past five years? I haven't done any autopsies in my current job," Parten replied.

"And when you did autopsies, before five years ago, how many were done on children?"

"None. The hospitals where I worked before were adult hospitals, where there were no pediatric patients," he said.

"So, you really haven't done any autopsies on children with head injuries or anything else, for that matter, right?" Mary said.

"Yes, ma'am," he said.

"Yet you claim to know a lot about head injured children from the pathologist's point of view," Mary said.

"Yes, because I've made a study of head injury in childhood and consider myself an expert in this area. And I've been qualified as an expert in a number of courts both here and in Canada and in England. As a pathologist you don't have to actually perform autopsies to have learned about them in training and to keep up with the literature on the subject," he said.

"Are you a pediatrician?"

"No."

"Are you a neurosurgeon?"

"No."

"When Mr. Feingold was questioning you, you said that shaking can't cause the things we have seen in Luke Talbot because," Mary paused, looked at her yellow legal pad and quoted, " 'shaking can't cause these injuries because it's been proven biomechanically that shaking can't do these things. It would take much more force than a human being can generate to cause these injuries. Besides, there were no injuries to Luke's neck, and if a baby were shaken there would have to be injuries to the neck.' Do you remember saying that?" Mary asked.

"Yes, that's what I said," Parten said.

"Are you a biomechanical engineer, then?" Mary said.

"No, but I've read the literature about the biomechanics of head injury. The literature's pretty clear about this, you know," Parten said.

Mary then took Parten through the same hoops about the biomechanical literature that she did with Boyd, with the same kinds of responses from Parten.

"Now since we've heard that the biomechanical literature you rely on doesn't support your theory, is it fair to say there's no scientific evidence that shaking *cannot* produce these injuries?"

"I suppose not direct evidence, because that's hard to come by. It's hard to prove the negative. But all of the indirect evidence says that shaking can't do these things," he said.

"Are you aware that many other researchers have criticized the dummies used in experiments as too crude to be taken seriously?" Mary asked.

"They're the only ones we have and so far the conclusion is that the forces needed to do these injuries can't be produced by shaking," Parten said.

"But Doctor, do we really know what forces are required to cause the damage to all of these tissues—the bridging veins, the brain itself, the skull, the scalp, the dura? How can we know that?"

"By extrapolation. We take what we know, subject it to experiments, and voila! We have the answers," he said. "The pediatricians are guessing at this diagnosis based on the triad. They claim when the triad is present it can only be shaken baby syndrome. They never consider the other countless possibilities. They want to get the perpetrator convicted. The pediatricians hate me because I take this position, but I really don't care about that. They're wrong about shaking causing this thing. They don't believe what we forensic pathologists believe," he said.

"Do you mean all forensic pathologists believe as you do, that shaking can't cause these injuries?"

"All of them that I talk to on a regular basis," he said.

"Who are these forensic pathologists? Can you corroborate that they agree with you with any data, a survey, or something like that?" Mary said.

"You'll just have to take my word for it. I haven't done a survey, but I correspond with a lot of pathologists and they all agree with me about this," he said.

"Let me ask you this another way: what proven evidence do you have that a certain amount of force causes damage to tissue unless we experiment with real children?"

"We can't experiment with children, obviously, so we have to study models. And the models are getting better all the time. Someday we'll have a perfect model to experiment on and we'll have definitive answers, and I think I'll be proven right about shaking not being able to produce these injuries," he said.

"What proven evidence is there now?" Mary pressed on.

"Asked and answered, Your Honor," Nate cried out.

"Move on, Counselor," Judge Carlsson said.

"Dr. Parten, do you believe short falls can kill children?" Mary asked.

"Yes indeed, I do. Studies have clearly shown that," Parten said.

"Do you mean this study?" Mary said, handing him an article.

"Yes."

"Can you describe to the jury what this study showed?" Mary asked.

"This author described thousands of playground falls, some of which resulted in death from short falls. It is a seminal paper, and it proved that short falls can, indeed, kill children," Parten said.

"But isn't it true that none of the children in the study was younger than 12 months of age?" Mary asked.

"Yes."

"Do you recall that Luke Talbot was 7 months old when he died?" Mary said.

"Yes."

"And isn't it also true that some of the falls in that study were accelerated because the children were swinging from playground equipment?"

"I don't remember that part of the paper," Parten said.

"And some of the falls were from seven feet, and therefore not 'short falls'?" Mary said.

"That's possible. I don't remember all the details of the paper," Parten said.

"Well, can you recall that several of the children had pre-existing conditions that may have increased their risk of death?"

"Don't recall that part, no," he said.

"And isn't it true that, even accepting that author's conclusions, the rate of death was less than 0.02 percent, making death from short falls an extraordinarily rare event?" Mary asked.

"But it happens!" Parten shouted.

"Are you aware of the paper in a pediatric journal that states that the risk of death from short falls is less than one in a million?" Mary asked.

"I don't believe everything in pediatric journals. They can be very biased," Parten said.

"Do you think the journal *Pediatrics*, which is published by the American Academy of Pediatrics, would publish a biased paper?" Mary said.

"As I said earlier, pediatricians think differently than forensic pathologists. The American Academy of Pediatrics is their organization and they publish a lot of things I don't agree with," he said.

"Does that make the research wrong, just because you don't believe it?" Mary asked.

"Well, you're a lawyer and you wouldn't understand what goes into the acceptance of research by journals. A lot of it is rigged," Parten said.

"In what way is it rigged?" Mary asked, sensing a big opening.

"Certain people are more respected than others and their stuff gets published and the others don't, especially if it doesn't agree with the peer reviewers who are making recommendations about accepting or rejecting an article," Parten said.

"Isn't it true that the peer review process is done anonymously, that is, the reviewers don't know who wrote the article and the authors don't know who the reviewers are, a so-called 'blind review'?" Mary said.

"Yes, that's the way it's supposed to be done, but I think the reviewers sometimes know who wrote the papers and give them a lot of leeway," Parten said.

"So what you're saying is that the peer review process is not working for *Pediatrics* but working perfectly for the pathology journals?" Mary said.

"Well, to some extent that's true. Pathology papers are more scientific than pediatric papers," he said.

The jurors were stirring around, scrutinizing him as he crossed and uncrossed his legs in the witness box. The jurors' expressions indicated his carping was not going down well. Dr. Parten's face flushed red as he spoke, perspiration sprouting from his forehead. He shifted his weight around, looking over at Nate, hoping that he'd object to the questioning, hoping to be rescued from this predatory woman. But Nate was looking skyward. Janet had her head down, concentrating on some papers before her, and neither looked ready to rescue him from the hole he had dug for himself.

Mary turned around and looked at the ceiling in exasperation. Sweat was apparent, soaking through his tan suit under Parten's arms. He looked like a man who would write a large check to be somewhere else. It was up to Mary as to whether she would go for the jugular or let him depart. She didn't want an Appeals Court to judge her as abusive to a witness, so she allowed the tension to rise for a few minutes. She flipped through her notes, while the jury regarded Dr. Parten, judging him. The longer she waited, the more Parten moved about, adjusting his tie, and applying tissues to the sweat on his forehead.

"There is one other question I have for you, Doctor. You mentioned something called a "lucid interval" in your testimony on direct examination by Mr. Feingold. Have "lucid intervals" ever been described in a seven-month-old baby?"

"It's what I think happened in Luke's case. He had a fall, injured his head and that caused a subdural hematoma. He was in a lucid interval until the hematoma bled again after his temper tantrum. Then the increased pressure in his head caused him to lose consciousness and then later, he died," Parten said.

Mary locked eyes with Parten for what seemed like an eternity to Parten.

"Dr. Parten, do seven-month-old infants walk or talk?"

"No."

"So how do you measure normality in a seven-month-old infant if they are in what you call a 'lucid interval'?"

"Oh, if they are acting normally," he said, looking away from Mary, beginning to cringe from what he knew was going to be another difficult question.

"Isn't the literature on 'lucid intervals' exclusively from adult patients?"

"No, not exclusively. There have been some reports in children," he said.

"Can you cite the publications that describe lucid intervals in infants?"

"Well, I didn't memorize those. But they're out there," he said.

"Doctor, isn't it true that lucid intervals have never been described in the pediatric infant population, ever?" Mary said in measured tones, looking at the jury.

"Oh sure they have. I just don't have them at my fingertips," Parten said.

By now some in the jury had put down their notepads and iPads, and looking downward, seemed embarrassed by this display of evasive prevarication.

Finally, Mary said, with a clear note of disdain, "I have no further questions for this witness, Your Honor."

"Mr. Feingold? Any further questions?" the judge asked.

"No, Your Honor," Nate said, a touch of weariness in his voice.

"Court adjourned until two PM," Judge Carlsson said.

28

"Out the side door. I don't feel well," Nate whispered in Janet's ear.

Janet looked at her father, saw his pallor and understood why he hadn't done a redirect examination on Dr. Parten. Not that it would have done much good since Parten had buried himself. But she was surprised that he didn't give it a try.

They brushed by the bailiff and headed to Hanrahan's. Nate asked the greeter for a private spot upstairs where they wouldn't be disturbed. Once they were seated, Nate said to Janet,

"I'm not feeling hungry. I've got a bit of a bellyache. Really tired. Can you do the direct on the biomechanics guy this afternoon? Let me go home to rest?"

"Good God, Dad, what do you think is going on? You've never been sick your whole life. You need to see a doctor–right away. Do you even have a doctor?"

"No. Well, there's Dr. Berman, but I don't see him often. I need to go home, take a nap and I'll be fine. My question is, can you do the direct on Dr. Szabo?"

"Sure, if you give me your notes. Don't worry about that for heaven's sake. More importantly, you have to go to an emergency room and see a doctor. I'll be a basket case if you don't do that. Promise me you'll go there now. You look terrible. Promise?"

"OK, I'll go, if you insist. This is probably just some indigestion. Too much coffee and doughnuts this morning. My diet's been for crap for the last week or two. Where do you think I should go?"

"To St Joseph's Hospital. OK?"

"It's a total waste of everyone's time, but if you'd feel better, I'll go. So, here're my notes," Nate said as he pulled a sheaf of papers from his briefcase.

"Can you read my writing? If you can't, call Nina and she can type it out. She's used to my scrawl," Nate said.

Janet looked at his legal pad. What a mess–chicken scratches, with arrows zigging and zagging across the pages.

I hope Nina can figure it out. Maybe I should ask for a recess. I sure can't figure out what these notes say. Nina could also make sure Dad goes to the hospital, Janet thought.

"Dad, I'm going to ask for a recess. I'm sure the judge will grant it if he knows you're sick. Then I can get Nina to decipher your notes and maybe this evening we could go over them together."

"I hate like hell not to proceed. Szabo is waiting to testify and the longer it takes to get him on the stand the more money it's costing me. Maybe I'll just press on this afternoon. I'll eat something and then I'll feel better," Nate said.

"Not a chance," Janet raised her voice. "You don't look good and you're not going back to court today. This is your daughter speaking to you," she said.

Janet had lost her own appetite. She hurried Nate into a taxi and off he went. She went back to the court and got a recess with no argument from the prosecutors or the judge.

"Dr. Szabo? This is Janet Feingold, Nate's daughter. Dad's sick and on his way to the hospital so we won't need you in court this afternoon. Can you stay an extra day?" Janet said.

He agreed to stay another day. Janet then called Nina, told her about her Dad's illness and then drove to her father's office.

"What in the world could be wrong with him?" Nina said. "I've never known him ever to be sick in any way. This isn't like him at all."

Janet gave Nina a hug. She knew how close Nina and her Dad were. In short order, Nina broke away from Janet and took the notes into her office to make them discernable.

Nina must have a Rosetta stone to untangle his scrawl, Janet thought, anxious to receive the translation of Nate's hieroglyphics.

As she settled into her father's chair, she thought of Jared. *I wonder what he's up to?*

"Jared, this is Janet. Can you talk?"

"Well, what a pleasant surprise. Thought you'd be in solitary confinement in the courthouse. Glad to hear from you," Jared said.

"There's bad news and good. Dad's sick and at the hospital. That's the bad news. The good news is that we've got a recess in the trial because of Dad's illness and I have this evening to go over the questions he had prepared for tomorrow's witness."

"Your dad? What's wrong with him?" Jared asked.

"Don't know yet. I just packed him off to St. Joseph's Emergency Department. He looked terrible–all pale and clammy. He didn't want any lunch. He was uncharacteristically passive in court this morning and I wondered why he wasn't his usual aggressive self. Turns out he was feeling horrible. So unlike him. He never gets sick. I'm really worried about him. Thank heaven I could talk him into going to the hospital."

"Anything I can do?"

"Not now. I'm going to see how things are going," she said.

"Janet?" Jared said. "I'll be thinking about you and your dad. Sure I can't do anything?"

"Thanks, I don't think there's anything to be done right now," Janet said.

Nina came in with the translation.

"Gotta, go, Jared. Hope to talk to you soon," Janet said and hung up. "You're a wizard, Nina, I couldn't make heads or tails of it."

"That's what comes with working with him forever," Nina said, looking distraught. "He seemed OK yesterday. He never complains, so naturally I'm worried," Nina said.

"We won't know much 'til later, I guess," Janet replied.

Janet looked over the questions Nina had typed out for her. They seemed straightforward enough. She glanced at her watch and saw that it was four o'clock already, so she headed to the hospital.

"Bye Nina, and thanks a lot," she said as she left. "I'll let you know when I find out what's going on."

"OK," Nina said, as her throat constricted and she filled her lungs to calm herself.

Janet went through the maze of the Emergency Department and finally found her father. He'd already been seen by three doctors, had gone for an MRI, had "two gallons of blood drawn and an ECG," according to Nate, and was waiting for results in the holding room of the Emergency Department.

"How're you feeling?" Janet said.

"They haven't killed me yet," Nate said. "I guess they don't know I'm a lawyer or they would've already done me in. But the pain in my belly's not as bad." He grinned. "I thought bleeding was no longer a medical treatment but since they did that I feel better. Maybe those docs 200 years ago knew what they were doing."

At that moment, the curtain to the cubicle was pulled back and the intern, who looked about twelve years old, came in, accompanied by a tall, dark-skinned man with angular features, who introduced himself as Dr. Krishnamoorthy.

"Good afternoon, sir, I'm one of the gastroenterologists here at St. Joseph's. I've reviewed your lab studies and your MRI." Turning to Janet he said, "Might you be his daughter?"

"Yes, I'm Janet Feingold."

"I'm pleased to meet you, Ms. Feingold," he said with a lilting, Indian-accented baritone. "The laboratory work and MRI suggest pancreatic disease of some sort. This could be a number of things, such as an inflammation called pancreatitis or it could be more serious."

Turning to Nate, he said, "I think we should bring you into the inpatient service to do further assessments."

"You mean stay in the hospital?" Nate said. "No way I can do that. I'm a lawyer in the middle of an important trial. I can't take time now for 'further assessments' as you put it. I'll come back after the trial is over and we can go from there."

"I hear where you're coming from but please understand that I don't think that would be the best plan at this point. The sooner we get a diagnosis the better off you'll be. I strongly advise you to allow us to help you now," Dr. Krishnamoorthy said, as quietly and unexcitedly as he could.

"Well, I appreciate your advice, Doctor, but I just can't do that. Janet, find out what they've done with my clothes. Thank you, Doctor, you've been swell, but I really have to go," Nate said.

"I don't think you've comprehended what I'm trying to tell you, Mr. Feingold. There's a very real possibility there's cancer in your pancreas. Time is of the essence. This could rapidly progress. With the pancreas, it often does. We need to intervene as quickly and as aggressively as we can to prevent its spread to other organs."

The doctor looked at Janet. "Ms. Feingold, do you understand what I'm saying?" he said, in hopes of getting her help in convincing this recalcitrant man to cooperate.

Janet grasped the chair in front of her as she took in what Dr. Krishnamoorthy had said. She felt light-headed, but knew she had to push her father to make the right decision.

"Yes, I do understand," Janet said. She looked squarely at her father. "Dad, you have to be admitted. You're in no shape to go home, or to do anything more in court until you're better. This time I'm going to tell you what to do for your own good. You have to take the doctor's advice. He knows what he's talking about. This is not the law. This is medical science, and if he's analyzed your lab tests and your X-rays and thinks this is what the diagnosis may be, then we have to listen to him." Janet was surprised at her own resolve and strident tone.

Nate looked back and forth between Dr. Krishnamoorthy and Janet.

He glanced at the intern, whose face was inscrutable. He focused on the monitors and medical equipment around him, heard the beeps and whistles and general din that define an emergency department. He was vaguely aware of the murmurs of voices from other cubicles; he could hear a baby crying somewhere in the cavernous room that surrounded the cubicles. This was a new experience. For once, he was not in control. He weighed his options carefully, trying to analyze his case the same way he would look at legal cases, arguing within himself–on the one hand, then on the other hand–and slowly, very slowly, he decided that the doctor and Janet were right, damn it, and he should submit to their judgment. Then he got scared.

What if it's cancer, the "Emperor of All Maladies"? he thought, fidgeting and moving his arms and legs restlessly, looking furtively at the medical equipment, the beds, the floor of the cubicle. He wanted to deny that he was even sick, put on his clothes and get the hell out of this noisy, confusing and terrifying place.

At length, he said, "I give up. Go ahead and admit me."

Janet exhaled deeply. "Dad, I love you so much. I know this is the right thing to do. Don't worry about the case. I'm a big girl and I'm a good lawyer because you've taught me so well. Nina deciphered your notes. I can talk to the other witnesses and develop my own questions for them. You concentrate on getting well. I know you'll be in good hands here. I'll stay with you until you get settled upstairs and then I think you need to rest."

After Janet saw that her father was ensconced in his room, she arranged to meet Jared—the only person she wanted to see—at Luigi's. As soon as she saw him, her composure evaporated and tears dropped down her cheeks, as the events of the day finally bubbled up to a conscious level. She held onto Jared for a very long time.

"I'm sorry," Janet said. "I usually don't act like an emotional basket-case."

"Don't apologize. What's the story?" Jared asked.

"Everything has gone wrong in one day." She described what had happened in court during the morning, and then the events of the afternoon.

"The doctors think it's pancreatic cancer. From what I know about that disease, it's not good. Something like 90% mortality," she said.

"Isn't that the cancer that Ruth Bader Ginsburg had? She had surgery and was cured. So that 90% figure may be old. Maybe it's not quite that bad," Jared said.

"That's true about Justice Ginsburg. I guess we have to stay hopeful. Listen, I'm sorry but I'm not going to be able to spend much time with you tonight. I have a pile of work to do to get ready for tomorrow. We can make it up later. I'm really sorry," Janet said.

"Of course. But if you want I can come to your place while you work and we can at least be together," Jared said.

"Oh, no you don't," Janet laughed. "I know myself well enough to know that if I did that, tomorrow I'd walk into that court totally unprepared."

"Never hurts to try," he grinned.

After a quick pizza, Janet gave Jared a long kiss and hug, and said goodbye. She needed to get her head around questions on Nate's sheets that Nina had deciphered. She knew almost nothing about biomechanics. Would she be able to absorb enough by morning?

29

Janet bolted down three cups of black, industrial strength Verona coffee to rouse her brain from the torpor of her restless night. A tenuous emotional strand hung between the twin stresses of Nate's illness and the challenge she faced in court a few hours hence.

What do I know of Newton's Laws? How do they apply to shaken baby syndrome? How can I extract information from an engineer that would mean something to a jury?

Scraps of thoughts rattled through Janet's mind as she hurried through morning ablutions and fumbled into her sensible lawyer suit.

Rushing out the door, she grabbed her phone and called her Dad's hospital telephone number. An unfamiliar voice answered.

"Mr. Feingold's line. He's out of his room right now. Please leave a message."

"Dad, this is me; I'm going into court now. Your notes were terrific, and Nina was so helpful to transcribe them. I'll do my best. Hope you're feeling better. I'll stop by after court. Love you."

Perhaps more tests or X-rays? What could be going on?

Janet frowned as she put her phone away. Then she compartmentalized, but it was a strain to focus on the task at hand.

She found Dr. Zoltan Szabo in the courtroom corridor. His large, stocky frame was wrapped in a dark, oversized suit. His large brown eyes studded his swarthy face, whose cheeks, though recently shaven, were almost coal black, giving him a Nixonian look. Dominating his face was a large hooked nose, below which hung large wide lips. When he greeted Janet, his Eastern European accent was prominent.

"You are Mr. Feingold's daughter," his sonorous voice boomed. "He well described you. I'm Dr. Zoltan Szabo. How is your father today?"

"Yes, I'm Janet Feingold. I'm not sure how he is today. He wasn't in his hospital room when I called a few minutes ago. He could be having more tests. I hope he's doing OK.

"Bear with me this morning," Janet said, leading Szabo into the courtroom. "I'm using notes he wrote when he talked with you. I hope I ask you the right questions in the right way."

"My testimony should be short. Maybe I get an early flight?" Dr. Szabo said.

"You're first on the list of witnesses. Can you tell me what your main points will be?" Janet asked.

"Shaking alone cannot make subdural bleeding, based on published literature and experiments. No neck injuries shows shaking didn't happen. That's about it," he said.

They sat down at the defense table. Mary Egan and Albert Polcari came over .

"How is your father?" Mary asked.

"When I left him yesterday evening he was at least comfortable," Janet said, touched that they would be solicitous.

"Listen, if you want a continuance because of his illness, we have no objection to it. I think Judge Carlsson would allow it," Albert said.

"Thanks. Maybe after I've finished with my first witness I can decide. I have Dr. Szabo here. I'd like to get his testimony in today so he doesn't have to come back. How would that be?" Janet said.

"Fine with us, just let us know after Dr. Szabo is done," Mary said.

Janet called Dr. Szabo to the stand, and after he was sworn in Janet said, "What is your profession?"

"I'm biomechanical engineer. I work in Department of Engineering at the AutoSafe Corporation, in Landsdowne, Maryland."

For the next few minutes he recited his background, education and degrees.

"What does a biomechanical engineer do?" Janet asked.

Now on familiar turf, Szabo lost some of his accent.

"The science of biomechanics uses physics, structural mechanics and biology to study why certain body parts fail under certain stresses," he said. "We determine the mechanical causes of trauma to find out ways to prevent harm. In our shop it usually involves automobile crashes, but we also study the biomechanics in other trauma, like falls from heights, violent acts, and so on," Dr. Szabo said.

"Have you been qualified as an expert witness in courts to testify about these issues?"

"Occasionally," he said.

"After you reviewed Luke Talbot's records, did you come to conclusions based on your expertise in biomechanics about his injuries?"

"Yes."

"Please tell the court what those conclusions are."

"His subdural hematoma and skull fracture were caused by impact trauma, not by shaking," he said.

"On what studies do you base your conclusion that the subdural hematoma was not caused by shaking?" Janet said.

"Numerous biomechanical studies tell us about what forces are required to cause bleeding in the subdural space. The studies of the dummy model confirm these conclusions. They all show that injury thresholds can't be reached by shaking," he said. "One study also proved that there would be injuries to the neck if shaking was so forceful that it made subdural bleeding. This matter is settled."

"Thank you Dr. Szabo. I have no further questions."

Mary began her cross-examination by saying, "Dr. Szabo, are you a physician?"

"No."

"Have you ever cared for a child with a head injury?"

"No."

"So, would it be accurate to say that all of your conclusions are based on your reading of the literature developed by others?" Mary asked.

"I've done my own experiments and have come to the same conclusions," he said.

"Are your experiments published?"

"No."

"Do you believe that the models used in the studies you rely on are biofidelic, that is, have head properties very close to human infants?" Mary said.

"No dummy model is perfect. We can use some animal models as comparisons," he said.

"Turning to animal models, do you believe in the concept of mass scaling to extrapolate data from animal studies to human infants?"

"Yes, mass is mass regardless of whether it is a rat brain, a pig, or a monkey," he said.

"Are you aware of the biomechanical study that showed the piglet toddler brain can withstand over three times greater strains than the infant piglet brain before injury results?" Mary said.

"I know only a little about that research," Szabo said.

"Here is the paper. Would you read the highlighted paragraph for us?"

Szabo looked at the paper Mary handed him. It confirmed that mass was not the issue in brain damage but that tissue vulnerability was greater in the younger piglet brain.

"Doesn't that study refute your theory about mass scaling?" Mary said.

"I still say that it all has to do with mass."

Mary paused and looked toward the ceiling for effect. "Alright Dr. Szabo. Let's go back to discussing studies using dummy models. Isn't it true that these models were only shaken in a single direction because the models had a crude hinged neck?" Mary said.

"That was a long time ago. The models we use now are much better," he said.

"But you said you relied on these studies to inform your opinion. Aren't you contradicting yourself?" Mary asked.

"We have to use the data that's out there," he replied weakly.

"Are you aware of the study that demonstrated that by altering the materials used in the dummies they could achieve acceleration levels that exceeded those found in the earlier studies?"

"I've heard of that study and I told you the dummies are not perfect, but they're all we have right now," he said.

"Do you think we'll ever have any model–a biofidelic model–that will accurately simulate all the complexities of the various tissues of various ages of infants and children?" Mary asked.

"Someday, but not now."

"And if we can't model them, how can we know what forces are involved in damaging these tissues?" Mary asked.

"In science, we have to rely on what we can study. At the present time, the things that I have said are what science has provided us," Szabo answered, shifting his large body in the chair. His face was distorted as he answered, and he lost his earlier equanimity.

"Do we have accurate data on what forces are required to cause damage to the bridging veins, the structures in the infant brain, and the skull, under the circumstances of shaking and/or impact?" Mary asked.

"Accurate? What is accurate?" he growled, his accent more pronounced. "We have only what we have. Are we sure? No. But it's as close as we can come. We can't shake babies, and even if we could, it would be hard to calculate the forces being brought to bear," Szabo answered, with increasing agitation and surliness.

"Now, regarding that biomechanics study you cited. Are you aware that others found significant numerical errors in that study that rendered its conclusions erroneous?" Mary asked.

"But other studies show cervical spinal cord injuries are common in whiplash injuries. So if they're absent in shaken baby cases, which are like whiplash, then the babies weren't shaken," Szabo said dogmatically.

"But isn't it true, Dr. Szabo, the spinal cord injuries in those whiplash cases were only in fatal cases using specialized techniques to show those injuries during postmortem examinations? "

"Yes, these injuries have only been shown in fatal cases. You can't do dissections like that in live patients," he shouted.

"But most cases of abusive head trauma don't die, do they?" Mary asked.

"Yes, but that doesn't disprove my statement."

"Isn't it true that most studies have shown the absence of neck injuries in abusive head trauma?" Mary asked.

"I can't answer that, since I don't know what you mean by 'most studies,' " Szabo said.

"Thank you, Dr. Szabo, I have no more questions for this witness, Your Honor," Mary said, deciding that presenting additional research papers showing the absence of neck injuries in shaken baby cases wouldn't budge this dogmatic man.

Dr. Szabo is a toss-up. The more discerning jurors will see he's unfamiliar with some literature and his certainty is based on his beliefs rather than published research. But he wasn't as bad as Parten or Boyd. That's a plus, Janet thought.

"Ms. Feingold, do you have any further questions?" Judge Carlsson asked.

"No, Your Honor," Janet said.

"Lunchtime. Court adjourned until 2PM."

Janet called her dad at the hospital. This time he answered on the first ring.

"Hi, how'd it go this morning?" Nate said.

"I'd say Szabo was just OK. But I don't think he hurt us too much. How're you doing?"

"Well, the good news is that I feel a whole lot better. The bad news is that my cancer is inoperable. More good news is that I can go home this afternoon. I commence therapy next week. But in the meantime I can help you again."

"What? Inoperable?" she said. "What kind of prognosis does that suggest?"

"I'm taking this all day to day. I don't know what the long term outcome will be, so I want to get back on the horse and help you win this case," Nate said.

Janet was incredulous that he was intending on jumping back into the fray.

"Yes, I'm looking forward to working on the case later today."

"Jesus, Dad, give me a minute to get my mind around this. Should I get a continuance? I can ask for that. The prosecutors are being really decent about it. I think Judge Carlsson would grant it if you think we should."

"Hell, no, don't get a continuance. I'll be back at your side tomorrow morning, ready to go. I feel fine. Next week I may not feel so good. So let's press on."

"I don't know; are you sure?"

"Janet, listen to your father."

"If you say so, Dad." Janet said. She knew there was no point in discussing this. "When can I see you?"

"I've already called the taxi to take me home. Come to the house after you finish in court today. Bring supper, maybe Chinese or Thai. I think I could tolerate one of those," Nate said.

"OK, see you there," Janet said.

She didn't tell him that she was going to get a recess for the afternoon. She spoke with Judge Carlsson and he'd already decided to postpone the next court session until the following morning. He asked if she wanted a longer recess, but she told him what Nate had said, and the judge just chuckled.

"I knew that would be his attitude. He's the type that'll run all the way to the autopsy table."

Not funny, Judge, Janet thought.

"Hi Nina. I talked to Dad, and as he said, there's good news and bad. The good news is that he's being released from the hospital this afternoon and going home. I'm going to take him some supper and see that he's settled. I'll stay there tonight," Janet said.

"And what's the bad news?" Nina said, knowing deep in her heart that it would be terrible news.

"He has inoperable pancreatic cancer," she said without embellishment. Silence.

"Did they say how long he has?" Nina asked.

"No, most doctors nowadays don't make predictions like that but pancreatic cancer is one of the worst. I think we have to be prepared to accept that Dad will die soon," Janet said quietly, surprising herself with her equanimity.

"What can I do?" Nina said.

"I suppose from the office standpoint, you ought to alert clients they'll need to postpone their appointments until further notice," Janet said. "Anything I can do for you?"

"I'll be fine. I had a hunch he was very sick. Now at least we know why," Nina said, trying not to let the catch in her voice show, before saying goodbye and hanging up.

Janet then sat down to call Jared.

"How's it going?" he said.

"Not very well. The news about Dad is terrible. He has inoperable pancreatic cancer."

Finally the tears came, falling onto her blouse as she told Jared the details about his illness. She had hoped to be able to hold it together, but Jared was so sympathetic, she cried until she was choking on words and hiccups.

"I'm so sorry. I don't know what to say. Of course I'll do anything to help," Jared said.

After a moment of silence, he said, "What happens now with the trial? How did that go today, with all that's on your mind?"

Janet sniffed, regaining control.

"Just OK. Some of these witnesses don't seem as well prepared or knowledgeable as I'd hoped." Her voice grew stronger as she went on. "I'm also getting a sneaking feeling that this controversy about shaken baby syndrome is exaggerated. Most of the docs I respect have little doubt about it and the stuff I'm hearing from these medical experts sounds more like belief than science. Their ideas seem poorly supported by the research.

"You know, Dad is such a true believer. He rejects all doubt. I'm not convinced. Having these guys as witnesses makes me feel…a little soiled. I know that's terrible for a defense attorney to admit, but I can't help it," Janet said.

"One of the reasons I respect you so much is that you're honest and really care about truth. I don't have a clue about all that stuff so I can't offer any opinion. Sounds like you need a hug or a shoulder. When can I see you?" Jared said.

"Let's hope this trial will be over in a week to ten days," Janet said.

"I'd rather not wait that long. Go to plan B," said Jared.

"OK, maybe the weekend. By that time I hope most of the testimony will be completed and I can relax a little," Janet said. "Of course, that depends on Dad. Tonight I have to take food to him and see how he's doing at home," Janet said.

"Do you want me to come with you or do you need solo time with him?"

"I better make sure he's settled, not the best circumstances for you guys to meet," Janet said

"Give him my best. Even though I don't know him, he sounds like a good man," Jared said.

"He is that. But I'll call you tomorrow and make more definite plans. I'm sorry to be so tied up. You know I'd rather be with you than working," Janet said.

"Certainly hope so. Not much of a choice there," Jared said. "Talk to you tomorrow."

"So, who's up tomorrow?" Nate asked after sitting down at the kitchen table and opening the cartons of Chinese food.

"The ophthalmologist, Ralph Constant, from Alabama," Janet said.

"His main message is that retinal hemorrhages are caused by high pressure in the head," Nate said. "Beyond that, I wouldn't get into too much with him because he's pretty old and gets off on tangents. I talked to him by phone once and it took me forever to get off."

"What about the neuropathologist–what's his name–from Boston?" Janet asked.

"Frans van Hooven. He's not coming," Nate said. "He's also pretty old and has had problems with his testimony being contradictory from jurisdiction to jurisdiction. His thing is re-bleeding from old subdurals, but Boyd covered that in his testimony. I can't remember the infectious disease expert, what's his name, Langone?" asked Nate.

"Yes, that's his name, but Nina told me he's not coming either. Which is just as well because I found out he's become a lightening rod for child abuse pediatricians. They hate him, have called for revocation of his medical license and censure by medical societies for unethical behavior in testifying. The societies and the university hospital where he worked won't say anything to criticize him though. They're probably worried that he'll sue them if they discuss his activities outside of the hospital, especially his anti-vaccine rants.

"He's a prominent spokesman for the anti-vaccine crowd whose crusade against vaccines of all kinds is scaring a lot of young parents into withholding vaccines from their kids. Langone has claimed subdural hematomas can be caused by Diphtheria-tetanus-pertussis vaccine. His other theory is that subdurals are caused by venous sinus thrombosis, an infection in a big vein in the head. But prosecutors have successfully shot down both of these theories. The first, about DPT vaccine, is pure hogwash, has no scientific merit. The second condition, venous sinus thrombosis, is rare and usually occurs in terribly sick infants in the first couple of weeks of life," Janet said, surprising herself that she knew that much about him and his testimony.

"Sounds like you should skip him," Nate said. "The only other guy you should get is that general pediatrician. Grasbauskas is his name. He's on our witness list and the prosecutors know about him. He's got this theory that abnormal bleeding is caused by vitamin C deficiency. The best thing about him is that he's a pediatrician. The prosecution might argue that pediatricians are the ones who actually see and treat most of these cases. It's a good idea to have at least one pediatrician who'll argue that shaken baby syndrome doesn't exist and the doctors aren't considering all the possible reasons for these symptoms," Nate said.

"So we could finish with our witnesses tomorrow if I get Grasbauskas to come tomorrow. You think?" Janet said. "Awful short notice for Grasbauskas isn't it?"

"He told me he would drop everything and come at a moment's notice. He doesn't have much going on. I think he's mainly retired," Nate said.

He continued, "What about Chrystal? Think we should put her on?"

"God, I don't know. I think jail has totally squashed any soft spot she might have shown the jury. She has such a tough persona, if she comes across as a surly teenager she won't help herself much. I'll ask her if she even wants to testify. The prosecutors might crucify her," Janet said.

"I'll call Grasbauskas," Nate said. "I'll try to come in tomorrow. While you examine the eye specialist, I'll prep with Grasbauskas and do him in the afternoon. OK?"

"Are you sure you feel up to it for tomorrow? I could do both of them, but I wouldn't have much time to sit with Grasbauskas and get the questions developed," Janet said.

"I feel fine and I want to be there tomorrow. I'll get a cab over in the morning. I'll see if Grasbauskas can get here tonight and I'll get with him in the morning," Nate said.

30

A female attendant brought Chrystal to the defense table. Janet gave her a quick hello, and a shudder of guilt ran through her.

"Chrystal, my father is very sick. He won't be with us today," Janet said. "I'm sorry I haven't been in touch." She received a blank stare in return. She turned away from Chrystal.

I know she's young, lived in an abusive home, she's in the middle of an enormous crisis, she's in jail, confused and scared out of her mind. Why should I expect her to react to Dad's illness, given all that? And maybe she's scared even more that Dad won't be helping me, Janet thought. *But I wish she was more open, more likeable—it would really help me plead her case.*

Today Janet noticed that Judge Carlsson wore a carefully selected yellow bow tie with his judicial black robe, a style statement proclaiming he was no mere gray eminence on the bench. He got the proceedings underway with his usual dispatch.

"Ms. Feingold, will you please approach the bench?" he said.

Confused by this request, wondering if she had somehow offended the judge, she promptly went to the side of the bench furthest from the jury.

He leaned over. "How's Nate today?"

"Oh, he's better. He may even come in later today. Thanks for asking," Janet stammered, surprised that he would bother to inquire.

"Good. That's all I wanted to know."

Janet returned to her table and before she sat down Judge Carlsson said, "Ms. Feingold, please call your first witness."

"Defense calls Dr. Ralph Constant," Janet said. As she turned, her eyes swept the courtroom, and she noticed June again in the back row of the gallery. Chrystal and June locked eyes. No Daryll. Janet wondered what conversations went on in their house. She also saw "The Professor."

Dr. Constant, an overweight, grandfatherly, ruddy-faced man waddled from behind the gates to the witness stand. His tinted glasses added to his difficulty navigating this short distance. His wispy hair barely covered his glistening head. He wore a rumpled gray suit and a dreadful red paisley tie. Janet hoped he'd be a wily, folksy, brilliant witness, a sort of medical Clarence Darrow, but she didn't know what to expect. She had discussed his testimony briefly with him, but she hadn't grasped what his main theme might be.

"Please state your name and occupation," Janet said.

"Ralph, no middle name, Constant," he said and spelled his name. "I'm an ophthalmologist, an eye specialist," he said.

"Where do you practice, Dr. Constant?" Janet asked.

"I'm retired. I was in private practice in the great state of Alabama, in the best town in the world: Tuscaloosa," he said smiling and looking at the jury.

Janet asked about his education, training and experience in the field of ophthalmology, all predictable. He recited the list of Luke's medical records he'd reviewed, looking frequently at the jury to establish rapport. Dr. Constant had obviously done this before. He knew how to work the jury and enjoyed being the center of attention.

"Dr. Constant, what were the eye findings you consider important in Luke Talbot?"

"This poor child had lots of retinal hemorrhages, blood in the vitreous humor, retinal folds, and more bleeding underneath the membranes surrounding the optic nerves. All terrible stuff," he said in a mournful voice.

"Let's take these one at a time, Doctor. Tell us about the retinal hemorrhages first," Janet said.

"Well," he said, turning to the jury to give them the full benefit of his teaching experience and his radio announcer's voice, "The retina's made up of ten layers of tissue. Different kinds of tissue, but all having a particular function, you see."

"There's lots and lots of tiny little blood vessels in these layers," he said, pinching his thumb and forefinger together. "When these little blood vessels burst, blood leaks out and that's what we call retinal hemorrhages. These were all over the retina, in many layers," he said.

"What could cause these retinal hemorrhages, doctor?" Janet said, glad he was talking medicine now instead of flirting with the jury.

"Many things can cause retinal hemorrhages and that's the whole problem in this case. A lot of doctors–especially pediatricians," he peered with great seriousness at the jury as he said this, "don't consider all the possibilities in these head injury cases. They jump to the conclusion that retinal hemorrhages are always caused by shaking. But there are many, many reasons we see retinal hemorrhages. Infections can cause them, even just giving birth–pushing that baby out–you ladies in the jury who've had babies know what I'm talkin' about here."

He turned his attention back to Janet.

"High pressure inside the head can cause them. Blood clotting abnormalities can cause them. Vitamin C deficiency can cause them. Accidents can cause them. Cardiopulmonary resuscitation–you know–what we call CPR for short–when you give mouth to mouth and push hard on the chest to get the heart going–that can also cause them. Convulsions can cause them. The list goes on and on. And if the doctors don't check out all these reasons, they're not doin' their jobs right and they can make awful mistakes, messin' up whole families, sending innocent people to jail," he said.

Mary Egan jumped to her feet. "Objection!" and Judge Carlsson immediately admonished Dr. Constant to restrict himself to answering the questions and not editorializing. *"Once the bell has rung, you can't un-ring it,"* Janet thought of the old legal cliché.

"In Luke Talbot's case, in your expert opinion as an ophthalmologist, what caused his retinal hemorrhages?" Janet asked.

"Increased pressure in the head due to the subdural hematoma and brain swelling. The retinal hemorrhages happen because of back pressure in the veins of the retina. Just like your pipes backing up in your house that cause leaks," he said, eyes turned directly toward the jury.

"Not shaking or impact?" Janet asked.

"No, shaking doesn't cause retinal hemorrhages and neither does impact," Constant said categorically.

"What about the vitreous hemorrhage? Oh, let's back up. What is a vitreous hemorrhage, Doctor Constant?" Janet said.

"The vitreous humor is the jelly-like stuff inside the eyeball. A vitreous hemorrhage is bleeding into that jelly," he said. "In this case, the vitreous hemorrhage was caused by high pressure in the head."

"Can you tell us about the retinal folds?"

"That's a little confusing, but I'll try. Retinal folds are lines along the edges of little cavities of split layers of the retina. Some ophthalmologists who believe in shaken baby syndrome mistakenly call retinal folds diagnostic for shaken baby syndrome, but they're not."

"What do the hemorrhages around the optic nerve tell you?" Janet asked.

"More pressure. More leakage due to ruptured veins," he said.

"So let me ask you this: Do you think that Luke was shaken, causing his retinal hemorrhages?" Janet asked.

"Absolutely not. His retinal hemorrhages came on, as I said, because of increased pressure in his head due to brain swelling and the blood under the dura. And as I said, the back pressure on the veins of the optic nerve caused those tiny little blood vessels in the retina to snap and leak," Dr. Constant said. "I believe this whole thing was due to an accident, probably a fall onto his head, that happened several days before the day the babysitter took care of him. The blood clot from that accident got stirred up when Luke had his temper tantrum and the rest is history," he concluded.

Dad prepped these expert witnesses so their testimony would be identical. They all claimed old injury and reactivation on the day he was brought to the hospital. Very neat, very plausible to a lay jury. The very definition of a specious argument. But was it true?

"Thank you Doctor, no further questions."

"Ms. Egan? Your witness," Judge Carlsson said.

"Good morning, Dr. Constant," Mary said.

"Good morning to you, Counselor," Constant said with a wide grin.

"In your practice of ophthalmology, did you care for children?" Mary asked.

"Sure did. Loved seein' the little ones," he said.

"Were these children seen in your office, or did you see them in the hospital?"

"Both places."

"Did you consult on cases of head trauma in children?" Mary said.

"Yes."

"How often?"

"Oh, I can't remember things like that," he said.

"Well, let's ask this a different way, then. Did you consult on infant head injury cases once a week?" Mary asked.

"Not that often," he answered.

Mary went on to try and establish some frequency of his involvement but he was hard to pin down.

"Well, over the course of your career, would you say you have personally seen, maybe, five cases altogether?"

"About that."

"But you're still sure of your position that shaking and impact doesn't cause the injuries we've heard described in Luke Talbot?"

"Dead sure," he said, completely unaware that the colloquialism was inappropriate.

"You said in the direct examination by Ms. Feingold that Luke's retinal hemorrhages were caused by pressure in the head. Is that right?" Mary asked.

"Yes."

"So is it your theory that the high pressure within the head prevents blood in the retinal veins from getting out of the eyes?" Mary asked.

"Yes, you can't force blood back out of these veins if the pressure in the head is high. The blood just won't flow," he said.

"Are you aware of this recent article addressing how intracranial pressure is unassociated with retinal hemorrhages?" Mary asked.

"Not sure I know that article," he said.

Mary went to her table, picked up a reprint, and took it to Dr. Constant.

"Will you please tell the court what the conclusions of this articles are?" Mary said.

"Well, it says that lots of retinal hemorrhages in babies are not due to high intracranial pressure," Dr. Constant said. "But in the first sentence they talk about just what I've said–alternatives. Besides, one paper doesn't change the whole field," he said.

"Here's another paper I'd like you to see. Please read the conclusions of this article that I've highlighted there," Mary said as she handed him the paper.

"Increased intracranial pressure is accompanied by papilledema," he read.

"Doctor, can you tell the court what papilledema is?" Mary said.

"Sure. Papilledema is due to high pressure in the head causing the optic nerve at the back of the eye globe to swell up. You can see that with an ophthalmoscope," he said, turning to the jury.

"Did Luke have papilledema either clinically or at autopsy?" Mary asked.

"No. But...."

Mary cut him off. "Just answer the question, doctor. Did Luke have papilledema?"

"No. At least it was not described in the medical records. Of course it could've been missed."

"Please read the next passage in the second paragraph that is highlighted," Mary said.

"Experimentally, increased intracranial pressure in animals does not cause retinal hemorrhages at all," he read.

Mary handed Dr. Constant another paper.

"Will you tell the court the results of that study?"

"Nearly all the children with subdural hematomas from accidental head injury had no retinal hemorrhages. Only two children had retinal hemorrhages and they were few in number and were in only one layer of the retina," Dr. Constant read.

"Don't all those papers contradict what you just told the court in your direct testimony?" Mary asked.

"It's the exceptions that prove the rule," he said.

"Doctor, please answer my question: Don't these papers clearly show that increased intracranial pressure does not cause multilayered, extensive retinal hemorrhages?" Mary persisted.

"Three papers don't make this true," he said.

"Alright, Dr. Constant. Let's go about this in another way. Can you cite recent scientific, peer-reviewed papers that prove your claim that raised intracranial pressure causes such hemorrhages?" Mary said, rising incredulousness in her voice.

"Proof? What's proof? I can't quote papers like that. Most of this depends on clinical experience, not studies," he said.

"So now you're saying your conclusions come from your 'clinical experience,' and yet you've seen a miniscule number of these cases person-ally–five perhaps, over the course of an entire career. Is that what you're saying?" Mary thrust back.

"Clinical experience of mine, plus that of my colleagues with whom I speak," he said.

Dismissing this with no comment, Mary went on. "Here's another paper I'd like you to see. What does this paper say?"

"Well, it says that raised intracranial pressure only rarely causes retinal hemorrhages," he said.

"Doesn't it also say that when retinal hemorrhages *are* seen in cases with raised intracranial pressure, that they are intraretinal hemorrhages, the kind of retinal hemorrhages present accompanying papilledema?"

"Yes."

"Again, did Luke have papilledema?" Mary asked.

"No."

"You also said in your testimony that doctors–especially pediatricians–fail to consider all the possibilities. Please look at the medical record at Children's Hospital," Mary said. "How many possibilities do you see in the admission note, in the part called 'Impressions'?" Mary asked.

"There are eleven listed," he said, after looking at the record.

"Did you check to see if all of them had been investigated and ruled out?"

He paged through the record, and after several minutes, said, "In this case, they did look at these possibilities."

"And it's this case we are talking about, right?" said Mary.

"Yes."

"I have no other questions, Your Honor."

Janet stood up. "No questions, Your Honor."

"You may step down, Doctor.

"Thank you," Judge Carlsson said. "Court will reconvene after lunch."

Janet looked over at Chrystal to gauge her response to the skewering of this key defense witness by the prosecution. She gave no indication of realizing how feeble his testimony had been, making Janet wonder if she hadn't paid attention or simply that she didn't understand any of the testimony.

As Mary walked back to her table, she was gratified to see some relief on the Talbots' faces as they watched Dr. Constant being revealed as a fraud.

"The trial's not over, by any means, but today belongs to us," Mary said to Albert.

31

Janet tapped in Nate's phone number once out of the courtroom. He picked up after the first ring.

"Dad? How're you doing? Where are you?" Janet said.

"I'm fine. I'm sitting over at Hanrahan's right now, upstairs, and I'll buy you lunch if you're ready," he said.

"I'll be right over. We just finished with Dr. Constant," Janet said.

"How'd it go?" Nate asked.

"Tell you about it over lunch. See you in a few minutes," Janet said.

Nate was dressed for court. His illness wasn't going to constrain his mission to disprove the theory of shaken baby syndrome. He was going over the notes he'd made during his morning with Dr. Grasbauskas when Janet walked in. They hugged and she exhaled deeply as she ran her fingers through her hair, realizing that this would be a meeting with her father, the defense attorney, not her father, the cancer patient. She would have to be honest.

"Dr. Constant was a smarmy bag of wind," she said.

"Really? That surprises me. His CV was good and the conclusions he sent in his letter seemed credible. I talked with him on the phone; he seemed great. What do you mean, 'smarmy bag of wind'?"

"Oh, he was so treacly with his folksy manner. He stopped just short of winkin' and blinkin' at the jurors. He also doesn't know what he's talking about. Mary undressed him on the stand and his testimony was worthless. Sorry, I know you thought these experts would be spectacular and win the case for us, but so far they're not convincing, even to me. What do you do when you feel a case is slipping away?" Janet asked, nearly in tears.

"You pull up your socks and keep fighting! That's what you do! Don't let the bastards grind you down! We're gonna win this case because the truth is on our side!" Nate exclaimed, at high volume.

Janet looked around to see if anyone was eavesdropping but, to her great relief, they were the only patrons on the upper floor. She hadn't seen her father this worked up since his clients went to jail for money laundering in a case ten years ago.

"I'm sorry, Dad. I know how strongly you feel about shaken baby syndrome, but I have to tell you—I'm not sure Chrystal didn't shake and slam this baby. I know you're not supposed to conclude guilt or innocence of your clients, but I can't help it in this one. Chrystal is a royal pain in the ass. She can barely manage a civil word to me. I know she's had a horrible life with that monstrous stepfather, and now she's standing trial for murdering a baby. But I've tried everything to penetrate her shield and nothing works. I thought I saw a glimmer of humanity in her, but that spark was temporary. I hate to think of her in jail for years. But I'm beginning to think she did this and she can't admit it even to herself. Or maybe she's a pathological liar, I can't tell," Janet said.

Nate winced.

"Look, I'll do Grasbauskas this afternoon," he said. "Then we can talk about the closing argument. I could do it if you go on feeling this way. What do you think?"

"I don't know. I hate to be a quitter like that. If you weren't around I'd have to see it through. But I admit: I'm down on Chrystal. I hate this diagnosis and these so-called medical experts. I know Chrystal deserves a strong defense, but I may not be able to give it to her. That's the worst failing of a defense attorney."

Nate didn't answer right away. He had always preached that a defense attorney should never, ever let personal feelings enter into the work, and never, ever come to a verdict about a client. But this was his daughter, and he was dying. He didn't want some of his last words to be hurtful ones. He also didn't want Janet to decide whether to close right now; that decision could wait. This afternoon's examination of Grasbauskas was immediate.

"I'll do Grasbauskas this afternoon. Then we'll talk, OK?" Nate said.

"OK. Thanks. You think I'm foolish?" Janet asked.

"Of course you're foolish. You're a defense attorney. Only foolish people do that. I'm foolish too—but what a life I've had being foolish!" Nate said, showing some of the old exuberance and charm that had made him so successful.

They went down the creaky stairs at Hanrahan's out into the bright wintry day. When they got back to the courthouse, Janet and Nate hurried past the press. Nate waved them off. He didn't want to field any questions about his absence in court, get into the whole issue of his illness. He didn't know whether they even knew about that yet, but he didn't want to make that the headline of the day. He'd talk to them after he'd finished with Grasbauskas.

When the court reconvened, Judge Carlsson winked at Nate as he rose up onto the bench and asked Nate to call his next witness.

Nate rose and in a strong voice said, "Defense calls Dr. Neil Grasbauskas."

Neil Grasbauskas strode briskly to the witness box, took the oath, and seated himself, adjusting the microphone upwards.

He stated his name, and then Nate said, "Tell us about your education and training, Dr. Grasbauskas."

"I went to State University and their medical school, then did my pediatric residency at St. Anthony's Hospital. Since then I have been in the private practice of pediatrics in Charleston, West Virginia," he said.

"Are you Board Certified in Pediatrics?"

"Yes, since 1987."

After Grasbuaskas detailed the medical records he'd examined, Nate said, "On the basis of the records you have examined, and your training and experience as a pediatrician, do you have an opinion as to the cause of Luke's fatal outcome?" Nate asked.

"Yes, I do."

"And what is that opinion?"

"I think Luke had a pre-existing condition that made him more vulnerable to injury; namely, he had vaccinations prior to this fatal event that predisposed him to a bleeding disorder and that was complicated by vitamin C deficiency. He had a prolonged prothrombin time when he was tested at the hospital indicating a clotting disorder. Then he had a head injury from a short fall two to three weeks prior to his hospitalization causing a subdural hematoma. He had a lucid interval during those intervening weeks. Then the struggling during his bath disrupted that subdural and it bled again. This raised the pressure in his head and that led to his retinal hemorrhages and, ultimately, to his death," Dr. Grasbauskas said.

"Are you saying that a vaccine Luke got caused a bleeding disorder?" Nate asked.

"Yes, hepatitis A vaccine has been shown to be associated with thrombocytopenia, a deficiency in platelets that can lead to bleeding disorders. Not only that, but encephalitis has been shown to be associated with DTP vaccine, and Luke had both of those shots. There have even been cases of respiratory arrest following vaccine administration!" he emphasized.

"How does vitamin C deficiency enter into this?" Nate asked.

"Vitamin C is necessary for collagen formation. If it's not in sufficient amounts in the diet or supplements, collagen doesn't develop properly. A lack of collagen makes blood vessels weak; they can rupture and hemorrhaging takes place. This accounts for the subdural hematoma secondary to the short fall two to three weeks before Luke became seriously ill and was hospitalized," Grasbauskas said.

"How do you account for the skull fracture?" Nate asked.

"Well, the skull fracture undoubtedly occurred when he fell. I have no doubt that that fracture was two to three weeks old. The CPR by the emergency medical crew could've produced the retinal hemorrhages, but I really think the retinal hemorrhages were more likely due to low platelets secondary to the hepatitis vaccine abetted by vitamin C deficiency-induced poor collagen development in the tiny vessels of the retina. Any small trauma could have caused the retinal hemorrhages with that combination of clotting disorder," he said.

"Thank you Dr. Grasbauskas. No further questions, Your Honor," Nate said.

Mary Egan had been furiously making notes on her legal pad when Nate finished questioning Grasbauskas and was not quite ready to begin her cross examination. She was surprised that Nate finished so abruptly and rose slowly from her chair.

"Judge, can you give me a minute, please?" she said.

"Perhaps this is a good time to have a short break," Judge Carlsson said. "Let's take a 15 minute recess."

Mary turned to Albert. "Have you ever heard such malarkey? I did find some articles about these weird theories he's talking about. Unfortunately, they're on my desk in the office. I didn't anticipate that I'd need them but it looks like I will to cross-examine him. Can you get them for me? I'll go ahead with him once we're back in session, even if you're not back," she said, handing the references to him.

When court reconvened, Mary stood at the lectern and said, "Good afternoon, Doctor. My name is Mary Egan, I'm one of the Assistant District Attorneys prosecuting this case."

"Hello."

"You're a practicing general pediatrician, right?" Mary opened.

"That's correct," Grasbauskas said.

"In the course of a year in your practice, how many cases of head injuries would you care for?"

"Oh, it varies from year to year. Hard to put a number on it," he said.

"Please try, Doctor," Mary said.

"In the course of a year? I guess…I don't know…maybe five?" he said.

"Is that a question, or your answer?" Mary asked.

"OK, let's say five as a fair estimate," he said.

"And of those five, how many are accidental?"

"Maybe three?"

"Again, is that a question, or your answer?"

"That's my answer, Counselor," he said.

"Then are two of them something else, like vitamin C deficiency or a clotting disorder?" Mary asked.

"My private practice is not a fair population to ask about since…"

"Just answer the question, Doctor," Mary said, interrupting.

"I don't keep a record of things like that," he said.

"Doctor, let me try to understand what you said when Mr. Feingold was questioning you. Did you say you believe the hepatitis and DTP vaccines Luke got caused him to have poor clotting, and vitamin C deficiency caused his blood vessels to be fragile and then leak. Is that correct?" Mary said.

"That's correct," Dr. Grasbauskas said.

"Did you also say Luke had a pre-existing subdural blood clot in his head that was stirred up by his temper tantrum? Is that about right?" Mary asked.

"Yes, that's a fair summary of what I said," Grasbauskas said.

"What research do you rely on when you claim vitamin C deficiency causes subdural bleeding and retinal hemorrhages?" Mary asked.

"An article in the *United Kingdom Medical Journal*, in which the author said that vitamin C deficiency led to capillary fragility and rupture and was responsible for subdural and retinal hemorrhages in infants," he said.

"Was this a scientific study of this problem?" Mary asked.

"That's right," Grasbauskas said.

Mary glanced at the prosecution table to see if Albert was back. He was, nodding to her. She hurried over to the table to get the papers he had brought back.

Ruffling through, she found the paper in question. She looked at it for a minute and then handed it to Grasbauskas.

"Is this the publication you're talking about?" she asked.

He looked at the paper, paused a moment and said, "I think so, yes."

"Isn't that really just a letter to the editor expressing the author's opinion about vitamin C deficiency and capillary fragility, not a research publication?" Mary said.

"Yes, but it's based on his research," he said.

"Can you tell me where his research findings are published?"

"I think it's unpublished data, but I've talked with him and I believe his conclusions," Grasbauskas said.

"Are you asking the court to believe that a letter to the editor expressing an opinion based on unpublished data should be considered evidence?" Mary asked, her voice dripping with skepticism.

"Yes, I am."

"Thank you, Doctor."

Mary allowed a few beats to pass for the full impact of her question and Grasbauskas' answer to register.

"Are you aware of the large number of papers about head injury–both accidental and abusive–that link abnormal prothrombin time to the actual trauma to the brain?"

"Yeah, that's one explanation. But I think in Luke's case it was due to low platelets and vitamin C deficiency," he said.

Mary picked up the hospital record and turned to the laboratory reports section.

"Doctor, look at the report of the platelet count done at the time of Luke's admission to the hospital and tell me if it's abnormal," Mary said.

He looked at the lab report.

"Well, the platelets are normal but on the low side of normal, and that, combined with his vitamin C deficiency, led to his bleeding," he said.

"If Luke had something wrong with his blood clotting apparatus why is it that the only places he was bleeding were in his head and eyes? Wouldn't a generalized clotting disorder cause bleeding all over the body, say in the kidneys, or the skin, or the joints where kids with hemophilia bleed?"

"Because it's in his head where he bled before and that clot disrupted," he answered.

"Isn't it true that there is no evidence that he had an old subdural hematoma?" Mary said in a louder voice.

"He got that at the same time he got the skull fracture, and that's three weeks old," he said.

"How do you know that the skull fracture is three weeks old?" Mary asked.

"That's my opinion," he said.

She stood there, hands on hips, glaring at Grasbauskas, then decided to move on. She handed Grasbauskas another paper. "Returning to your assertion that CPR might have caused Luke's retinal hemorrhages, would you please tell the court what the researchers did in this study?"

He examined the paper for a few minutes.

"They looked at the retinas in the eyes of patients with clotting disorders who had gotten CPR in their hospital," he said.

"Now will you please read the conclusions of the paper?" Mary said.

"Well, they found a few retinal hemorrhages in one patient. So they concluded that retinal hemorrhages are rare after chest compressions in patients with bleeding disorders."

"Doesn't that refute your argument that CPR might have caused the retinal hemorrhages?" Mary said.

"One paper doesn't refute my argument," he said.

She went to the prosecutor's table and gathered up four more papers. "Well, here are four other papers that say exactly the same thing," Mary said, shaking the papers in the air. "Would you like to see these and read the results?"

"No, you wouldn't bring papers into court that say otherwise," he snapped. "There are still the vitamin C and hepatitis vaccine influences," he said. "And also the DTP vaccine, don't forget that!" he said.

Mary returned to the prosecution table and brought another document to Dr. Grasbauskas. She paused and walked to the end of the jury box. "Doctor, please read the conclusion of this enormous national vaccine study, that looked at a half million children."

He read the conclusion that stated that the study did not show that Diphtheria Tetanus Pertussis (DTP) vaccine caused damage to the brain.

Mary quickly turned her back on him, walked to the lectern, wheeled around and said, "Dr. Grasbauskas, have you ever diagnosed a child with shaken baby syndrome?"

"Never. I don't believe there is such a thing. I don't think you can shake a baby hard enough to cause all that damage and not have neck injuries. And biomechanical engineers tell us that you can't generate enough force to cause subdurals. So I've never made that diagnosis," he said.

"What studies tell you that neck injuries have to be present in these cases?" Mary asked, knowing what his inevitable response would be, since it was the standard response of all the defense witnesses.

Grasbauskas cited the same studies the other defense experts had used in their testimony, and of course Mary was able to discredit them using the same arguments she had used with the other witnesses. She focused on the one with the math errors in it, but Grasbauskas merely dismissed this.

"I don't think the author intentionally misled anyone," he said.

"But, Dr. Grasbauskas, aren't his paper's conclusions just plain wrong because of his bad math?"

"If you want to view it that way," he said.

Janet sank lower in her chair. She tried to look busy by making notes on her legal pad as Grasbauskas became more undone. She glanced at Nate to see if he was going to object to any of these questions, but knew there was nothing in the questions that was objectionable. Unless, of course, if you're a defense attorney and you're watching another highly paid expert melt down on the stand.

"I have no further questions, Your Honor," Mary spat out.

Nate got up and said, "Dr. Grasbauskas, the prosecution is trying to turn the jury's attention away from your basic testimony. Will you please restate your theory of the case so that jurors can hear it once more?"

"Objection, Your Honor. Asked and answered earlier. No need to repeat that testimony," said Albert.

"Sustained. Any other questions, Mr. Feingold?"

Nate hesitated, looked down at his notes, and finally said, "No, Your Honor."

"In that case, I need to know if either side has any more witnesses?" the judge asked.

"Your Honor, I have a rebuttal witness I'd like to present," Mary said.

The judge looked hard at Mary for a few seconds.

"Will all the attorneys please visit me for a side bar conversation?"

When they had gathered at the sidebar out of the jury's earshot, Carlsson said, "We've had enough medical testimony to choke a pig. Over a dozen medical experts. What can possibly be added by having another doctor testify? More medical testimony will only confuse the jury. I'll think about this overnight and decide in the morning."

Mary flushed, Albert clenched his fists and they both spoke at once.

Judge Carlsson shushed them and said, "One at a time."

"Our medical testimony was from fact witnesses," Albert said. We haven't presented one independent expert. We have Dr. Thomas Sturgis, a child abuse pediatrician, who's come all the way from Los Angeles to testify. I don't think it's fair not to let our expert testify, the same way the defense had their independent experts."

"While it may be true that your doctors were all fact witnesses, they're also experts in their fields, and I accepted them as experts. So the two sides have each had their experts testify. I repeat, I'll make my decision known to you tomorrow morning. That's it," Judge Carlsson said.

Knowing that further argument was futile, and that it could even alienate and irritate Judge Carlsson, both Mary and Albert turned and returned to the prosecution table. They gathered up their paraphernalia and headed out right after the judge adjourned court for the day. Even in the hall, they had to keep their cool since the press was eager to get their take on the day's events. In one corner of the hallway, a clutch of reporters was interviewing Janet and Nate. Several rushed over to Mary and Albert.

"Who's your rebuttal witness gonna be?" yelled the TV reporter.

"Judge Carlsson will decide tomorrow if we'll be allowed a rebuttal witness. I'll name him then if he's allowed to testify. The judge wants to get the case to the jury as soon as possible," Mary said evenly.

"How do you feel about that?" taunted the wag from the tabloid paper.

"It's the judge's call. Of course I hope we're given the opportunity to present our rebuttal witness," Albert said.

In the other corner, one reporter asked Nate about Grasbauskas' testimony.

"I thought he handled it real well. Hard questioning, but he knew the answers and I thought he made his points," Nate said.

"Looked to me like he was struggling," the reporter said.

"He did fine," Nate said.

"Are you going to put Chrystal on the stand?" another reporter asked.

"Of course, we'll offer her the opportunity, but I think she won't want to testify. She's been under so much pressure," Janet said.

"Thanks for your questions," Nate said. "We've work to do and we'll talk to you after closing arguments tomorrow. Thanks!"

His upbeat steps toward the door were counter to how bushed and in need of a drink he felt. Janet took his arm and they left amid a chorus of questions, heading to his office to discuss how they'd handle the closing arguments.

While the lawyers were occupied in court, dreadful things had been afoot at the Watts household. When Janet glanced at her cell phone, she saw a message from Sue Edgerton, a social worker at St. Joseph's Hospital. The message: "I need to talk to you–urgent." She left no details.

32

"Today you're not goin' to court," Daryll said. "I need you at the store. What good are you doin' there anyhow? Ask Chrystal what happens. You get one phone call a day with her. So get your ass in gear and come along."

"I'm not coming to the store. Chrystal needs to see me in court. No one else cares about her. I have to support her even if it's only sitting in the back row. She's got no one else. Nobody, not even you, can make me desert my own daughter in her time of need," June said.

Her uncharacteristic insistence on going to her daughter's trial every day had compelled Daryll to manage the store by himself since the trial began. With each day of her absence his anger had grown.

Without warning, Daryll erupted.

"God damn you! You don't give a shit about me, only that little bitch of a daughter! I'm gonna have to teach you a real lesson!" Daryl screamed. His arms whirled, his fists landing savagely on June's eyes, her cheeks, and her mouth, dislodging several teeth. He pounded her back when she turned away to flee and drove her into the wall, crushing her shoulder. She ducked under his fist, which crashed into the wall with such force that it broke the plasterboard. The back of his hand bulged as he drew it back from the hole in the wall.

June ran to the bedroom. With fumbling fingers, she locked the door.

"Come back here!" Daryll shrieked, holding his swelling hand. "Let me in!" He pounded on the bedroom door. June cowered against the far wall, praying that the hinges would hold. "You better be here when I get back or there'll be hell to pay! You hear?" Daryll shouted. Then he did what habit dictated: he went to the store.

Eyes swollen and bruises spreading down her distorted broken nose, June trembled. Her lips were bloodied, looking like slabs of liver. She could scarcely move her arms because of exquisite pain in her shoulders. When she breathed, a bolt like lightening radiated from her shoulders and chest. Her rib cage protested every breath.

The silence in the house let June know Daryll was gone. She dialed 911. After years of insults and abuse, she mustered newfound courage to call the police.

"Knock. Knock," sounded on her door a few minutes later.

She opened it carefully and saw the officer standing on the front stoop. "Someone called the police. Said there was a problem at this address," the cop said as he scanned June's face and knew why he was there.

"I called," June said. "I've had enough. My husband beat me up. I need a doctor. I hurt all over. My shoulder hurts real bad, and I think I got a couple of busted ribs."

"Your husband here?" the cop said.

"No, he went to work at the store."

"I'll need a statement from you. How this happened, who did it, and where I can find him. We'll arrest him, but you'll have to bring charges and testify that he did this to you. Otherwise it's pointless. If you're planning on getting back together, this is a big waste of time," the cop said, betraying a weariness born of many such encounters.

"I'll testify. I can't live this way anymore. He's done this before, not as bad, but I never want to see him, ever again."

The cop nodded. An old story. Once the acute pain was gone, the perpetrator would sweet talk the victim into taking him back. He'll say "one last time-I'll never do that again"-and then the cops would have to respond to the next call. He could only hope this woman would stick to her statement.

The cop called an ambulance to transport June to the hospital. She got her purse and quickly packed a bag. When the ambulance arrived, the EMT's put her on the gurney. June glanced around, hoping none of the neighbors were watching.

After being treated at the hospital and giving the police her statement naming Daryll as the perpetrator, Susan Edgerton, the hospital social worker, talked with her. Within an hour Sue had secured a bed for June at Lori's Place, one of the larger shelters in the city for domestic violence victims.

Sergeants Kevin Murphy and Tim Coogan drove to the convenience store. Daryll, always hyper-vigilant, watched the police car park across the street. Never a good sign when two cops walked into the store. One cop, different story. One cop would buy a pack of cigarettes or a candy bar, but when they came in pairs, it was business. He wasn't taking any chances. He opened the drawer under the cash register and took out his Glock, checked to see that it was loaded, took off the safety, and waited until the cops came in the front door.

"Good morning. I'm Officer Coogan and this here is Officer Murphy. We're looking for Daryll Watts. Is he here?" the officer said.

"I'm Watts. Whaddya want?"

"Is June Watts your wife?"

"Yeah, what's it to you?"

"She's at the hospital. She says you beat her up. Is that true?"

Daryll was back in Iraq. The two Arabs who had come out of nowhere stood in his path, both with knives. Daryll summoned all his speed, all his training in killing, and sprayed so many bullets into them that their bodies were shattered. In his maniacal state, he continued to fire his automatic weapon until it was empty. He frantically looked around and saw four more hate-filled fighters surrounding him, glaring at him. He was powerless with no more rounds. At the last moment, all four collapsed from gunfire from his buddies hiding behind a crumbling wall. Daryll was saved from certain death but scarred by terror.

This time, he wasn't going to be caught without defenses. He pulled the Glock from under the counter, aimed it at Murphy.

"Get the fuck outta here or you're dead meat!"

Coogan whipped out his service revolver. "Drop it, or I'll fire."

Daryll turned on him and fired one shot that struck his arm, the gun clattering to the floor. In a millisecond, Murphy drew his gun, squeezed off a round as soon as it was out of his holster, fired point blank at Daryll, killing him instantly with a bullet through his chest. Murphy quickly dropped to his knees to find out how badly wounded his partner was.

"Tim, are you OK?" Murphy said.

"Hurts like hell," Coogan said. "But I'm not bleeding bad. Think it's pretty minor."

Murphy called for an ambulance, checked Coogan again, dialed the station, and reported what had happened. Within minutes, numerous police arrived, the ambulance came for Coogan, and the convenience store was turned into a crime scene.

June was still talking to the social worker when the message came about Daryll.

"Oh God, I didn't want him dead. I just wanted to be away from him," she sobbed. "Oh God, Oh God. What've I done? Oh Jesus, Mary and Joseph. I'll burn in hell."

Sue Edgerton put her arm around her and grasped her hand, but June was inconsolable. She wailed and groaned and each time she took a deep breath, her broken ribs ripped with searing pain. Her shoulders ached and her face hurt. She was desperate. One of the Emergency Room doctors heard her keening and finally injected her with Valium. Within minutes, she was asleep.

When June woke up, she asked to talk to Sue.

"My daughter is Chrystal Begley, the girl who's on trial in that Talbot baby case. You must've heard about it on the TV. I got to get word to her about what's happened. And where I'll be."

"Let me think," the social worker said. "How can I get in touch with her? Do you know her lawyer's name?"

"Name is Janet something. Her father's helping her in the case. Two of them with the same last name. Maybe I can find her card," June said, and emptied the contents of her purse onto the table. "Here it is. Janet Feingold. And that's her number right there."

"I'm looking for Sue Edgerton. This is Janet Feingold returning her call."

"Oh, Ms. Feingold. Thanks for returning my call. I'm here with June Watts, Chrystal's mother. She says she was beaten up by her husband

Daryll. She has a lot of facial bruises, some broken ribs and shoulder injuries. As you can imagine, she's distraught. She's patched up enough that she won't have to stay in the hospital. She's scheduled to go home when they release her medically. And there's more…"

Janet said, "I'll be right over. Where can I find you?"

After jotting down Susan's phone number, Janet jumped into a taxi and headed to St. Joseph's Hospital. She was getting familiar with this Emergency Department, the same place Nate had been. She raced to the admitting desk, identified herself, and asked for Sue Edgerton. She was led into the typically small office the hospital set aside for social workers, and in a few moments Sue appeared. She looked the part: fortyish, plump, brown hair pulled back in a bun, pleasant smooth face, and a look that said, "It's all right. Let's talk."

"Hi, I'm Sue Edgerton."

She filled Janet in on the sequence of events. She also told her the news about Daryll's death and some details about what happened with Coogan and Murphy. Coogan was also brought to St. Joseph's, and the news was all through the Emergency Department.

"Where's June now?" Janet asked.

"She's down the hall in the chapel. She wanted time to pray and gather herself," Sue said. "I'll bring her here."

As soon as June saw Janet, she began weeping. Janet cradled her head on her shoulder and gently rocked her.

"How can I tell Chrystal?" June asked.

"Want me to tell her?" Janet heard herself saying.

"Would you?"

After talking for a few more minutes with June and Sue, Janet headed to the jail. She was hungry but that could wait. She needed to tell Chrystal what had transpired.

When Chrystal came into the lawyers' interview room, her face was blank as usual.

"I have some bad news, Chrystal," Janet began. "I guess I'll get right to it. Your mother was beaten up by Daryll. Your stepfather is dead, shot by the police when he resisted arrest at the convenience store. As you can imagine, your mother is devastated. She wanted me to tell you."

"Is Mom OK? I mean, was she hurt bad?" Chrystal asked.

"She looks terrible, but the doctors say she'll heal pretty well. Some broken ribs, a broken shoulder, and a lot of bruises on her face. She was released from the hospital and is probably home by now.

"Daryll's dead?"

"Yes. He shot at one of the cops and the cop's partner shot and killed him," Janet said.

Chrystal's eye narrowed. "I'm glad he's dead. He's the worst kind of animal. June always said he had PTSD from the war, but he was screwed up before he went in the Army. That PTSD stuff was just an excuse for being mean and bullying my mother and me. I hope he rots in hell," Chrystal said.

"Your mother feels guilty because she called the police and reported his assault," Janet said.

"She always feels guilty about everything. She needs to see somebody, other than a priest. They tell her to say a few 'Hail Mary's,' put some money in the box, and pray to Jesus–that'll take care of everything. Such bullshit. I've tried to talk to her, but she never listens. Says I'm just a kid and I don't understand about life. She's the one that doesn't understand about life."

After a few minutes of silence, Chrystal said, "I was listening to those doctors that testified. They all seemed to say the same things, like they were rehearsed or something."

Janet didn't reply.

"You know, I had a dream last night," Chrystal said. "I dreamed Daryl was whipping my boobs and my belly with his belt. I was so pissed I wanted to fight back. And then there was this screaming little brat, with his red, screwed-up face, all smeared with cereal, and I lost it. I grabbed him under his arms and shook the shit out of him, back and forth, over and over again, until my arms got all rubbery and I couldn't hardly breathe. Then I hit the back of his head against the bathtub. I did all that 'cause I was mad as hell that he kicked me in my boobs, reminded me of Daryll,"

Janet and Chrystal stared at each other.

Now tearful, Chrystal said, "Could that have been what really happened? They say that dreams do tell you about stuff that happens when you're awake. I woke up in a cold sweat, and I'm still nervous wondering if I did that to Luke."

Janet sat mesmerized. This was the most Chrystal had said about what might have happened since the beginning of this dreadful case.

Was she describing a dream, or was she making a veiled confession? What she was saying was the exact scenario the hospital doctors had described. So, does this mean that she IS guilty? If she's saying she did this, what now?

"Chrystal, was that a dream? Or is that what really happened?"

"Well, if it happened that way" her old defenses had returned – "and I'm not saying it did- what are you going to do? The trial's almost over."

"If it did happen that way, you would have to say that in your testimony if we put you on the stand. Let's talk about the possibility of changing your plea. If you changed your plea from not guilty to a plea of guilty to a lesser charge–like manslaughter–it's possible you would get a lesser sentence," Janet said.

"But I'd still go to jail, right?"

"I don't know what the sentence would be, but it'd involve some jail time. Less than if you get convicted on a second degree murder charge, and frankly, I'm afraid your chances of getting a not guilty are not great right now."

Chrystal looked out the window. Janet let her silence drift in the air. Raindrops splattered on the windowsill. A starling landed outside the window, head jerking around, then flew away. The wind made music as it passed the window. The guard outside the interview room moved and keys clattered.

At length, Chrystal said, "I'll take my chances with the jury. I been watchin' them. Don't think they're so sharp. I only need one, right, to get off? Isn't that what your father said?"

"Yes, technically, it only takes one juror to side with you."

Chrystal looked up at Janet, losing the bravado she'd been showing. Her face was pale, her eyes wide open. Her hand trembled as she reached up to brush hair from her forehead. The pulse in her neck was thrumming faster and a blush was forming at the base of her neck.

At length, she said "Nope, I'm not changin' my plea."

"OK, if you're sure," Janet said.

"Have a message for your mother?"

"Yeah, tell her she's better off without Daryll and she shouldn't get all choked up about him being dead. Not her fault. He was stupid, thought he could bully the cops the way he bullied us. He got what's coming to him. I'm glad he's dead. Tell her I'm holding up OK and not to worry. I'm getting used to jail and I'm not getting such a hard time now. They got some new girls that just came in they're harassing now."

"I'll pass that on to June," Janet said. "We'll be doing the closing arguments tomorrow."

"Tell them I'm innocent and young and have my whole life ahead of me," Chrystal said, biting her lower lip, once again in her self-protective mode.

Janet picked up her briefcase and walked out of the room. She knew she'd need an actor's skill to pull off a good closing argument. She also knew she needed Nate's encouragement and advice to do this job. Maybe he should do it after all.

"Dad, heard the news about Daryll Watts, Chrystal's stepfather?" Janet asked when she called Nate. "I'm on my way to the office to talk about tomorrow."

"It's all over the news. Too bad the jury can't know about this, stoking up sympathy for Chrystal, her terrible environment, an abusive stepfather, and all that," Nate said.

Ignoring her father's words, Janet said, "I'm thinking you should do the closing argument tomorrow. What do you think? You feeling OK?"

After only a few minutes of discussion the decision was made: Nate would do the closing argument. Janet had crossed a line and she knew it. She couldn't circle back far enough to argue convincingly–to herself or to the jury–that her client was not guilty.

Chrystal shows no remorse or guilt. She's interested only in self-preservation. Does she inherently lack empathy? Was she born that way, or is this something that you learn from your life's experience, from victimization? Or a combination of the two? Reams of mental health literature has been written about this dichotomy, but no consensus seems to exist. Looks like human behavior is still poorly understood, despite all the research that has been done.

33

Mary Egan and Albert Polcari wanted to have Dr. Ellen Barker, the pediatrician from the university, as their independent medical expert, but she was ill and unavailable. Albert had found and retained Dr. Thomas Sturgis, a pediatrics departmental chair and recognized child abuse pediatrics expert from California, to be the prosecution's rebuttal witness. Dr. Sturgis had testified in a number of high profile cases and was respected on both sides as an objective, honest and effective witness.

Mary and Albert were furious that the judge might not allow his testimony, but they had no recourse. When Mary met with Dr. Sturgis, who had arrived recently from Los Angeles, they explained the situation as objectively as they could. He was surprised, but showed no emotion.

"What was the judge's reasoning about rebuttal witnesses?" he asked.

"He said there'd already been too much medical testimony and he wanted to get the case to the jury. He implied that the jury couldn't understand the complexities of medical testimony and more would just get them further confused. Of course, he's sure he understands all those complexities. He's always had the sense that he's the smartest one in the room. I think he's already decided what should happen with Chrystal and he's in a hurry to conclude this trial," Mary said. "But there's still a small chance you'll get to testify, so we should go over your testimony. Is that OK with you, even knowing that you might not get on the stand?"

"I'm here, so I'll do whatever's needed. If I don't testify, that's no skin off my nose. But it does seem unfair for the judge to deny the opportunity to present your experts when the other side has had—what was it—five outside experts testify? Any idea of why he won't allow the prosecution an opportunity to refute the defense testimony, much of which was patent nonsense?"

"Well, of course that's the way we feel too, but he has that power. I don't know what his rationale is."

"So let's get to work. If I do testify, I want to do a good job. I have no doubt that this is shaken impact syndrome," Sturgis said.

"OK, what's your opinion about a short fall causing Luke's head injuries," Mary said.

"Well, before we get into the specifics of this case, let me make a few points about the–quote–medical experts–unquote–who have testified," Sturgis said. "These guys are notorious for their irresponsible testimony. They're hired guns and they recite from the same playbook. They're peripatetic and get paid outrageous sums of money for their testimony. For some of them it's their major source of income. Most of them have little or no clinical, hands-on experience with childhood head injury.

"But they're not stupid. They can be articulate and convincing. In the past, some did reasonable work within their specialty, before they morphed into professional defense head injury whores in court. They cite only medical literature that supports their point of view, the very definition of confirmation bias. They misquote medical literature, sometimes simply invent information, and they're slippery. They charge that mainstream medical people rely on 'junk science' despite the mountain of strong evidence in the literature supporting the diagnosis of abusive head trauma, with shaking and impact as mechanisms of injury. More to the point, none of them has published any significant research on abusive head trauma.

"These professional witnesses always testify for the defense, whereas true experts will present objective scientific information, regardless of which side calls them to testify. What these guys say in court is reprehensible and they shouldn't be allowed to give such testimony. Professional medical societies have difficulty disciplining them and courts have low standards for qualifications of an expert. Anyone with an MD can come into court and be qualified as an expert in any area of medicine, the way it was 75 years ago before specialization occurred. This is beginning to change but it's a slow process and it varies from place to place."

"It's very frustrating for us," Albert said. "We try to discredit these faux experts by pointing out those deficiencies."

"So, let's talk about what you can rebut," said Mary. "The defense claims that a short fall caused the things we saw in Luke."

"There's a huge literature on falls in childhood commencing in the mid-1970's and with a couple of exceptions they show that short falls seldom cause serious head injuries in infants and young children. One injury exception is called epidural hematomas. These are primarily arterial bleeds ABOVE the dura, not UNDER the dura. They are easily distinguishable on CT scan," Sturgis said.

"Defense experts always cite that paper on playground falls, and Mary, I heard you did a good job breaking that down when you crossed Parten. That playground paper is of little value in trying to understand abusive head trauma in infants since there weren't any infants in those thousands of cases. Most importantly, the information in those archived records was accepted as definitive, even though it varied from a line or two to maybe a paragraph describing the history of the events leading up to the head injury. Think of it—that many records with rushed entries and it was all lumped together and accepted as though there was some uniformity to the gathering of information. A later paper blew a hole in this when the data showed that fatal outcomes in short falls were less than one in a million."

"Tell us about the re-bleed phenomenon?" Mary asked.

"Here again, the defense experts make this stuff up. There's no evidence that a previous, old subdural hematoma can re-bleed enough to cause collapse and death. Any re-bleeding of a subdural is from veins. As Dr. Coughlin said, more of an ooze than active bleeding seen from an artery. This slow oozing doesn't lead to a fatal outcome unless other factors are involved."

"Neck injuries?" Albert asked.

"First of all, consider that the neck is made up of several things: muscle, blood vessels, vertebral bones, ligaments, nerve roots, and spinal cord. Injuries to neck muscles are extraordinarily rare in abusive head trauma cases. My theory—un-provable because it really can't be studied—is that neck muscles in infants are so under-developed that they're under no tension during shaking and not vulnerable to injury. They're sort of like loose cables. That's why we support the baby's head when we hold them at this age.

"Then there are the bones. In the infant spine the bones are soft. Since they're not brittle, they seldom fracture during shaking.

"The one area where you might see injury is in the small nerve roots coming off the spinal cord. These may bleed slightly but it's clinically insignificant. You can't see this bleeding on MRI or CT, but special post-mortem examinations have demonstrated it."

"What about the argument biomechanical engineers make that you can't shake a baby hard enough to cause subdurals, brain damage and retinal hemorrhages?" Albert said.

"The values for forces they cite are based on very old experiments on monkeys. There are no animal models, or dummies, or computerized models that are true representations of a human infant head. We don't have good data about the injury thresholds for these different tissues–the blood vessels, brain, bone, scalp, and so on. So putting numbers to this is the worst kind of guesswork. The biomechanics people are good at measuring forces on things like ligaments, muscles and bone. But they don't know what the numbers are for the infant head and the good ones will admit that. The defense biomechanics 'experts' who testify will simply state their opinion as if it were fact, and it isn't."

"On to retinal hemorrhages," Mary said. "Does raised intracranial pressure cause retinal hemorrhages?"

"Not all retinal hemorrhages are the same," Sturgis said. "The ones we see in shaking cases have three unique characteristics: they're multiple, usually 20 to 30 in number; they occur in several layers of the retina; and lastly, they cover the entire inside surface of the globe of the eye, going all the way out to the area just behind the lens of the eye.

"Now, as to the cause of retinal bleeding. Current thinking, based on a number of good clinical and pathological studies, is that these are shearing injuries that occur during the commotion of shaking, sort of like the tectonic layers of the earth sliding over each other during an earth-quake. Raised intracranial pressure is no longer thought to be a factor in producing this. Mary, you brought this out with Dr. Constant, who clearly doesn't know–or doesn't want to know–any medical literature since 1980.

"The other important thing to remember in these cases is that we're talking about repetitive, acceleration-deceleration, rotational injuries. The head goes back and forth a number of times and the head describes an arc or curved line as it bobs back and forth. The forces developed this way are much different than straight line forces that occur just once, like falling and bumping your head."

"What about the vitamin C theory causing fragile vessels and clotting disorders?"

"Pure nonsense. Any expert who will testify like that is a crackpot. There're simply no studies showing this," he said.

"Anything else if we get the chance to put you on the stand?" Albert said.

"Well, there are other cockamamie theories. One is that low oxygen causes leakage of blood from within the dura into the subdural space. The vast majority of researchers reject this theory. The trial courts in England won't even allow this testimony. Some 'experts' here are still trying to slip this stuff into our courts, and in some jurisdictions it will fly. But it's bad science and hardly worth talking about," Sturgis said. "The media love this kind of manufactured controversy because it sells papers and gets television viewers all pumped up. These defense 'experts' can be charming and persuasive, but if you scrutinize what they're saying, it's apparent they don't know what they're talking about, or worse, they're just plain lying."

"I sure hope we can get you on the stand tomorrow," Albert said. "You'd be a breath of fresh air. Even I knew some of the stuff we've been hearing was absurd, and I barely passed my science courses in college."

The next morning, after everyone was in place in the courtroom, Judge Carlsson summoned the lawyers to the sidebar.

"No rebuttal witnesses. I've thought about it and have decided against more medical testimony."

Mary and Albert asked for a ten-minute recess. Once they had extinguished the flames of their fury at this decision, they huddled around the prosecutor's table with Sturgis to tell him of the decision.

"I'm so sorry to have gotten you all the way from California and then have this decision. As you know, we have no control over it. We're outraged. But that really doesn't matter, does it?" Mary said.

"I'm sorry too, not for me, but for you and Albert and for Luke and his family. I'm also sorry that justice isn't being served when a ruling like this comes down. It's easier for me than for you and the Talbots, because I get to go home this afternoon," Sturgis said, as he picked up his things and headed out of the courtroom. "Let me know the outcome." He shook hands with Mary and Albert.

Janet noticed that Sturgis paused to say hello to "The Professor." If the prosecution medical expert from California stopped to chat with "The Professor" in this courtroom in Kansas City, "The Professor" must be someone with clout in the child abuse field. Janet wondered once more: *Who is that guy?*

Mary and Albert paused a moment at their table.

"Let's get to work on our closing argument. We can't stand around licking our wounds because the judge has made the wrong call. Let's just hope he doesn't throw another curve in this trial," Mary said.

34

Janet and Nate settled down in his office to craft their closing argument. Mary and Albert were pacing at Mary's house, firing phrases at one another as they rehearsed for the final act.

Closing arguments can be like the oculist's lens as changing pieces of glass click into place in the refraction instrument. A particular lens can sharpen the outlines and details of the case or blur them. If your job is to defend a client whose crime is blatantly obvious, you want to obscure clarity. Nate planned to martial every argument of the deniers to push aside the vast array of medical opinion and research, claiming its invalidity. A master weaver of arguments, Nate had honed these skills over years of lonely advocacy for felons and murderers. Glossing over nuance, and even the truth from time to time, was his forte.

The next morning, the courthouse was abuzz with reports about Daryll Watts. The *News* identified him as "…the stepfather of Chrystal Begley, the young babysitter on trial for the death of seven-month-old Luke Talbot. Watts was shot and killed by the police in a face-off in Watts' convenience store. The case is under investigation." Predictable editorials complained about police being "trigger-happy" and demonstrating "no restraint in dealing with a citizen."

"The police officer who shot and killed Watts should have adhered to the department's own protocol for self-defense. Instead of lethal force, they should have immobilized him by a shot in the arm or leg," one paper proclaimed.

Officer Murphy was put on administrative leave as the police department began its internal investigation. June's whereabouts were not disclosed, but it was leaked that she was the victim of domestic violence that precipitated Daryll's deadly confrontation with the police. Social columnists used the domestic violence angle to question its relationship with the allegations of murder that Chrystal faced. Pop psychology theories went viral, claiming Watt's violence toward June was indicative of his poor parenting of Chrystal. One Op-Ed columnist claimed that if Chrystal Begley had harmed Luke it was because of Daryll's abuse of Chrystal and her mother.

Janet and Nate walked into the melee of excited reporters covering Chrystal's trial, admixed with a heterogeneous crew of clients and their lawyers waiting for their day in court.

"We'll talk after the court session, later today," Nate told the media. "We have to keep our focus on the task at hand."

Mary and Albert avoided this scrum by entering the courtroom from a back door. They heard the commotion outside when the courtroom doors opened and watched as Janet and Nate, on their way to the defense table, escaped the horde of journalists. Bailiffs then blocked the doors to all but the officers of the court. After some of the confusion abated, on instructions from the judge, spectators, some members of the press, and a handful of young lawyers from the DA's office who wanted to watch and learn, crowded into the courtroom.

"I'm impressed that the Talbots have come to every session," Mary said to Albert. as they took their place at the table.

"The media have been really cruel to them for some inexplicable reason. Both have held up pretty well, considering the stuff they've had to listen to," Albert said.

Judge Carlsson took his seat on the bench. "Mr. Feingold, please proceed with your closing argument."

Nate stood, and without a legal pad or any notes, walked toward the jury box, head down, a man deeply troubled by what he was about to say.

"Ladies and gentlemen of the jury, you have a difficult task before you. You've heard the prosecution's medical witnesses from our beloved Children's Hospital give mainstream medicine's account of the death of an infant. They say Luke died of shaken baby syndrome. They say that our client, Chrystal Begley, who was taking care of Luke Talbot on that awful day, did this to him. Ladies and gentlemen, the prosecution has presented absolutely no evidence she did this. No one saw her do this. She says she didn't do this. She said that Luke 'went limp' in her arms when she finished bathing him. Chrystal called 911 right away, acting responsibly to get help. This is not the behavior of someone who just hurt a baby. She didn't try to cover anything up because she didn't do anything that needed to be covered up. She didn't harm Luke in any way.

"Shaken baby syndrome. This diagnosis has been made many times and yet–and yet–the doctors cannot tell you for sure that shaking actually causes these head injuries. They make the diagnosis because of certain findings they say cannot be caused by anything else. But have they really looked carefully enough? Some thoughtful doctors, who used to make this diagnosis, now are seriously questioning its validity. Some, being totally honest with themselves, admit they were wrong. New evidence is being published daily that shows that the previous foundations for this diagnosis are falling apart. Now that we have evidence–based medicine, we see that older research is seriously flawed.

"Biomechanical engineers–true mathematical scientists who rely on numbers, not feelings and guesswork–are demonstrating in their research that a person shaking a baby cannot generate enough force to cause this kind of damage inside the head. You heard this from Dr. Szabo who has studied this problem. We also know from studies and experience that short falls can indeed kill babies. You heard that from Dr. Boyd, a neurosurgeon with years of experience in taking care of infants and young children with head injuries and from Dr. Parten, a pathologist who's given much thought to this problem."

Nate was in his element. He spoke to the jury in the manner of a kindly grandfather telling his grandchildren a favored bedtime story. As he proceeded, however, he projected impatience with mainstream medicine, implying they hadn't kept up with the latest findings.

"We now know that old, undetected blood in the head can be disrupted with just a little bump and can lead to serious consequences. We now know that predisposing conditions–things the baby may have had but nobody knew about–can lead to this outcome. Dr. Grasbauskas told us about how vaccines and vitamin C deficiency can compromise clotting of the blood and how this contributes to bleeding in the head. We now know that the previously accepted diagnostic triad of subdural hematoma, brain swelling, and bleeding in the eyes, is not really diagnostic at all. The American Academy of Pediatrics has even removed the term 'shaking' from the title of this condition.

"So, please remember in your deliberations that shaken baby syndrome is rapidly falling out of favor. It hasn't been proven with evidence-based medical research.

"Look at my client: eighteen-years-old, with her whole lifetime ahead of her. Chrystal loved little Luke. And now she's falsely accused of killing this poor baby."

Alison looked at Fred, whose face was flushed as his hand tightened around Alison's. They twisted in their chairs, but were able to contain themselves, once again. Chrystal, for the first time, had red blotches on her neck, creeping up her face, when she heard Nate proclaiming her "love" for Luke.

"But medical experts have told you that Luke wasn't shaken and his condition had to have been caused by something else. Remember what the experts have told you.

"Luke had an earlier injury, probably from a fall that no one thought was anything, but that caused his skull fractures and subdural bleeding. That was made worse by vaccines he got, and a vitamin C deficiency that led to easy bleeding. Then when Luke had a tantrum coming out of his bath, that commotion disrupted the clot and led to his collapse. The increased pressure in his head from the bleeding and the swelling caused his retinal hemorrhages, aided and abetted by his bleeding disorder. Remember all of this as you deliberate. When you do, you'll have to find Chrystal 'not guilty.' Thank you for your kind attention."

Nate walked back to the defense table. Janet looked up at him as he sat down and marveled at how he had put the argument together so seamlessly from memory. She also was aware of how much of what he said was just not true.

Fred and Alison glared at Nate Feingold as he eased himself into his chair. Chrystal crossed her arms, quietly breathed out and sat up in her chair.

"Ms. Egan?" Judge Carlsson said.

Mary was dressed in a somber blue suit with a faint pinstripe, a white cotton blouse open at the neck, black shoes and, as was her custom, no jewelry. Her handsome features were not embellished with lipstick or other makeup. As she stepped to the lectern, the jury saw a serious lawyer who was about to give the most important closing statement of her career.

Mary moved towards the jury box, fixing her gaze, one by one, on the juror's eyes. Her voice carried passion and intensity as she began her monologue.

"Ladies and gentlemen of the jury, the defense would have you believe that Luke Talbot had an old injury that suddenly exploded while he was in Chrystal Begley's care and this led to his death. But both his parents and his pediatrician knew that Luke was in excellent health on the morning of that fateful day. Chrystal's girlfriend, Carol Smith, testified that he was in good spirits, his laughing and chortling coming over the phone as she and Chrystal spoke. He was taking his feeding, playing with his cereal, tossing it about, the way seven-month-old babies do. He was not vomiting or crying or giving any indication of being in pain or distress. Yet only a few hours later he was at Children's Hospital near death when admitted and dying soon after that. Recall his injuries: a three-inch skull fracture in the thickest part of his head—the occiput, in anatomical terms; bruises resembling fingers on his upper back; bleeding under the membrane covering the brain, called a subdural hematoma; severe brain swelling; multiple retinal hemorrhages over both retinas, and retinal folds in his eyes. The Children's Hospital doctors, who actually take care of sick children regularly and took care of Luke, unanimously say he died of shaking and impact injuries. They said that these injuries could only *be inflicted.*"

Alison and Fred could no longer hold back their tears, falling silently onto their hands. Both recalled their happy Luke before that morning, recalling smiling pictures of him. They also recalled him immobile in his hospital bed, head bandaged and heart monitor beeping.

"These doctors, using their years of study, training and experience, looked for other possibilities, in medical parlance: the differential diagnosis. They could find nothing—*nothing*—to explain these injuries other than the trauma that was the result of abuse, of violent shaking and impact to the head. The only person who could have caused these injuries is

Chrystal Begley because she was the only one with Luke after his parents left him–in good health–with her. Yet she denies it.

Chrystal stared at a spot on the floor, just as she had during most of the testimony. She now stole a quick look at Mary Egan. Her palms were sweating, her heart racing as she listened to Mary.

"The defense hired, at great expense, several–what they call–'expert witnesses'–to come here and try to convince you that shaken baby syndrome doesn't exist and couldn't cause these injuries. One after another sang the same tune. Dr. Szabo, the biomechanical expert, says that a person couldn't shake a baby hard enough to injure the infant brain but when pressed, he couldn't tell us what forces would be necessary to cause this degree of trauma. Dr. Boyd, who seldom even treats children with head injuries, claims with amazing certainty it was an old injury. But there's not a shred of evidence that Luke had an old injury. These experts–every one of them, as though they had been rehearsed–stated un-categorically that they were sure the skull fracture was old, despite the fact of any evidence supporting that contention. They said this even though the CT scan showed new blood under the scalp overlying that fracture and the fracture was called 'fresh' when directly viewed at the autopsy.

"The severe brain swelling was due initially to brain injury, then made worse by hypoxia–low levels of oxygen in the blood-because of Luke's disrupted respirations and poor blood supply to the brain tissue due to the extreme brain swelling. The many retinal hemorrhages seen in several layers of the retina are considered by *real* experts to be unique to shaking injuries. They're not due to increased pressure in the head, a theory that has been disproven by many researchers in this area, but research apparently left unread or ignored by the defense medical experts, because they don't fit into their pet theories.

"Does shaking cause these lesions? Defense wants you to believe there's a raging controversy about this. But these deniers of shaken baby syndrome are armchair experts. They never have the primary responsibility to take care of children like Luke. They spend much of their time traveling and testifying for the defense for exorbitant fees. The doctors at Children's Hospital, who are in the trenches and actually put their hands on patients like Luke every day, made the diagnosis of abusive head trauma due to shaking and impact, based on their careful diagnostic analysis. And they received no money for their time in court.

"A tiny minority of doctors has fabricated this phony controversy. The vast majority of sober, intelligent and objective physicians, who take care of patients, study the problem, publish research on the issue and read all of the literature on the subject, know there's no controversy.

"Chrystal Begley lost her temper–badly–on that day and took it out on Luke. When he was unconscious, she panicked and called 911. Luke had all the criteria for shaken impact syndrome. He died of shaken impact syndrome. Chrystal Begley did this to him. Justice demands that she be convicted of this awful crime. This won't bring Luke back. But we must send a message that says emphatically that this kind of behavior won't be tolerated by a civil society and those who do this to children will be found guilty and punished.

"I ask you to find Chrystal Begley guilty."

Mary strode back to the prosecutor's table and sat down. The courtroom was as quiet as a desert. No one stirred.

Alison and Fred paid close attention to Mary as she spoke. When she finished they lifted their heads, locked eyes and nodded, acknowledging that she had spoken for Luke.

Chrystal's eyes were now moving quickly between Judge Carlsson and the jury, as she knew the climax to this case was near at hand.

Will I go to prison or go free?

The silence seemed endless.

Finally, Judge Carlsson turned to the jury to instruct them about the relevant laws to guide their deliberations. He described the issues in the case and discussed the standard of proof needed in coming to their decision.

"First, let me tell you that your decision must be based on *only* the evidence presented at this trial. The opening and closing arguments are not evidence. You as jurors are required to adhere to the law as it applies to this case. You may not agree with the law, but it is the law.

"In order to prove murder in the second degree, the State must prove beyond a reasonable doubt that:

"The defendant, Chrystal Begley, caused the death of Luke Talbot.

"The defendant, Chrystal Begley, committed an unlawful killing with malice aforethought. Malice aforethought can be considered as having three possibilities, or 'prongs' as it is referred to. The first is that she had a specific intent to cause death; the second is that she had a specific intent to cause grievous bodily harm; or three, she intended to do an act which a reasonable person would have known created a plain and strong likelihood that death would result."

Judge Carlsson continued for another twenty minutes, discussing arcane and puzzling legal theories, but most of the jurors' eyes glazed over. He then sent them off for deliberations. After they filed out, he banged his gavel and dismissed the court.

Albert turned to Mary and gave her a handshake. "Terrific close. Now let's hope the jury listened and understood."

"I'm bushed. I wonder how long they'll take," Mary said. "Let's go upstairs."

Janet and Nate walked out of court to the gaggle of reporters. Janet sidled away from them but Nate wanted to talk. He put up his hands for quiet.

"Now it's in the hands of the jury. God grant them the wisdom to do the right thing."

"What's the right thing?" several said, almost in unison.

"Why, to find our client not guilty, of course. She didn't do this. She couldn't have done it. All of the experts told us that shaking can't do these things. Did you hear the testimony? I'm confident the jury will find her not guilty."

Janet worked her way out of the crowd. She grudgingly had come to the conclusion that her father was wrong and the hospital doctors–from Tom Baxley on–were right. She and her father needed to talk about the next phase–sentencing–in case Chrystal got convicted, a likelihood that would now not surprise her. But that could wait until tomorrow. She needed a break. She waited until Nate was finished with the press and then made sure he was OK to go home. As she helped him into the taxi, she decided to call him later to check on him after he had gotten home.

35

The jury was sequestered, so there was nothing to do but wait. In her office the following day, a Saturday, Janet sat disconsolate, reflecting on the past few weeks. *At least I have a boyfriend I can call.* "Jared? Have time to talk?" she said.

"Sure. What's happening?" Jared said, laying down his sax.

"Jury's out and we're all waiting for their verdict. I needed to talk. Do you feel like a good sponge?"

"For you, always. Vent away."

"Well, OK, here goes. I'm so glad this case is finished. I hated every part of it–my client, dishonest testimony, and even some of my dad's tactics. I've always held Dad in such an exalted place, probably too exalted. Most kids denigrate their parents during adolescence, but I didn't, so coming now, it's a surprise. Even he has blind spots and biases. But why should he be different from the rest of humanity just because he's my father? I guess it's because he always preached fairness and justice and equality and all those moral high ground principles at the dinner table, in conversations at the cabin, while we were out in the boat, fishing together..."

"I think you have to consider his entire body of work and life rather than his latest behavior. From what you've told me, he's gotten a little overwrought about shaken baby syndrome," Jared said.

"I don't understand what's made this subject so important to him," Janet said. "Where did this passion for proving mainstream doctors wrong come from? Is this current penchant for twisting facts to fit his defense strategy a new development in his character or has it always been there? Maybe it's been hidden behind the screen of my admiration? Does he have any insight into his self-delusion? He's swum against the tide his whole life, do you think he feels infallible?"

"Those are questions I can't answer since I don't know him. But I don't know my own parents that well either. It's hard to know one's parents," Jared said.

"I guess so. But I thought I knew him; we've been so close, especially with my mom so sick, no sibs..."

She paused. "But then there's Chrystal. My animosity toward her–my professional responsibility–only got worse during the trial. She's a totally self-absorbed teen, I get that, but that and her hostility were so hard to penetrate. Was her attitude because of Daryll's abuse? If she's found guilty, will my animosity towards her be one of the reasons for the jury's verdict? If she goes to prison, will she get effective therapy there?"

"Stop beating yourself up, Janet. I bet you were better than anybody dealing with her. Give yourself some credit for doing your best. When this is over we can get together, maybe go someplace for a few days, and let you get over this. OK?" Jared said.

"OK, thanks. Oh, my other phone is ringing. Gotta go. "

"Hey, can you come over to the office soon?" Nate said.

"What'd you think of Mary's closing argument?" Janet said.

"Meet me at the office. We can talk about everything," Nate said.

"OK, should I bring over lunch?"

"Get something for yourself if you want. I don't feel great, no appetite. See you in about an hour?"

"OK, see you then," Janet said. She closed her eyes, feeling the full weight of guilt. How could she deal with this negativity towards her father? She never felt these doubts when with him. Nate's very presence had a way of dispelling criticism, charming even the biggest skeptics.

"I think we put on a great case," Nate said when she got to his office. "The jury will have a hard time convicting Chrystal with all that confusing medical testimony. I thought our experts did a great job, didn't you?"

"Well, to be perfectly honest, Dad, I wasn't that impressed with their logic and how they responded to cross," Janet said. "You're more ready to believe what they said."

"What part didn't you like?" Nate asked.

"Dad, do you mind if we don't go over it right now? I'm really tired and I need time to process it. Let's have a regular conversation about other stuff. You said you don't feel great. Are you in pain?"

"Well, I hate to mention it, no big deal, but when I was sitting there, listening to Mary Egan, my back was killing me. And I felt nauseous and light-headed. But then it passed and I could talk to the press. When that was over though, this damned backache returned. Maybe it hadn't actually stopped." He winked. "Maybe I was so eloquent with the news people, I forgot about my pain." He exhaled. "Yep, no appetite. The very thought of food makes me want to gag."

Janet looked at her father. He was wan and thinner, something she hadn't noticed before. How could she have been so unobservant? Was she just focusing on this case? The other thing she noticed was a faint yellowing of his eyes.

He coughed a bit. "I think after the verdict is announced–and we've prevailed, of course–I'm going to call the doctor and get something for the nausea and back pain. Up until now, I haven't taken anything. I'm a virgin about drugs," he said.

"Good idea. I hope the verdict is soon so we can get you some rest," Janet said. "But why don't you call the doctor now? No need to wait, is there?"

Nate hesitated. "I guess you're right."

36

Fourteen weary jurors – the twelve who would vote and two alternate jurors–assembled around a table in the jury room. In this cramped room thousands of arguments had settled out, in consensus or in dispute. Here the legal guilt or innocence of Chrystal Begley would be determined.

Those charged with making this decision had passed through many screens before arriving in this place. Each had unique personal baggage. The collective verdict about Chrystal hinged largely on what they had heard in court. They would also be influenced by their world-view, as well as their age, gender, emotions, intellect, belief systems, and by unconscious factors, large and small. Some had perhaps already made up their minds. Still, no one knew going into that room what might be said that might alter one's opinion.

The Foreman, Earl Prentiss, opened the discussion with a question: "How would you like to proceed?"

They looked at one another, hoping someone else would commit to speaking first.

At length, Henry Bryant, an African-American retired riverboat captain and the oldest juror at age 69, said, "Why don't we go from the beginning and talk about the little fella's injuries, how they were described at Children's Hospital?"

"I hope we can make the discussion short. This trial has dragged on for way too long," George Butler, the dentist said.

"Yeah, my shop needs me back. A lot of decisions need my attention," said James DeFiore, a small business owner.

"I think we ought to do as Mr. Prentiss suggested. We can't rush this thing. A young girl's future is at stake," said Margaret Claiborne, a retired elementary school teacher. "We need to give this the proper amount of thought. Think if this were your daughter. You'd want the jury to take its time and get it right."

A collective sigh went around the table as they acknowledged she was right. So began the process of sorting through the medical testimony of the Children's Hospital doctors, each juror looking at notes they had written at the beginning of the trial.

"I'm pretty convinced that what the doctors said about Luke was accurate," said Sarah Coleman, an African-American nurse. "I've been a nurse for almost 20 years and what the hospital doctors said seemed right to me."

"Yeah, but the things that were said later by some of the defense experts contradicted what the hospital doctors said, and frankly, I can't see how an eighteen-year-old girl could or would do such an awful thing," said James Hinckley. "I use my body doing landscape work. I know a little about what forces it takes to do things. Some of what that biomechanics guy said made a lot of sense to me."

"What impressed me, though, was that Luke was perfectly OK when the parents left and two hours later he was nearly dead when they brought him into the hospital," said Virginia Roche. "How can you go from well and happy to nearly dead without some intervening event?"

All heads turned toward her. She had an air about her that commanded respect. She seemed calm and reasonable.

"I am so freaked out by what happened to that poor little baby that I have trouble even thinking about it," said Laura Howell. "But I'm not sure that Chrystal did it. Maybe the defense experts were right, maybe he had some old head injury that got jostled during his temper tantrum. My two kids both had temper tantrums when they were that age and I can see if the baby already had blood in his head that it could've bled again when he had his tantrum."

"Speaking as a dentist, I do think the Children's Hospital doctors may have jumped the gun when they made that diagnosis. Some of those defense experts had pretty good credentials, you know. The neurosurgeon gave a lot of information when he spoke. I thought the DA gave him a really hard time and he did pretty well under fire. So I guess we have to go over all the testimony before we decide. I hate to do that, but I agree we have that obligation as a jury," Dr. Butler said, realizing his earlier impatience made him seem insensitive.

The deliberations went on for several hours, with the balance shifting back and forth. Food was brought in from a local deli, and the jurors ate as they deliberated. When the fifth hour of discussion commenced, nine jurors indicated they were leaning toward a guilty verdict and three toward a not guilty one. The three holdouts were Butler the dentist; Hinckley the landscaper; and Laura Howell the young mother. They all said the defense experts had persuaded them that there were too many possible alternative reasons for Luke's head injury.

"Let me say a few things," said Virginia Roche. "I'm not a doctor of medicine, but I think I was able to follow and understand the medical testimony of both sides. I don't think the logic of the defense experts passes my test. I think a lot of what they said was programmed and rote. Some of the things they said were absolutely refuted by the medical articles the prosecutors used to question them. Those defense witnesses were too dogmatic about their answers.

"More than that, I repeat what I said earlier. I'm a mother and I can't believe that a baby goes from being completely well to devastated in two hours. There was no history of any old injury. The defense experts simply made that up to use as a reason for his current problem. If that baby had had an injury that caused bleeding in his head, wouldn't he have had symptoms the parents would have noticed? And what about the skull fracture? A big fracture in the back of the head couldn't have escaped notice. I think the defense experts were putting a spin on everything they said, like politicians who say black is white. So I'm voting guilty."

When she finished, silence descended over the jury room. Everyone had listened attentively.

"I just want to be sure we're taking into account all of the arguments," said Butler. "If the court qualified these people as experts they must be accomplished professionals or the court wouldn't recognize them as such.

But I have to admit it's worrisome that the hospital doctors and the experts for the defense are so far apart on their positions."

""If both sides have experts who know what they're talking about, why are they so different in their opinions? They can't both be right. It's very confusing. I hate to see that poor girl go to jail. I know what it's like to get mad at a kid when they're having a tempter tantrum. I sympathize with Chrystal. I've been there," said Laura Howell.

"You say you've been there. But you didn't shake and slam and kill your child. I sympathize with her too, but we can't acquit her because we feel sorry for her. If she did this—and I think she did—she should be found guilty. We can't just excuse behavior that kills a child because we feel sorry for the person who does it. Otherwise we might as well just let everyone go for committing any crime," said Earl Prentiss, who had said nothing up until now.

"Yeah, I agree that feeling sorry for Chrystal isn't enough to vote for acquittal. But that biomechanics argument keeps bugging me. Can we go over that testimony again? I hate to put everyone through that but I'm still troubled by it. If it's biomechanically impossible to cause these injuries, then we have to find her not guilty," Hinckley said.

Line by line, the jurors read over the testimony of Dr. Szabo.

"So he said that shaking can't get up enough force to make the head injuries, that the baby would have to have neck injuries. And this baby didn't have neck injuries, right?" said Hinckley.

"But when Mary Egan questioned him, he admitted he'd done no research himself and that dummy models aren't close enough to real babies to prove anything," said Sarah Coleman, the nurse.

"And he didn't know the research he was asked about, and he's never taken care of babies with this kind of injury," said Tabitha Jenkins, the secretary.

"That's true. And he did get mad when the DA pressed him on that. That bothered me," Hinckley said.

"Maybe we need to go over all the experts' testimony, to be sure we're doing the right thing," said Prentiss, the foreman.

Everyone groaned but they finally agreed that they should. For the next several hours, they pored over transcripts of the testimony and their notes. They got into heated discussions, and it was clear that fatigue had begun to blunt their thinking.

"How 'bout we adjourn for the day, get some sleep and resume in the morning?" suggested Prentiss.

"No wonder he's the foreman," said Hinckley.

"Are you sure we can't just agree right now?" asked Roche.

"Ugh, I hate to go one more day, but I guess we should," said Butler. Grumbling, the others acquiesced.

"At least this gets a unanimous decision," said Roche as they exited the jury room.

In the morning, the jurors felt refreshed and ready to tackle the problem anew. They finished reviewing the testimony, but then Rose Jimenez, who had been quiet but attentive during the previous day's discussion, spoke up.

"I'd like to bring up another point. When the judge gave his instructions, I wasn't clear about the term 'malice aforethought.' I wonder if that girl meant to cause that much harm to that child."

"As I understand it, what applies in this case is that a reasonable person would have to know that shaking a baby and hitting his head hard enough to cause a skull fracture would cause 'grievous bodily harm' or death'," said Henry Bryant.

Silence. Each withdrew into their own private thoughts, struggling with the gravity of their responsibility.

Finally, Prentiss said, "Does anyone want to ask the judge for clarification of his instructions, or anything else in the proceedings before we take a vote?"

No one spoke or raised a hand.

"So, shall we take a vote?"

The jury had done their job. They had weighed the evidence, discussed and argued about it, reasoned through the arguments, and taken a vote. It had not been easy, but they had come to a decision.

37

Nate's phone rang. He answered, mumbled a few words and hung up.

"We got a verdict," he said. "Jury's coming back."

Janet and Nate hurried to the courthouse and swam through the reporters. Nate shouted that he'd talk with them right after the verdict.

Mary, Albert, Chrystal, Nate and Janet sat in their respective chairs and waited. The Talbots were in their usual spots. Soon, the judge entered and the court was called to order. The jurors filed in, their tired and blank faces betraying nothing. The foreman, Earl Prentiss, stood.

Judge Carlsson asked, "Have you reached a verdict?"

"We have, Your Honor," Prentiss said.

"What is your verdict?"

"Guilty of second degree murder, Your Honor. Unanimous vote."

Judge Carlsson then polled individual members of the jury, each of whom affirmed the verdict.

Janet blinked once, but felt calm, almost relieved, at the verdict.

Nate glared at the jury, his eyes wide, pupils dilated. Mary and Albert looked at one another, trying not to display any emotion.

"How can you do that to me?" Chrystal wailed in misery. Janet moved quickly to catch Chrystal as she slid nearly out of her chair.

Behind the rail, the Talbots embraced each other, tears flowing onto each other's shoulders. Fred turned to watch Chrystal's reaction. His face hardened when he heard her screaming. He squinted, as he took in the enormity of what just happened. He wanted to stand up and scream, "You should rot in hell!" but his habitual self-restraint prevented such an outburst.

Once the commotion surrounding the verdict subsided, Judge Carlsson declared, "Sentencing will take place two weeks from today at 9 AM." He thanked the jurors for their services and intoned, "Court adjourned."

38

F red and Alison Talbot had just put David to bed when they sat down in their living room and looked at each other for several minutes.

"I don't know whether I can do this," Alison said, "I can barely stop crying when I'm sitting in the courtroom, let alone having to get up and…" Alison paused, took a deep breath, and went on, "talk about how this has affected us. No matter what we say, someone will misinterpret it. You know the terrible things the press has said about us from beginning to end. Maybe we shouldn't give a statement."

The press, on more than one occasion, had characterized Fred and Alison Talbot as more interested in their professional lives than in their children and that they had not paid enough attention to possible signs of an original injury. The Talbot's avoidance of the press had a predictable effect on the media: they turned on them. "No comment" implied some sinister motive. Lost in all the media hype was the searing tragedy of Luke's death from being shaken and killed.

"It's really hard. I know that. But I think we should try to give the judge, the jury, the lawyers on both sides, and the witnesses—and Chrystal—some idea of how this has been for us," Fred said.

"How do you talk—in public—to another human being who tore your heart out with what she did? How do you coolly read a statement about how much grief and pain she inflicted? Does she have any idea of the depth of despair she caused? Does she even care? She never admitted she'd done anything to Luke, doesn't seem to have any remorse. Why say anything to her? Will it do us any good? Sure won't bring Luke back," Alison said, weeping again.

"Let me work on the statement. You can read it over, add to it or subtract from it, and then we can decide if it's worth doing," Fred said.

Fred Talbot rose when asked to deliver the victim impact statement. Alison stood beside him. His hand was fluttering as he held the paper.

"Thank you for this opportunity to address the court, Judge Carlsson. Alison and I appreciate it.

"First I'd like to say 'thank you' to our friends, family and co-workers at the school who have supported us through this ordeal. We couldn't have survived this without you."

He paused, took a deep breath, and swallowed.

"Alison and I struggled with what we should say here today. Are there words that can describe how it feels to lose our precious baby? How it feels to move through the horror of this reality, so raw that it is difficult to breathe, or 'be' without crying? Our sweet little baby Luke. We will never get to watch his talents emerge, whatever they might have been. We have lost the chance to watch the growth of his character as he learned to cope with success and failure. We'll never be able to listen to him sing, or see him dance, or solve an arithmetic problem, or kick a soccer ball into the net..." Overcome, Fred choked back tears. "Or do the many wonderful things that children do. We'll not see his graduation from high school and college, watch him fall in love, get his first job. His brother David will not get to teach him how to bait a hook, or build a tree house, or row a boat. This loss is permanent," Fred paused, "and time does not heal wounds like these.

"We have a right to feel angry. And we do."

He stopped again. He took a deep breath.

"Still, we know that unless we try to forgive, this wound will continue to fester. We will become constant victims if we do not try to forgive. We know that harboring anger and resentment, as tempting as that is, will diminish us. Our own mental, physical and spiritual health will be at risk if we do not forgive. We will make an effort to do this.

"Does Chrystal deserve forgiveness? That doesn't matter. We will try to give her the gift of forgiveness for our own sake. That does matter. And the impact of this tragedy on all of us will be less if we can forgive.

"Thank you."

Fred and Alison went to sit with their parents behind the rail. Most in the court were dabbing their eyes with tissues or the backs of their sleeves.

Sentencing someone convicted of second-degree murder in this jurisdiction required a life sentence. This was expected. Judge Carlsson was twenty minutes into his detailed ruling, a plethora of esoteric legal language, when he uttered a shocking decision.

"I am reducing the charge in this case to manslaughter and vacating the life sentence. I am imposing a sentence of two years, and during the time of incarceration, Chrystal Begley will be mandated to undergo psychological counseling."

"What?!" Oddly, both the Talbots and Chrystal looked frozen in confusion.

Mary looked at Albert, completely stunned. His jaw dropped open.

Nate was too exhausted to react. He turned to Janet. "Call me a taxi. I wanna go home. Can you clean up our stuff here?"

"Dad, are you nuts? I'll take you home. Wait a few minutes, I'll call Nina to come to collect our files," Janet said. "And I'm staying over tonight, don't even try to change my mind," she added.

"OK, deal." When Janet turned her back to him, he snuck a pain pill into his mouth and gulped from the water glass on their table.

Janet turned to Chrystal.

"Do you understand what the judge just said, Chrystal?"

"I think he said I have to go to prison."

"Yes, but for only two years. He changed the charge to manslaughter, so you don't get a life sentence. Do you understand that, although you have to go to prison, it's only for a couple of years, with maybe time off for good behavior?" Janet spilled out the words.

"You think that's a good thing?" Chrystal asked, this time not being sarcastic, just trying to understand this confusing outcome.

"Yes, Chrystal, it's good. Very good for you."

It's not so good for legal process, but I'll think about that later.

Both legal teams planned to appeal the verdict and the sentence.

"We have to appeal. The very idea that the judge set aside the jury's verdict and reduced the charge, then set his own sentence. It's outrageous," Albert fumed. "Carlsson has proved once more that he's a maverick and a contrarian. He's pissing nearly everyone off. I've had calls from the Children's Hospital doctors who say the judge is 'out of his mind.' I'm getting emails from prosecutors all over the country wondering what the hell we're doing in this state. As for Judge Carlsson, he couldn't care less."

"He assumes he's always right," said Mary. "He probably thinks he's the only one who could understand the medical testimony and the poor slobs in the jury couldn't possibly get it. His superior intelligence allowed *him* to see things clearly. Such hubris!"

"Got to appeal. What we want is a not guilty, not a reduced sentence. I want Chrystal to go free," Nate said to Janet.

39

After a restless night, Janet woke up around six AM when the
crows lifted their eerie caws. Her bleary eyes scanned her old
room, retracing years of waking up here. Her bed squeaked
when she swung her legs onto the floor. She felt that someone had come
while she was asleep and stuffed her mouth with chalk; she needed water, to brush her teeth and to shake herself out of the arms of Morpheus.
She walked down the too silent hall to her old bathroom. She found
toothpaste and a toothbrush in the closet and scrubbed out her grubby
mouth. She'd take a shower after she peeked in on her father.

She listened at his door to avoid waking him. No sounds. She cracked
the door slightly, just enough to get a look into the room. As she opened
the door, a pungent odor assaulted her. *Oh my God, did Dad soil himself?*
"Dad?" she whispered.

Approaching his bed, clarity struck; Nate lay in the fetal position
under a mound of covers. There was no doubt he was dead—no rise and
fall in the bedclothes from his breathing, his face an ashen gray.

She gasped, brought her hand to her mouth, biting her knuckles,
Nausea rose swiftly and unable to suppress it, she retched, bringing up
tiny bursts of yellowish fluid.

Her rational mind gradually took over. She called 911 to summon
help. The Emergency Medical crew arrived within minutes. When they
left, Janet was left alone in the house she had grown up in.

*I need to call people. Who should I call first? Of course, Nina. Then Jared.
I'll need to let the nursing home know, even though Mother won't comprehend.
Uncle Len, the cousins in Atlanta. A funeral home. Jeff at the PD office. Nina
will know who else to call.*

Nina saw to it that his obituary appeared the next day. He had been such a presence for the local media for so long, and as is the case for familiar figures in any community, the obituary writers already had his written, at the ready. True to form, Nate himself had composed it for them so they wouldn't miss anything or be too maudlin.

LONG-TIME DEFENSE ATTORNEY FEINGOLD DEAD

The *Kansas City News* declared on the front page.

Although there were no cliches about "battling cancer," or being a "beloved father and loving husband," there was an in-depth description of his life and accomplishments.

When Jared walked in the door, Janet molded herself into his frame. They stayed intertwined for several minutes

"Thank you," Janet said, without letting him go. Her body relaxed for the first time since she learned of her father's cancer.

"Tell me what I can do," Jared said.

"You've already done it. You're here. Can you stay a while?"

"Sure. I do have to play tonight, but I can come back after my gig."

"Can we go somewhere for dinner? Do you have time for that before you play? " Janet asked.

"Why don't I get some take-out and we eat here? I don't think either of us really wants to be out at a restaurant," Jared said.

"Sounds perfect, Jared."

The memorial service and week of sitting Shiva behind her, Janet welcomed the opportunity to return to work and normal routines. Her deepening affection for Jared was in stark contrast to the painful hollowness from her father's absence. Her mother had gone to the cemetery with her, but was so much in her own world, the feeling of being orphaned was palpable.

She needed to talk to Chrystal, an understandably neglected duty since Nate's death. Her old guilty feelings surfaced again.

The guards brought Chrystal into the familiar interview room. She slumped into the chair.

"I'm sorry about your dad. I liked the old dude," Chrystal said.

"He was a good man. He tried his best to get a 'not guilty' for you. I did too. But sometimes the evidence is too strong," Janet said.

Janet rustled some papers from her briefcase. She waited for Chrystal.

"So now I have to have a shrink! How would you like to have someone prying into your life? Can they make me do that?" Chrystal said.

"Try to look at it as if there may be some benefit to you," Janet said, knowing her words wouldn't change Chrystal's thinking.

"Yeah, right," Chrystal said. "And what's this crap about appeal?" Her bravado did not hide the fear in Chrystal's eyes.

"The prosecutors will argue that the judge went beyond his power by setting aside the jury verdict. *We're* appealing because we don't believe the prosecution proved its case on the evidence and you should be declared not guilty of all charges and freed."

"All this legal bullshit!" Chrystal snorted. "What are my chances?"

"Well, we don't know that," Janet said. "If the Appeals Court agrees with the prosecution that the judge exceeded his authority, they could reinstate the mandatory life sentence. So we have to do this appeal. No choice."

"Well, that really sucks. I have to wait even longer to find out what the hell is going to happen to me" she said, and got up to leave, ready to go back to her cell.

"Don't worry. I'll go right on advocating for you, because that's what I signed on to do. But I think your attitude stinks. So cut the crap, grow up and cooperate with me as I try to save your ass!"

Chrystal just stared at Janet, brought up short by this outburst.

She walked toward the door, then turned to look at Janet.

"OK, I'm sorry. I'll try to act better. But it's hard."

The attendant opened the door for her and she left.

Well, at least she said she was sorry, Janet thought.

The appeals of both the prosecution and defense were denied, leaving both sides irate. Judge Carlsson's decision to reduce the original charge to manslaughter and to impose a two-year sentence stood.

40

"I have a call for you from Dr. Raymond Lucyniak," the operator said.

"Who?" Janet asked.

"He says he's a pediatrician, wants to talk to you about the Begley trial."

Curious, Janet picked up. "This is Janet Feingold. Can I help you?"

"Thanks for taking my call Ms. Feingold. This may seem odd since we've never met, but I've been in the courtroom following the Chrystal Begley trial. I'm a retired pediatric child abuse specialist and I've testified in dozens of trials involving both physical and sexual abuse. In the course of those trials, and especially during the Begley trial, I've gotten increasingly worried about the medical opinions being accepted as evidence by courts. I see a serious problem in a judicial system that isn't discriminating between responsible and irresponsible testimony. These problems, it seems to me, are both medical and legal."

He paused, but hearing no response from Janet, pressed on.

"I considered calling Mary Egan and Albert Polcari to talk about an idea I have. But I thought perhaps the project I have in mind would have greater credibility if the defense side were involved. And you impress me as someone sincerely interested in justice."

Janet was both flattered and intrigued by the unorthodox nature of the call.

"I am interested in justice, that's why I became a lawyer. But what made you think that I was, as you say, 'sincerely interested in justice?'" Janet said, a little suspicious about where this conversation was going.

"Your body language, the way you questioned the witnesses, glances at your father during his questioning. Nothing in particular, I guess, just the gestalt."

"Can you tell me more about yourself?" Janet asked, still wondering what this guy was all about.

"I've worked in child abuse diagnosis since the early 1970's, mostly in California. I've headed up several hospital child protection teams, done research on child physical abuse. I've published in peer-reviewed medical journals, have edited several child abuse texts. I will immodestly tell you that I'm pretty well-known in the field. I got your email address from your secretary and I'm emailing my CV to you as we speak," he said. "I was hoping we could meet so I could discuss ideas I have to address the ethics of the situation."

"Are you still in Kansas City?"

"Yes, I'm visiting colleagues here a few more days," he said. He gave her his cell phone number.

"I'll think about it and get back to you," Janet said. "Thank you for calling."

Janet called Tom Baxley to see if he knew who this fellow was.

"He's only one of the most well-known child abuse specialists in the world," Tom said.

Janet opened her email and found the attachment with Lucyniak's CV. He was, indeed, highly qualified. *Okay, why not?* She called him back and they arranged to meet at her office.

The next day, when he came into her office, she recognized that Dr Lucyniak was "The Professor." Now his presence in the courtroom and call made sense.

"Dr. Lucyniak, we obviously can't do anything about this trial," Janet said, "but I've been pondering the serious generic problems you've brought up. I got quite an education on shaken baby syndrome–I mean shaken impact syndrome–or should I say abusive head trauma? I know we're both aware of the caliber of expert witnesses in the Begley trial, I'm sorry to say. I'm sure they will go on presenting their theories in courts everywhere and defense attorneys will welcome them. Do you see any way out of this morass?"

"Well, I do have some ideas. It'll take a two-front strategy," Lucyniak began. "The first is to revise the rules of professional medical organizations governing medical expert witnesses. Several of them already have rules governing ethical testimony. Spotting irresponsible medical testimony is not hard. But getting professional organizations or licensing boards to discipline members who have violated these rules is. Physicians who should be sanctioned are extraordinarily self-righteous. They'll go to great lengths for retribution when they feel wronged. They are litigious in the extreme. So that issue needs to be addressed somehow, perhaps with some kind of immunity from frivolous lawsuits for professional organizations and licensing boards that legitimately sanction doctors. That's tricky.

"The second front is the justice system. Because the rules are so vague and there is always fear by judges of overturned decisions, judges give wide latitude in qualifying even marginal witnesses. In trials I've testified at, judges are more likely to admit testimony than to exclude it. I've also observed the judges as susceptible to becoming amateur scientists—deciding they know what testimony is valid and what's not."

Lucyniak got up from his chair and walked over to the window overlooking the river. He took off his glasses and went silent for a moment.

"Of course, as you know, defense experts need only introduce doubt, not solid evidence. And the expert is allowed to introduce hearsay evidence and other questionable factoids. He doesn't need to have real or personal knowledge of the subject matter. What we need are rules with teeth for expert witness testimony. Expert witness testimony should be made part of the practice of medicine, so those who give irresponsible testimony should pay the price by losing their licenses to practice. Then we need a commitment from the judiciary to be stringent about who gets qualified to testify. No small feat."

"This sounds really difficult. Any strategy to approach this?" asked Janet

"I think what is needed is a task force of representatives from the major medical and legal professional bodies and licensing boards to develop a roadmap out of this jungle. Someone like you—and a couple of respected judges—could get the ball rolling from the legal side. There will be opposition, I'm certain of that. Some of it from your own colleagues from the criminal bar, but I believe the ones with integrity will see that such a move would benefit both sides in these cases.

"I've already begun to beat the drum within my professional organizations. Hospital staff privileges committees will need to do their part. This is a long-term project, but the sooner we get going, the sooner true justice will prevail relative to this heinous crime. Maybe in a few years we'll get a handle on this problem," Dr. Lucyniak said. "Of course, it would also be advantageous to get the media on our side, they often do tremendous damage perpetuating false information. Their participation would be a way to atone for that."

"You've certainly given me a lot to think about," Janet said.

"I hope you're interested in helping," he said.

"I'm not sure how much I can do. Let me do some soul-searching and talk to some of my colleagues, both on the defense side and on the prosecution side. Maybe later we could organize a meeting between the legal and the medical societies to set up a task force to address this." Warming to the idea, she said, "It really is intriguing."

"I'm so glad you feel that way. I think my instincts were right that you were the person to approach," he said. "Thanks for the conversation. I've taken up enough of your time."

He got up, shook Janet's hand and headed for the door. Janet was impressed with this man and with the mission he was advocating, a mission she could embrace.

"Thanks for meeting me, Nicole," Janet said to the psychologist sitting across from her. "I wasn't sure if I should make an appointment in your office, instead of this tea room."

"This works for me, Janet—now I get a free hour of legal advice, plus, you'll love the black currant tea."

The server placed their order on the table and quickly departed.

"I'm so sorry about your dad, Janet. I know how close you were, how much you loved and admired him," Nicole said.

"Thank you, Nicole. It's so strange to not see or talk to him. Especially because of that case—we were together almost every day," Janet said.

Their conversation drifted into more mundane matters for a while, then Janet got to what had been preying on her mind.

"You know that my defendant, Chrystal will be in prison for two years since the judge discarded the verdict of the jury."

"Yes, and I know there was quite a backlash against his decision."

"I feel conflicted about what the judge did, even though I never got close to Chrystal. Truthfully, I grew to dislike her more and more as the trial went on. I think she's self-centered way beyond the usual adolescent narcissism." Janet took a deep breath. "I found out, though, half way through this, that Chrystal's stepfather had sexually and physically abused her since she was fifteen years old. Would that hideous experience explain her attitude and behavior? I feel guilty for not liking her if it's not her fault that she's the way she is. Can you shed any light on this?"

"You've just asked one of the more vexing questions in psychology. A lot of literature has recently been written on the complex interplay between heredity and environment, especially as they affect the development of empathy. Events in one's life may play into a genetic vulnerability, or compensate for it, or a combination of the two. In other words, it depends."

"You sound like a lawyer," Janet said.

"Well, both of us are working in areas of ambiguity."

"But to explain this a little more, many kids are resilient when awful things happen to them but others, maybe a third, have varying degrees of negative outcomes. It sounds like Chrystal needed her defenses–ways to keep people away since, in her experience, most people will hurt you."

"Do you think therapy could help her?" Janet said.

"Maybe. Her behavior sounds pretty fixed, but therapy's always worth a try. It's her best shot to not ruin her life when she gets out of jail. Unfortunately, lots of kids with her background don't ever improve. They act out sexually, get involved with substance abuse, don't know how to treat themselves in a loving way. It's sad."

"Well, I hope she gets a good therapist. Sounds like we need a modern day version of Sigmund Freud," Janet said.

"The last thing she needs is a modern day version of Freud. When he published his paper about fathers abusing their female children, his colleagues were so harshly critical that he changed his position and said that women who claimed to have been sexually abused were 'hysterical', a term that's persisted for years.

"I'm sure the therapists in the prison sysytem have experience dealing with abused women. So therapy could be one of the few good things that come out of jail time," Nicole said.

"So what's next for you, Janet?"

"Hmm. This case made me question whether I want to continue with criminal defense work. Now that Dad's gone I don't have that impetus to prove myself to him, although I still feel the urge to defend poor people who get into trouble. I guess I should re-read Dershowitz's book to get my batteries recharged," Janet said.

"Give yourself some time to figure it out," Nicole said. "What are your options?"

"One possibility is to leave the Defender's Office and do private practice in my father's office. Ready-made. Well–known office, a great secretary if she'd stay on. Jared suggested I teach, since I've accrued a good number of court hours. He thinks law students would appreciate a young professor."

"That's a great idea," said Nicole.

"Not so easy getting a job in a law school, though it might be a good fit for me. I could do it part time with a little private practice to keep bread on the table," she said. "Especially if I was particular about the cases I took on.

"But what has the most charge for me is working with a well-known child abuse specialist who wants me to help him create a combined medico-legal task force to analyze the way courts qualify expert witnesses. If I were at a law school it could increase the possibility of getting heard. Write some law review articles. Donna Quixote herself!" she said, with a big smile.

They walked out of the tearoom into bright sunshine.

"Let's get together soon!" Nicole said." I want to hear more about Jared and what you decide to do with your life."

41

"Hello, Ms. Feingold," Chrystal said as she sat down opposite Janet.

"Hi Chrystal," Janet said. "Tell me how things are going for you."

Chrystal sat upright in the chair and looked directly at Janet. "Well, they hooked me up with a pretty cool counselor. She's young and knew all about the trial. We've only had a couple of meetings, but she's not what I expected.

"The other thing is," she began hesitantly, "I know I've told you about this before, but I've woken up a bunch of nights with the same bad dream. I'm shaking Luke and hitting his head on the bathtub. Maybe I did do that. I'm thinking I did. I couldn't have a dream that real, with all the parts, if I hadn't done it, could I? I told my counselor about this and she wants to talk more about this when I'm ready."

Janet sat stone still in her chair as she listened to Chrystal try to untangle her web of self-deceit and denial. She could hardly believe that in just the few weeks since the trial Chrystal had come this far. Now Janet had the story. It reinforced her firm belief that Chrystal had killed Luke Talbot by shaking and slamming his head. And now she saw that the court proceedings had been a charade and the defense medical experts were wrong in so many ways.

"I hope you can get to a better place, Chrystal. I wish you good luck," Janet said, meaning it this time.

They shook hands and Chrystal left. Janet would see Chrystal once more mid-way through her sentence.

After several weeks, Janet made the transition to her new life in her father's office. Nina, almost sixty-seven, agreed to stay on for a year but wouldn't make a commitment beyond that. She needed some transition time to work through her own grief having lost the only man she had truly loved. Of course, she had known Janet since, as a little girl she came to her father's office and poked around in his library. Now she was watching Janet mature into a competent lawyer, but she didn't really want to see her take Nate's place.

On the third day of her new life in her Dad's old chambers, Nina told her to pick up on line 1.

"Gould here. Got a minute?" he said. Bill Gould was one of her old buddies at the police station, the one who had originally told Janet that she had been assigned to the Begley case.

"Always for you, Bill. What's happening?"

"The Chief was asking me about good defense lawyers for one of our cops accused of excessive force during an arrest. So I thought of you," he said.

"Would that be Kevin Murphy?"

"You guessed it. Even though you defended the stepdaughter of the deceased, the Chief didn't think there's any conflict of interest since you had no legal relationship with Daryll Watts.

"I'll be glad to talk to the Chief. I'm surprised he wants me since I've given the police such a hard time in court," Janet said.

"We all know you're a helluva good lawyer and that's what Kevin needs."

"Tell the Chief or one of his minions to call me," Janet said.

She welcomed the case. She was now active in the ACLU, taking after her father and she had also wangled a job as adjunct professor of criminal law at the University School of Law. She had already begun work on organizing the project that she and Dr. Lucyniak were calling "Post Daubert."

There was already a fair amount written about this, especially by a young brilliant man who was both a physician and a lawyer. Polarization of opinions within medicine and law had made this pediatric condition the subject of intense heat but very little light. She hoped that the adversaries might become more flexible and that cool heads might prevail. A lot was at stake.

EPILOGUE

Janet visited Chrystal before her release from prison. What she heard from Chrystal was so unexpected, she didn't know how to respond.

"I don't know how to say this but…" she looked down, then in a rush said, "I'm sorry I was such a jerk during the trial. I'm glad you came to see me so I could thank you for what you did for me."

Chrystal continued, "Things have changed since I've been in therapy. Mom's also much stronger now that…you know, since Daryll's gone. When she visits me she smiles a lot, says she's making new friends and the store is busy. She's happy for the first time since I can remember."

This was indeed a different Chrystal than Janet had seen before. Janet gathered herself and said,

"That's really good to hear. What are your plans when you leave here?"

"I got my GED. I really didn't want to go back to my old high school. When I get out, I'm leaving Kansas City, going to Los Angeles where no one knows me," Chrystal said.

"What'll you do there?"

"Wait tables in a restaurant is what I think. I really dunno for sure, but that's what I think I'll do," Chrystal said.

Janet nodded her head in approval. Each of them was quiet for a moment. Janet wondered if Chrystal would say more.

"I also wanted to tell you that my counsellor and I have had some pretty heavy sessions. She thinks—and I guess she's right—that I had some-thing she calls diss-…" she stopped.

Janet said, "Dissociation?"

"Yeah, that's it. That I dissociated when I shook and hit Luke's head on the bathtub that day."

Chrystal looked down.

"Do you think I should write to the Talbots?" she said.

Janet considered this for a moment.

"That's up to you, Chrystal. They still live at the same place if you want to send them a letter."

They looked at each other for a while, and then, as if on cue, they both rose and shook hands. Janet was not sure Chrystal would write such a letter.

Janet thought it would help her. Perhaps it would even help Alison and Fred.

ABOUT THE AUTHOR

Robert M. Reece, MD, was Clinical Professor of Pediatrics at Tufts University School of Medicine (now retired). Additionally, he served as the Director of the Child Protection Team at Tufts Medical Center and as Consultant to Child Protection Teams at the Massachusetts General Children's Hospital, University of Massachusetts Medical Center, and the Children's Hospital at Dartmouth.

Reece edited nine pediatric textbooks: three editions of Child Abuse: Medical Diagnosis and Management, and two editions of *Treatment of Child Abuse: Common Ground for Mental Health, Medical and Legal Practitioners.* Reece co-edited *Inflicted Childhood Neurotrauma* published by the American Academy of Pediatrics. He has published 48 peer-reviewed medical articles and contributed 27 book chapters. Reece edited *The Quarterly Update*, a review journal, since 1993.

He has been honored by numerous professional organizations for his contributions to the field of child abuse diagnosis and treatment. Frequently called as an expert witness, Reece has consulted and testified in countless cases of abusive head trauma and has lectured extensively nationally and internationally on the subject.

REFERENCES

Note to my readers: in Chapter 12, Janet reaches Mike Greenbaum, a fictional expert on medical issues including SBS. Mike offers to send Janet a list of "50 or 60" articles he describes as good research. The referenced articles are real and appear for your benefit as follows:

1.   AAP Committee on Medical Liability and Risk Management. Policy Statement – Expert witness participation in civil and criminal proceedings. Pediatrics 2009;124:428-438.

2.   Adamsbaum (Ed.). Pediatric Radiology December 2014;44 (Suppl) S535-S659.

3.   Adamsbaum C, Grabar S, Mejean N, Rey-Salmon C. Abusive head trauma: Judicial admissions highlight violent and repetitive shaking. Pediatrics 2010;126:546-555

4.   Adams G, Ainsworth J, Butler L et al. Update from the Ophthalmology Child Abuse Working Party: Royal College Ophthalmologists. Eye 2004;18:795-798.

5.   Barlow KM, Milne S, Aitken K, Minns RA. A retrospective epidemiological analysis of non-accidental head injury in children in Scotland over a 15 -year period. Scot Med J 1998;43:112-114.

6.   Bechtel K, Stoessel K, Leventhal J et al. Characteristics that distinguish accidental from abusive injury in hospitalized young children with head trauma. Pediatrics 2004;114:165-168.

7.   Block RW. Child abuse – Controversies and imposters. Curr Probl Pediatr 1999;29:253-272.

8. Bonnier C, Nassogne MC, Evrard P. Outcome and prognosis of whiplash shaken infant svndrome: Late consequences after a symptom-free interval. Dev Med Child Neurol 1995;37:943-956.

9. Budenz DL et al. Ocular and optic nerve hemorrhages in abused infants with intracranial injuries. Ophthamology 1994;101:559-565.

10. Case ME, Graham MA, Handy TC, Jentzen JM, and Monteleone JA. Position paper on fatal abusive head injuries in infants and young children. Am J Forensic Med Pathol 2001;22:112-122.

11. Chadwick DL, Bertocci G, Castillo E, Frasier L, Guenther E, Hansen K, Herman B, and Krous H. Annual risk of death resulting from short falls among young children: Less than 1 in 1 million. Pediatrics 2008;121:1213-1224.

12. Cory CZ, Jones MD. Can shaking alone cause fatal brain injury? A biomechanical assessment of the Duhaime shaken baby syndrome model. Med Sci Law 2003;43:317-333.

13. Ewing-Cobbs L, Kramer L, Prasad M et al. Neuroimaging, physical, and developmental findings after inflicted and non-inflicted traumatic brain injury in young children. Pediatrics 1998;102:300-307.

14. Ewing-Cobbs L, Prasad M, Kramer L, et al. Acute neuroradiologic findings in young children with inflicted and noninflicted traumatic brain injury. Child's Nerv Syst 2000;16:25-34.

15. Fischer H, Allasio D. Permanently damaged: Long-term follow-up of shaken babies. Clin Pediatr 1994;33:696-698.

16. Forbes BJ, Christian CW, Judkins AR, Kryston K. Inflicted childhood neurotrauma (shaken baby syndrome): Ophthalmic findings. J Pediatr Ophthalmol Strabis 2004;41:80-88.

17. Gleckman AM, Bell MD, Evans RJ, Smith TW. Diffuse axonal injury in infants with nonaccidental craniocerebral trauma: Enhanced detection by beta-amyloid precursor protein immunohistochemical staining. Arch Pathol Lab Med 1999;123:146-151.

18. Gleckman AM, Evans RJ, Bell MD, and Smith TW. Optic nerve damage in shaken baby syndrome: Detection by beta-amyloid precursor protein immunohistochemistry. Arch Pathol Lab Med 2000;124:251-256.

19. Green MA, Lieberman G, Milroy CM, Parsons MA. Ocular and cerebral trauma in non-accidental injury in infancv: Underlying mechanisms and implications for paediatric practice. Br J Ophthalmol 1996;80:282-287.

20. Haviland J, Russell RIR. Outcome after severe non-accidental head injury. Arch Dis Child 1997;77:504-507.

21. Herman BE, Makoroff KL, Corneli HM. Abusive head trauma. Pediatr Emerg Care 2011;27:65-69.

22. Hymel K, Abshire T, Luckey D, Jenny C. Coagulopathy in pediatric abusive head trauma. Pediatrics 1997; 99:371-375.

23. Hymel KP, Rumack CM, Hay TC, Strain JD, Jenny C. Comparison of intracranial computer tomographic (CT) findings in pediatric abusive and accidental head trauma. Pediatr Radiol 1997;27:9:743-747.

24. Jaspan T. Current controversies in the interpretation of non-accidental head injury. Pediatr Radiol 2008;38(S3):S378-S387

25. Jenny C, Hymel KP, Ritzen A, Reinert SE, Hay TC. Analysis of missed cases of abusive head trauma. JAMA 1999;281:621-626.

26. Keenan HT, Runyan DK, Marshall SW, Nocera MA, Merten DF. A population-based comparison of clinical and outcome characteristics of young children with serious inflicted and noninflicted traumatic brain injury. Pediatrics 2004;114;633-639.

27. Keenan HT, Hooper SR, Wetherington CE, Nocera M, Runyan DK. Neurodevelopmental consequences of early traumatic brain injury in 3-year-old children. Pediatrics 2007;119:e616-e623.

28. Keenan HT, Runyan DK, Marshall SW, et al. A population-based study of inflicted traumatic brain injury in young children. JAMA 2003; 290:621-626.

29. Kemp AM. Investigating subdural haemorrhage in infants. Arch Dis Child 2002;86:98-102.

30. Kemp AM, Stoodley N, Cobley C, Coles L, Kemp KW. Apnoea and brain swelling in non-accidental head injury. Arch Dis Child 2003;88:472-476.

31. Kemp AM. Abusive head trauma: Recognition and the essential investigation. Arch Dis Child 2011;96:202-208.

32. Kivlin JD, Simons KB, Lazoritz S, Ruttum MS. Shaken baby syndrome. Ophthalmology 2000;107:1246-1254.

33. Levin AV. Retinal hemorrhage in abusive head trauma. Pediatrics 2010;126:961-970.

34. Maguire SA, Pickerd N, Farewell D, Mann MK, Tempest V, Kemp AM. Which clinical features distinguish inflicted from non-inflicted brain injury? A systematic review. Arch Dis Child 2009;94:860-867.

35. Maguire SA, Watts PO, Shaw AD et al. Retinal haemorrhages and related findings in abusive and non-abusive head trauma: A systematic review. Eye 2012, doi: 10.1038/eye.2012.213.

36. Narang S. A Daubert analysis of abusive head trauma/shaken baby syndrome. Part I. Hous J Health Law Policy 2012;505:538-539.

37. Narang SK. A Daubert analysis of abusive head trauma/shaken baby syndrome - Part II: An examination of the differential diagnosis. 13 Hous J Health L and Policy; 203 (2013).

38. Narang S, Clarke J. Abusive head trauma: Past, present, and future. J Child Neurol 2014; DOI; 10.1177/0883073814549995.

39. Morad Y, Kim YM, Armstrong DC Huyer D, Mian M, Levin AV. Correlation between retinal abnormalities and intracranial abnormalities in the shaken baby syndrome. Amer J Ophthalmol 2002;134:354-359.

40. Odom A, Christ E, Kerr N et al. Prevalence of retinal hemorrhages in pediatric patients after in-hospital cardiopulmonary resuscitation: A prospective study. Pediatrics 1997;99:p e.3.

41. Punt J, Bonshek RE, Jaspan T, et al. The 'unified hypothesis' of Geddes et al. is not supported by the data. Pediatr Rehabil 2004;7:173-184.

42. Reece RM et al. The evidence base for shaken baby syndrome: Response to editorial from 106 doctors. BMJ 2004;328:1316-1317.

43. Reece RM and Sege R. Childhood head injuries: Accidental or inflicted? Arch Pediatr Adolesc Med 2000;154:11-15.

44. Rooks VJ, Eaton JP, Ruess L, et al. Prevalence and evolution of intracranial hemorrhage in asymptomatic term infants. Am J Neuroradiol 2008;dpo 10.3174/ajnr.A1004.

45. Sandramouli S, Robinson R, Tsaloumas M, Willshaw HE. Retinal haemorrhages and convulsions. Arch Dis Child 1997:76:449-451.

46. Starling S, Holden JR, Jenny C. Abusive head trauma: The relationship of perpetrators to their victims. Pediatrics 1995;95:259-262.

47. Starling SP, Patel S, Burke BL et al. Analysis of perpetrator admissions to inflicted traumatic brain injury in children. Arch Pediatr Adolesc Med 2004;158:454-458.

48. The Ophthalmology Child Abuse Working Party (Chair: D Taylor). Child abuse and the eye. Eye 1999;13:3-10.

49. Vinchon M, Noule N, Tchofo PJ, et al. Imaging of head injuries in infants: Temporal correlates and forensic implications for the diagnosis of child abuse. J Neurosurg (Pediatr) 2004;101:44-52.

50. Vinchon M, de Foort-Dhellemmes S, Desurmont M, Delestret I. Confessed abuse versus witnessed accidents in infants: Comparison of clinical, radiological, and ophthalmological data in corroborated cases. Childs Nerv Syst 2010;26:637-645.

51. Watts P and the Child Maltreatment Guideline Working Party of the Royal College of Ophthalmologists and the Royal College of Paediatrics and Child Health. Abusive head trauma and the eye in infancy. Eye 2013, available on www.rcpch.ac.uk.

52. Policy Statements from the following organizations support the diagnosis of SBS/AHT.

The American Academy of Pediatrics
American Academy of Ophthalmology
American Association for Pediatric Ophthalmology and Strabismus
American Academy of Family Physicians
American College of Surgeons
American Association of Neurological Surgeons

Centers for Disease Control and Prevention, Department of Health and Human Services
Pediatric Orthopaedic Society of North America
American College of Emergency Physicians
Canadian Paediatric Society
Royal College of Paediatrics and Child Health (UK)
Royal College of Radiologists (UK)
American Academy of Neurology
World Health Organization

Made in United States
North Haven, CT
19 January 2023

31334545R00163